Business Clusters

Clusters of specialized business are being promoted around the world. Encouraged by high-profile examples such as Silicon Valley and Italy's industrial districts, cooperation with business neighbours appears to distinguish successful regions. But do clusters really drive the economies of regions and countries?

Drawing on studies by economists, geographers, sociologists and management specialists, *Business Clusters* explains and evaluates a wide range of perspectives. This multi-disciplinary assessment offers a real-world understanding of clustering and argues that the case for clusters has been exaggerated. Detailed case studies show the special conditions behind successful clusters. This book emphasizes clusters as a particular location condition and shows that cluster successes have relied on special conditions rather than being the product of universal trends. Perry concludes with three assessments of the present state of cluster theory: clusters as chaos, clusters as art and science, and clusters as a contribution to diversity.

This book, aimed at students of economic geography, management and business studies, as well as policy makers with an interest in industrial location, explodes the myths and misinformation surrounding the geographical concentration of business units.

Martin Perry teaches contemporary management and advanced business research methods in the Department of Management and Enterprise Development, at the Wellington Campus of Massey University, New Zealand. He is a research associate of the New Zealand Centre for SME Research and has acted as a consultant to the Ministry of Economic Development and the Workplace Productivity Working Group, New Zealand Department of Labour. He was previously an associate professor in the Department of Geography, National University of Singapore. His previous books include *Small Firms and Network Economies* (Routledge, 1999).

Routledge studies in business organizations and networks

Business Clusters
An international perspective

Martin Perry

Routledge
Taylor & Francis Group

LONDON AND NEW YORK

First published 2005
by Routledge
2 Park Square, Milton Park, Abingdon, Oxon OX14 4RN

Simultaneously published in the USA and Canada
by Routledge
270 Madison Ave, New York, NY 10016

Routledge is an imprint of the Taylor & Francis Group

© 2005 Martin Perry

Typeset in Baskerville by Wearset Ltd, Boldon, Tyne and Wear
Printed and bound in Great Britain by MPG Books Ltd, Bodmin

British Library Cataloguing in Publication Data
A catalogue record for this book is available from the British Library

Library of Congress Cataloging in Publication Data
A catalog record for this book has been requested

ISBN 0-415-33962-6

Contents

Tables

Boxes

Preface

In my youth, I lived in Workington in the north-west of England, a community that today would be known as a business cluster had its economic specialization survived. During the 1960s and 1970s, Workington was still an iron and steel town. About a century before, a steelworks had been relocated from Sheffield to take advantage of West Cumbria's supplies of iron ore, coal and port access. The town's iron and steel works could claim to have supplied many of the world's railways with track. I caught the rump end of this prosperity. Investment in railway infrastructure was well past its peak, the iron ore had been exhausted and the coal industry reduced to a single colliery that closed in 1986. As a schoolboy, this economic demise was less important than its reflection on the soccer field. Over a decade, as a die-hard fan of 'Workington Reds', I witnessed the town's professional football club slide from the heights of the Third Division to the bottom of the Fourth Division before being ejected to the semi-professional and amateur leagues. Standing on a rain-swept, barren terrace with a few hundred other fans hoping for a sudden change of fortune is an enduring memory of living in a cluster town.

This background did not produce a lifelong ambition to write about business clusters but it does leave a legacy when considering the claims made for encouraging local economic specialization. During the 1970s and 1980s, Workington was just one of many older industrial areas in Britain that were finding adjustment from past specialization to a new economy difficult. At school, for example, I was introduced to the idea of 'category D' villages. These were the former coal-mining settlements in north-east England that planners designated as being beyond the least chance of revival and so best encouraged to depopulate as rapidly as possible. In their case, public efforts to liquidate communities seemed to help their survival if only in stimulating resistance to the planner's blueprint. As a town of close to 30,000, Workington was forced to search for new activity. At one stage, plans were developed to designate land for high-risk chemical plants. That project failed to win approval but further down the coast another cluster helped bring much needed employment: the

Sellafield nuclear-fuel-processing plant. It also brought many other impacts and another perspective on how clusters can operate. In a community chronically dependent on its employment, local support was gained for activities that many suggest have been environmentally damaging and a source of fatal public-health risks. A more balanced economy than West Cumbria may have been in a better position to enforce upgrading of the plant's operation, if not its closure.

Both Sellafield and Workington (under its local-government district name of Allerdale) appear in a recent UK government map of business clusters (a study reviewed in Chapter 3), although only the former as a full cluster. The mapping of clusters was motivated by the belief that localized concentrations of industrial specialization aid business competitiveness. This book is motivated by the belief that such a claim, which is repeated widely, is not yet proven. In more recent years, I have lived in New Zealand where cluster advocacy is also well established. As with many other countries where enthusiasm for clusters runs high, the influence of the Harvard business professor and consultant Michael Porter has been strong. He was hired first by New Zealand's trade promotion agency for guidance on how they could most effectively engage with industry. Using his standard conceptual framework for assessing national competitiveness, he encouraged policy makers to give attention to clusters of related activity rather than individual industries. These clusters did not have to be concentrated in a particular locality but interest in discovering cases where this happened was stimulated. The Porter study itself identified a cluster of seafood activity around Nelson (in the north of the South Island) as New Zealand's best developed business cluster.

Following Michael Porter's ideas, a Nelson Seafood Industry Cluster Group was set up in 1991 to consciously exploit the advantages of being a cluster. In a research project not specifically dealing with clusters, I had the opportunity to review how the cluster was developing. The views collected revealed a project that was getting variable levels of support. Comments made by a chief executive of one of the larger fishing companies located in Nelson reflected one perspective:

> When the cluster proposal was announced we were interested because a cluster exists and is an important aspect of being in Nelson. [Our] operations are totally dependent on local services and infrastructure ... without whom this would not be the deep-sea fishing capital of the South Pacific. Within the cluster relationships work well, there is mutual interdependence ... This has not just been a case of tendering out services but also building up preferred providers and working with them for mutual advantage with long-term contracts.
>
>   At the same time, for [us] cooperation is essentially about national initiatives and relationships ... Geographical boundaries are not

important to cooperation. We have seen some opportunities for strengthening the cluster ... [but we] have several location options where there is spare capacity and do not need extra capacity in Nelson.

The cluster functions without being given a label. The cluster project has made no difference to the way [we] operate ... there is nothing the public sector can do to support the cluster ... it is a matter of good commercial relationships.

(in Perry 2001: 92–3)

This ambiguous perspective came from a company that could land and process fish in several New Zealand ports. It had different priorities to those companies based entirely in Nelson. Elsewhere in the Nelson community, 'stakeholders' in the cluster had expectations for dialogue with and access to businesses in the cluster. These expectations were problematic for the seafood companies. The sector has a poor image among many in the community, due to environmental concerns, the impacts of onshore processing and a reputation for low-status employment. The use of foreign crews and chartering of foreign vessels are further sources of resentment. Companies may understandably prefer a low profile in the community and not to promote Nelson's status as the South Pacific's 'seafood capital'. In contrast, stakeholders have had their expectations raised about the benefits that will accrue to them. They point out that there is no 'shopfront' for the industry such as a fish market or distinctive local seafood cuisine and no integration with tourism, organic foods or arts and crafts producers that are also an important part of the Nelson economy. A casual visitor, for example, is likely to remain ignorant of Nelson's importance as a seafood centre. Modern fishing methods and marketing do not generate the landscapes associated with traditional fishing ports but 'stakeholders' accuse seafood companies of being unwilling to provide opportunities.

These observations collected in the context of a particular type of cluster were an encouragement to take a larger look at the advocacy of business clusters. This book seeks to do that without promoting a particular definition of clusters. Rather its intent is to examine the proposition that there is a distinct advantage from business locating in close proximity to other businesses with which it shares the same specialization or is linked to in some significant way. This interpretation of clusters has encouraged policy attention and is the one that is given priority for this reason. At various times I have been attached to university departments of urban planning, land economy, geography, public policy and management. Reflecting this diverse background, the book offers a multidisciplinary perspective, aiming to avoid narrow theoretical arguments and communicate as widely as possible to persons wishing to examine the evidence that there is advantage in clustering business activity.

The book was written during the challenge of a new appointment teaching contemporary management and advanced business research methods to management students. I am very grateful for the patience of colleagues in the Department of Management and Enterprise Development, Massey University (Wellington) in accommodating my distractions. In this regard, particular thanks are due to Associate Professor Andrea McIlroy for allowing me time to complete this project.

Abbreviations

BIPIK	Program Pembinaan dan Pengembangan Industri Kecil [Project for Guidance and Development of Small Industry]
CEO	Chief Executive Officer
DTI	Department of Trade and Industry
FDA	Food and Drug Administration
ICT	information and communications technology
IT	information technology
ISTAT	National Institute of Statistics
MAR	Marshall–Arrow–Romer
MNC	multinational corporation
NBVC	non-broadcast visual communications
OECD	Organization for Economic Cooperation and Development
PTO	public telecommunications operator
SIC	standard industrial classification
SIMA	Surgical Instrument Manufacturers' Association
SME	small and medium-sized enterprise
TTWA	travel-to-work area

1   Introduction

The wave of interest in the possible advantage of business clusters has promoted interest in some well-known places as well as bringing attention to some unfamiliar ones. Dalton, Georgia in the United States is among the lesser-known places that has gained a new prominence. It figured in a story that was included in Paul Krugman's (1991a) introduction to his ideas about new economic geography. It has frequently since appeared as one of the places claimed to show how businesses that cluster with their industry peers can outshine those who remain as loners or who reside among unrelated enterprise. Krugman's interest in Dalton was to illustrate how a random event could kick-start a cluster. Once a place had started to move towards an industry specialization he could use economic theory to explain why more businesses should join that activity and squeeze out unrelated activity. The source of the initial push towards domination by a single activity was a gap in the theory filled by pointing to the possibility of random events. In this case, the making of a bedspread in 1895 by Catherine Evans, a young woman living close to Dalton.

The bedspread was made using a traditional technique that had gone out of fashion. The finished item was admired and more were asked for. To meet demand, Catherine Evans taught 'candlewicking' to others and then started to apply it to related products such as mats and bathrobes. Over 20 years after the first bedspread, the Evans Manufacturing Company was formed and sales expanded including an order from a leading department store in Atlanta. Production remained with home-based workers whose numbers had grown to around 10,000 in the 1930s, helped by the need for additional income during the Depression years. Factory production took over as machinery to do the 'tufting' developed. The bedspreads sold throughout North America but Georgian-made ones retained a status. From the 1930s, completed bedspreads drying on clotheslines visible from the Dalton–Cartersville highway led to the area becoming famous as Bedspread (or Peacock, from the most popular pattern) Alley. In the 1950s, tufting machinery began to be applied to carpet making, the product with which Dalton is now associated.

In 2002, the Dalton-based Carpet and Rug Institute estimated that

90 per cent of the carpet produced in the USA is tufted. The link back to the 1895 bedspread is even stronger given the Institute's calculation that 80 per cent of carpet sold in the USA comes from mills located within 65 miles of Dalton. Cluster enthusiasts usually leave the story there, with the implication that this concentration is an example of the benefits clustering brings to an industry. Close scrutiny of the locality's association with carpets has questioned whether Dalton's citizens might not have benefited from a more diversified economy than it has.

In the late 1990s, Dalton–Whitfield County had a population of 86,000 with an unusual employment profile. Close to half the workforce was in manufacturing, compared with a national share of 13 per cent, and around three-quarters of these worked in textile mills (Weinstein 2001). Much of this employment was provided by four companies who were the largest carpet makers in the USA, with three of the next ten largest carpet companies accounting for much of the rest. The popularity of carpets as a domestic floor covering has been dropping and this is reflected in declining returns to carpet makers. The Carpet and Rug Institute reports that from 1965 to 2002, the price of carpets in the USA rose by an overall average of 90 per cent, around half the income growth obtained by new car makers and less than a third of that for all commodities. The expected reaction in a 'mature' industry is ownership consolidation to maximize economies of scale and to rationalize production capacity. True to this, Dalton is now a big mill town with a share of the national industry that reduces if employment rather than output data are examined. In 2001, around 50,000 people were employed nationwide in carpet and rug mills (US Census Bureau 2002) of which, based on Weinstein (2001), no more than a fifth might be around Dalton.

Depictions of business clusters are usually coupled with images of large numbers of information sharing, innovative and highly competitive small enterprises. In contrast, Dalton has been described as a place controlled by a 'conservative power structure [that] has been focused more on hoarding the workforce for employment in the low-skill carpet industry than targeting resources toward upgrading the region's human capital' (Weinstein 2001: 340). In order to keep its carpet mills operating with their low pay and unpleasant working conditions, it has been necessary to recruit workers from far away. Meanwhile, opportunities to diversify the economy have not been taken, one sign of this being that the local community college had been restricted to vocational courses of no more than two years' duration. Reviewed in this light, the interpretation of Dalton as chance event leaves a large jump between the craft of bedspread making and the mass production of carpets. Dalton's association with carpets is more than an accident. Proximity to sources of raw material, originally cotton and later synthetics, the transportability of the finished product and the lack of competition for labour have given sound reasons for carpet making to concentrate around Dalton.

A close look at Dalton reveals why careful thought needs to be given before claiming the benefits of promoting business clusters. Clusters can be created through the consolidation of industry ownership as well as the stimulation of new enterprise. Especially in the former case, it may be questioned whether the failure to diversify is the more important economic issue than the specialization achievement.

The so-called Motor Sport Valley in southern England is another locality that has gained attention as a consequence of the revival of interest in clusters. The motor-sport industry in the United Kingdom is concentrated in and near to the Thames Valley west of London. It employs over 50,000 people, most of them highly skilled engineers and designers. In the late 1990s, around three-quarters of the world's single-seat racing cars were designed and assembled in the cluster (Pinch and Henry 1999). Breaking down the making of a Formula One car into four components (design, base, chassis and engine), nine out of 14 racing teams had three or four of these located in Motor Sport Valley. Unlike Dalton, therefore, this case is perhaps an unambiguous illustration of the benefit that clustering can bring but it still raises questions about the significance of the phenomenon.

The example has been researched in the belief that it is typical of other 'new industrial spaces'. To support this claim, a theory of learning that associates business clusters with the accumulation of 'architectural knowledge' has been proposed (Pinch *et al.* 2003). This theory makes a distinction between understanding of the overall significance of a technology and knowledge simply of the 'components' from which the technology is built. Component knowledge is open to anyone to acquire but, according to the motor-sport theorists, architectural knowledge tends to be acquired collectively among participants in a cluster. They illustrate this by the way designers in Motor Sport Valley became expert in aerodynamics while the Italian-based Ferrari team concentrated on engine power. The emphasis on aerodynamics proved to be the better choice but when this became apparent it was not easy to imitate. The components of aerodynamics could be grasped but not the full implications for car design without joining the cluster. Consequently, it is said, Ferrari located a design office within the valley and starting recruiting engineers from competitors with the insight that they were missing. Given that the office only remained open for a short period, the barriers to accumulating architectural understanding might be considered low, but not according to Pinch *et al.* (2003), even though the current world Formula One champion Michael Schumacher drives for Ferrari rather than a cluster-based team.

This cluster story is interesting but it may overlook that motor sport is not a 'normal' business. Cars are produced for races that are conducted against a uniform set of rules wherever the race takes place. A race in a tropical country such as Malaysia may have to contend with different weather conditions than encountered in Europe but such differences do not require design expertise to be located close to each race track. Design and construction teams can stay in one place while racing occurs around the globe. The appearance of the cluster has also to be seen as an outcome of the extensive regulation of car racing. Regulation produces the duplication of activity across race teams rather than the consolidation of ownership that would arise if cars were produced for the open market. For example, to prevent domination by one manufacturer, each team has to produce its own chassis (Pinch and Henry 1999). Neither are teams under much pressure to minimize on cost, so there is no pressure to relocate to where business costs would be lowest. Sponsors are generous and more motivated to see their logo on a winning team rather than to improve the efficiency of car racing. Indeed, for some teams at least it seems that there are no fixed budgets to constrain engineering operations (Pinch and Henry 1999: 819). Since cost savings arising from the proximity of buyers and suppliers are the usual way that economists seek to explain clustering (Chapter 5), the special conditions associated with motor-car racing are a challenge to standard theories of clustering. The importance of architectural knowledge was claimed to fill that explanatory void.

The shifting advantage between vertically integrated and disintegrated approaches to production is an aspect of Motor Sport Valley that perhaps does represent a general experience. England's current dominance of the motor-sport industry was at the expense of Italian companies who dominated up to the 1950s through companies such as Ferrari, Alfa Romeo and Lancia. The Italian companies were vertically integrated operations that built cars exclusively for their own team (Pinch and Henry 1999). The English industry includes scores of small companies that supply components to competing teams. This shift became viable in the context of the sport being overtaken by innovation and design modifications. Where technology is continuously changing it is hard for an individual company to keep pace in all areas, providing opportunities for independent suppliers linked to their own networks of specialist expertise. A complex question then becomes whether it is the industrial structure that generates the innovation or whether it is a structure that works within a particular context of innovation. Some credit for driving innovation must be given to the many small high-tech companies feeding the industry but peculiarities of the industry cannot be overlooked. Innovation is regulated by the specifications set by racing regulators which helps keep the industry within reach of small enterprises. As well, much innovation involves the application of technologies developed outside of motor sport. Arguably these conditions provide the context for Motor Sport Valley's success not the particular model of industrial organization that it represents.

Finland is another location that has gained attention from the presence of a cluster, although in this case a company (Nokia) is more widely recognized than the region which started the cluster (Tampere, or Pirkenmaa).

This case is associated with telecommunications equipment manufacturing and avoids the uncertainties that arise with activity not in the mainstream economy. Finland's success in building an ICT cluster has been interpreted using the cluster analysis proposed by Michael Porter, the single most influential cluster guru and seen by many as chiefly responsible for evangelizing policy makers to clusters (Martin and Sunley 2003). As well as illustrating Porter's approach, the case can indicate why it can be wrong to attribute causality to cluster attributes as Porter's methods tend to encourage.

At the end of the 1990s, ICT manufacturing accounted for around 7 per cent of Finland's GDP (Paija 2001). When software supply and services bundled with hardware are added, the cluster became of even greater importance. Over half the cluster measured by turnover or exports was accounted for by Nokia and overall Finland had the highest level of export specialization on telecommunications among industrial economies. In Porter's diamond model, local conditions shape international competitiveness mainly through four attributes:

- Factor conditions, such as a specialized labour pool, specialized infrastructure, and sometimes selective disadvantages that drive innovation.
- Home demand, or demanding local customers who push companies to innovate, especially if their tastes or needs anticipate global or local demand.
- Related and supporting industries, internationally competitive local supplier industries who create business infrastructure and spur innovation and spin-off industries.
- Industry strategy, structure, rivalry (intense local rivalry among local industries that is more motivating than foreign competition) and a local 'culture' which influences attitudes within individual industries to innovation and competition.

Finland's success in telecommunications has been seen to fit these conditions (Paija 2001). Factor conditions were provided by the liberalization of the capital market in the 1980s that allowed venture capital and foreign investment into the industry, providing resources for high-risk investment and expensive capital equipment. Government actions may also be seen to be part of the factor conditions. Unlike many countries, the Finnish telecommunications equipment market had always allowed competition and up to the 1980s had been dominated by foreign manufacturers. The Telecommunications Services Act 1987 was a further important liberalization. It took regulatory control away from the public telecommunications operator (PTO) that had opposed granting a mobile communications licence to a private operator. Demand conditions are present from the high penetration of mobile telephones. At the end of the 1990s, a fifth of households relied solely on mobile communications as one indicator of the way that the home market provided technology developers with a fruitful base for product and service experimentation. Supporting and related industries grew up to support the emerging specialization, focusing on highly customized inputs and allowing standard parts to be imported. Nokia is estimated to have had 300 first-tier high-technology partnerships with firms in Finland. With respect to the final diamond component, Paija (2001) does not emphasize intense firm rivalry as a feature of the cluster. Mobile-phone production started in Finland in the 1970s with four competitors including Nokia. By the early 1980s, two had been bought out by Nokia and the third by Ericsson, the Swedish telecommunications conglomerate (Maskell *et al.* 1998).

Even were the diamond completed, such rationalization does not explain how these mutually reinforcing attributes came about. Looking at the larger Nordic participation in telecommunications, a particular technological and regional context needs to be acknowledged (Maskell *et al.* 1998: 169).

Unusual among high-tech industries, telecommunications equipment evolved from earlier activity based on electro-mechanical technology. Nokia is well known to have once been big in trees and rubber. A more critical aspect of its inheritance was its taking over of a television company (Salora, established 1928), the Finnish Cable Works (Suomen Kaapelitehdas, founded 1917) and the State Electric Works (Valtion Sähköpaja, established 1925) (Paija 2001). Without the ability to draw on these established corporate structures and expertise, it is doubtful the Finnish telecommunications industry would have become as significant as it has. Even so, Nokia has made more use of 'off the shelf' standard technology than its competitors (Maskell *et al.* 1998: 175). This normally makes it easy for imitators to catch you up but it actually turned into a sound strategy. Components got progressively cheaper and plentiful, giving a cost advantage. The capacity to add new models and features gave scope to keep ahead through clever marketing. A further technological context was the way initial limitations holding back interest in other countries were not a disincentive for the Nordic region. The first systems were suited to serving comparatively small numbers of subscribers over large geographical distances. This suited a region with a sparse population and small urban centres.

The regional characteristics working to Nordic advantage were partly in the context of the particular inducements for cross-border cooperation. Among important consequences was the need to set standards for technology still at an early stage of development. Indeed, the launch of the Nordic Mobile Telephone (NMT) system in 1981 is generally taken as the single most decisive contribution to the industry's development. It increased the size of the market for equipment suppliers and gave a platform that Nordic firms further exploited when the GSM standard came into operation in 1992 (Bresnahan *et al.* 2001). Another distinctive component to the story was the need to integrate activity between equipment manufacturers and network operators. In the Nordic region, public–private 'development pairs' were particularly effective. Being small countries, it was not unusual to find strong personal connections between individuals on 'different sides of the table' and it has been argued that this contributed to levels of collaboration that would not easily arise in 'normal' market economies (Maskell *et al.* 1998: 171).

Against this bigger picture, Finland is a reminder not to assume that contemporary business structures explain why the cluster came about. This point has been raised as a weakness in Porter's interpretations of cluster advantage, including by one of his former collaborators Michael Enright (Glasmeier 2000: 567). The diamond model, Glasmeier points out, may provide an *ex ante* explanation of cluster composition but it lacks the ability to isolate characteristics that predict the creative forces which lay behind the formation of successful, integrated regional economies. A similar conclusion was reached and made more simply in a study that compared a sample of 'new Silicon Valleys' (including Finland) with the original Valley. This highlighted that many of the advantages thought to accrue to cluster participants are not able to exist at the outset of a concentration (Bresnahan *et al.* 2001). There are not, for example, other firms around in sufficient numbers to gain mutual advantage from. New clusters emerge as a consequence of 'old economy' attributes such as the sustained investment in education and research rather than 'new economy' attributes such as agglomeration economies (see Chapter 7).

The need to contend with overly optimistic assessments of existing clusters and their ability to sustain growth are a challenge to pinning down the significance of clusters. Any activity showing signs of growth and disproportionate presence in a locality seems capable of being turned into a justification for cluster promotion. Two contrasting assessments of the creative industry in Scotland illustrate the need to get beyond surface impressions. Scottish Enterprise, a government development agency, selected creative industry as one of its cluster projects in the mid-1990s. This followed the agency's recruitment of the Monitor Group, the consultancy firm co-founded by Michael Porter in 1983, to give advice on cluster development in Scotland. A positive assessment of the project is provided by Sölvell *et al.* (2003) following some standard methods employed by cluster enthusiasts. One technique is to draw the cluster boundaries as wide as possible to give an impression of the depth of expertise and particular attachment to place. Thus the contemporary creative industry is linked to Scotland's literary heritage, including the eighteenth-century nationalist poet Robert Burns, the presence of art galleries and museums as well as by drawing in activities as far apart as fashion design, computer games and architecture to augment the core creative industries of film, television and other arts. On this basis, the Scottish creative industries are estimated to contribute 4 per cent of Scottish GDP and provide 70,000 jobs. Added to this is the presence of new opportunities. In this case the emergence of digital media with its potential to 'transform all of the constituent industries' (Sölvell *et al.* 2003: 62). Meetings of representatives of organizations within the broad catchment of the creative sector are said to indicate interest in 'keeping people talking with each other'. Of course, more telling would be evidence further down the track that the talk remains productive.

A contrasting assessment of the creative sector in Scotland is provided by putting it in the context of the United Kingdom as a whole, focusing on activities that can most claim to be considered part of the creative sector and by examining the commitment of key organizations to the locality. Through this lens, the creative sector is small and its economic impact controlled more by national and transnational organizations and government regulation than by localized networks (Turok 2003). At the outset, for example, it is reported that concentration in London is the most striking aspect of the distribution of creative activity in the UK. Major broadcasters, studios, producers, distributors and specialized suppliers have their main base in the capital and key links to other creative activities are through London. The film-production industry in Scotland has had some individual successes but overall the throughput of activity remains too unstable to sustain the specialized services required for consistent quality. The number of foreign film productions is a misleading impression of creative activity. In some years, most are 'Bollywood' productions that make little use of local crews or facilities being drawn to Scotland simply to use 'Victorian buildings and parks as backdrops for song and dance routines' (Turok 2003: 557). Indigenous productions rely largely on public funding and often fail to get cinema or video release, meaning no reinvestment takes place. Television has had more impact than film production but involves organizations with centralized control. Public-sector regulation has been more important in influencing activity conducted in Scotland than local institutions or advantages. National television broadcasters based in London have been under pressure to diversify the location of companies that they commission work from. This has resulted in some inward investment from companies seeking to pick up non-London programme quota. Turok says that some local companies resent the newcomers although others are optimistic that they may help to improve the labour pool.

Under close inspection, Scotland's creative sector becomes less of a localized cluster and more of a satellite location for national organizations. In other cases policy makers may succeed in identifying a cluster but still mistake their ability to influence its development direction. Such is reported to be the case in Barre, Vermont (USA). This small city (population around 10,000) has been claimed as the granite capital of the world since the late nineteenth century. It is located above extensive granite deposits that in the late 1990s were mined by around 60 companies with many of the rest of the town's businesses supplying transport, machinery or equipment repair services to the miners. Most of the businesses have been in family ownership for generations. The town's specialization has been losing market share but, unlike Dalton, residents had little desire to see diversification. The stone industry paid good wages and the town was free of major crime. Officials and some industry leaders in Barre turned to cluster thinking for help to revive growth while remaining a granite town (Kotval and Mullin 1998: 314). Strategies adopted including the relaxation of zoning controls, more effort to ensure infrastructure and land was available for business growth, keeping taxes down, regulation to require the use of granite in all Vermont public buildings and encouragement for education and banking institutions to focus on the industry's needs. None of these strategies brought the desired upgrading of the stone industry away from comparatively low-value rough-cut stone and grave memorials. A key obstacle was that Barre's biggest firm was more inclined to act like a multinational corporation than a home-grown firm (Kotval and Mullin 1998: 315). It is a good citizen, participating in community events and operating a visitor centre, but its business strategies suggest greater interest in remaining the dominant business in the industry rather than in helping to grow the industry as a whole. Without its inclination to join, the effort to lever advantage from the concentration of activity was stymied. The final conclusion then becomes of wider significance: the presence of the elements of an industrial cluster does not automatically increase competitiveness.

Other researchers have pointed to the difference between physical clustering and functional clustering (Oakey *et al.* 2001). Physical clustering exists where businesses locate in proximity to each other without any functional linkages between them and without deriving any special benefit from their location. In this case, there is 'concomitance' in where firms locate but the presence of other firms plays little part in the reason for being there. Functional clustering arises where firms gain some benefit from being close to each other and these benefits explain why the co-location occurs. Against much of the reason for cluster enthusiasm, physical clustering is argued to be particularly prevalent among high-technology activities. In practice, these activities comprise a mix of often technologically sophisticated but functionally heterogeneous enterprises (Oakey 1995). Politicians and planners tend to see these activities as a single industry but in reality there is little in common between, say, a high-tech electronics company and a high-tech pharmaceutical company. As Oakey *et al.* (2001) investigate in the case of the non-broadcast visual communications (NBVC) sector (communications organizations utilizing Internet, multimedia, video conference and related media) in southern England there can even be much diversity within particular high-tech activities. Consequently, although NBVC firms are frequently clustered the benefits obtained from this are often minor.

Clustering arose partly from the frequency with which firms in the study had 'spun out' of some common research centre or other organization. It is a common assumption that these origins induce functional clustering, through linkages between the spun-off firms, the incubator organization or other local enterprises. In the NBVC sample, spin-outs did show a preference to remain close to their home organization but this was not because of functional ties. Whatever their origins, new enterprises like to stay close to home (see Chapter 3). The main cluster benefit can be that firms accumulating around the same location help to increase the availability of relevant labour-market skills. Aside from this, personal considerations were an influence on the origins of physical clusters. Common perceptions exist about desirable home and work locations and these help explain why clustering occurred. Moreover there is no reason to think that personal preferences coincide with the most economically efficient locations.

It should not be surprising that functional clustering can be weak among high-tech small firms as the inputs and outputs on which they rely are frequently of international origin and destination (Hendry *et al.* 2000; Oakey *et al.* 2001: 403). Reflecting on this, the present enthusiasm for clusters appears similar to the claims made for science parks in the 1980s. Influenced mainly by the concentrations of new enterprise in proximity to Stanford University in Silicon Valley and Massachusetts Institute of Technology in Boston, it was assumed that a functional connection caused the co-location of enterprise and university. Academic staff moved out of university to set up a company near by to maintain ongoing links with the university. This was taken up in the science-park model, offering business space near to universities to help high-tech ventures flourish by facilitating linkages to a university. Subsequent research revealed that science parks in the UK were best viewed as high quality real-estate projects, attractive to firms employing graduates but who rarely had significant contacts with their university neighbour (Massey *et al.* 1992). In the UK, the poor outcome was accentuated by the weak track record of academics becoming entrepreneurs. Interestingly in the USA, encouraging firms to locate around universities has been shown to slow down enterprise formation by academics as it gives the option of being a consultant to or director of an existing business (Chapter 3).

These six cases illustrate the general theme of this book. The growing identification of clusters does not of itself indicate universal trends are affecting the organization and location of business activity. Neither does the existence of a cluster indicate that a particular set of advantages are being gained by its participants. Of course, a need to recognize diversity has already been acknowledged by people who study clusters. As discussed in Chapter 4, there have been many attempts to develop typologies that distinguish clusters in terms of their enterprise profile (such as the balance of large or small firms), the types of linkages between cluster participants (including whether they exist at all) and the extent to which the cluster promotes competition or cooperation among its members. These classifications have sometimes been informed by investigation of particular cases (Markusen 1996; Coe 2001) but typically they are derived from theories that assume uniform processes are at work. This book seeks to encourage more extensive investigation of cluster experiences as the basis for theory building.

What is a cluster?

The case studies in the introduction assume that clusters are associated with a concentration of activity in a specific locality. Other conceptions of clustering are possible but this is a frequently understood interpretation, although clearly it needs elaboration to know how to determine when a cluster exists as compared with lesser forms of concentration. At the outset it should be stressed that this book does not seek to promote a particular definition of clusters. Rather the intent is to examine the proposition that there is a distinct advantage from business locating in close proximity to other businesses of the same specialization, connected through buyer–supplier linkages or through the use of common inputs. This is one interpretation of clusters that is significant because it encourages policy attention on promoting local economic specialization. It narrows the discussion compared with all the ways that clustering might be viewed as existing but it remains a problematic interpretation to examine because there are no agreed ground rules to know when a cluster exists.

To explain the focus of this book, it is first helpful to distinguish ways that the term cluster is applied and then consider how a cluster might be identified. The discussion of clusters can be confusing as there are at least four different perspectives on what an interest in clusters implies. These are not watertight categories but underlying any particular discussion one of these perspectives is usually dominant:

- *Cluster as a relative condition*: at the simplest level a cluster may simply be taken as a locality that has a relatively specialized economy or that contains a relatively high concentration of a particular industry or both. As summarized in Chapter 3, there are many studies that adopt this approach and simply rank locations according to their various degrees of economic concentration or diversification and take those localities at the top (or bottom) as clusters. This approach is one adopted by economists and has been applied in trying to determine whether relatively specialized cities outperform relatively diversified cities. Researchers taking this approach may not be overly concerned with restricting the search for specialization to a particular geographical area. If there are impacts from specialization, the reasoning is that they should be identified at any scale. The key thing is to be transparent and use data and methods that allow comparison among studies, even if this means that what is measured only approximates to the subject of interest.

- *Clusters as a particular location condition*: this perspective perceives clusters as a distinct industrial geographic grouping that has the capacity to obtain an advantage over alternative groupings of economic activity. From this perspective comes the need to 'nail time' the particular parameters of a cluster or at least to specify some minimum requirements. The value of a relative indicator is doubted partly because being the most specialized locality may not merit inclusion as a cluster if a threshold is not exceeded. Similarly, a low ranking may overlook clusters that exist at a finer geographic scale than that used in the ranking. The minimum requirement of a cluster is a scale with the potential to give advantages over more isolated firms. The maximum requirement is a scale that facilitates the attraction of resources that help firms produce efficiently and that can help individual firms optimize their individual activities. Translating this range into clusters that can be mapped remains a challenge, although people may vary in their assessment of the precision that needs to be aimed for. Similarly, while some argue for the need to keep searching for evidence that clusters offer advantage over other location patterns, others are convinced sufficient evidence exists already to confirm the advantage.

- *Clusters as a high performing economy*: a cluster is a locality where companies are locked together in various forms of interdependence, like organisms in a biosphere. Businesses compete with each other for market share, employees and resources, even more vigorously than those outside a cluster. At the same time, businesses rely on each other. Through their collective presence and willingness to cooperate with each other, information, skills and knowledge of their particular sector rises above the norm. As clusters grow, they begin to interact with the communities within which they are situated. Local universities and specialist industry associations become involved in providing specialist training and technical research. The critical mass of expertise makes a cluster greater than the sum of its parts and much more than merely a concentration of activity. Whereas the previous perspective struggles with the need to define cluster boundaries, when clusters are viewed as high-performing economies the boundaries are set simply by the area occupied by high performers.

- *Clusters as research strategy*: this interest in clusters denotes an approach to understanding business competitiveness rather than an interest in a particular form of economic geography. Clusters may exist at any geographical scale, from a single city to a country as a whole or even a group of neighbouring countries. Clusters vary in their state of development, their composition and geographical boundaries. Defining clusters and drawing cluster boundaries is a creative process unified only by the perceived importance of examining groups of interdependent businesses rather than individual enterprises or single industries. An interest in clusters is first and foremost an interest in a way of analysing the industrial landscape to reveal the linkages between businesses and between businesses and supporting institutions. The interdependencies are not limited to formal trading connections and so are only revealed partially through buyer–supplier linkages. Other forms of interdependence, such as a common labour market need or shared business-related local institutions, may be shown through the tendency for two activities to locate typically in proximity to each other. Clusters can be localized in a particular region within a national economy, and close physical proximity may assist a high-performing cluster but this will depend on the form that the interdependencies take.

This book is most affiliated with the second of these four perspectives: clusters as a particular location condition. Of the other perspectives, this book most disputes the idea of clusters as a high-performing economy. The identification of a model of cluster organization based on existing exemplar clusters is a worthwhile endeavour if the objective is to seek to identify any characteristics in common between high-performing localities. Chapter 7 includes a review of one such study in the context of an evaluation of the policy significance of exemplar clusters. That discussion stresses the challenges to replicating the experience of clusters such as Silicon Valley, partly as a consequence of the multiple advantageous conditions that were behind its emergence as a leading location of information technology innovation. As well, from the perspective of trying to identify a cluster model, the difference between cluster experiences is stressed especially in relation to the technology characteristics of the activity generating a cluster. Italy's industrial districts have frequently been taken as another cluster role model but, as shown in Chapter 4, a close look at these districts reveals a diversity of experience. Indeed it has been shown that the characteristics usually applied to a cluster exist among a minority of districts. Claiming a set of attributes particular to a cluster simplifies a complex range of experiences and downplays the interesting task of revealing the many different ways that clusters influence business behaviour. In short, this book is motivated by the perception that more investigation of a range of cluster experiences is needed before promoting clusters as a particular mode of business behaviour.

The perspective of clusters as a particular location condition encourages investigation of what, if anything, happens when activity is geographically concentrated. This approach relies on being able to produce a way of defining a cluster that enables their experiences to be contrasted with those of lesser forms of concentration. This is a challenge that has so far left a significant weakness in the discussion of clusters to the point where some researchers doubt the value of trying to proceed (Martin and Sunley 2003). As discussed in Chapter 3, the definitional challenge is reduced by regarding a cluster as simply a location input without assuming organizational consequences that have to be present. Location inputs such as a certain level of activity concentration within a specified geographic area are relatively straightforward to identify, although some complications need to be recognized. On the other hand, the assumed outcomes of clustering are more problematic to measure than are the concentration and location inputs to clustering.

Incorporating some measure of interdependence between cluster participants has especially contributed to vague conceptions of clusters. Accommodating interdependence raises the difficulty of identifying clusters for three reasons (Feser and Luger 2003: 13). First, business interdependence is potentially manifested through a wide variety of conduits and spatial scales and to varying degrees of intensity. It is not clear, for example, whether a threshold of interdependence needs to be crossed and, if so, what this would be and whether it could be measured. Second, simply by being co-located businesses are likely to share some local resources and possibly markets. This interdependence may not have influenced the original location decision or be significant in keeping a business in the location. Whether that interdependence is regarded as significant requires a judgement about whether actual evidence of interdependence is more or less important than evidence of potential for it. Third, dilemmas surrounding what is to be measured are confounded by their resistance to resolution through empirical research. Even in theory it is doubtful that many ambiguities can be resolved.

However the particular location attributes are defined, there is a need for more research to determine how clusters should be identified and what their significance to business behaviour is. Chapter 3 provides some guidance on how this should be done, working from the perspective that incremental investigation of differing degrees of activity concentration and their impacts ought to gradually reduce uncertainty about the appropriate starting points for cluster investigations. This is not to suggest that the aim is to restrict the cluster concept to a specified geographical size or scale. Rather that research can provide justification for narrowing the application of the term and provide understanding of what forms of clustering process are most likely to be observed at a particular level of clustering, among what types of enterprise. A further source of evidence can be obtained from studies that view clusters as a relative condition. The differentiation is that viewing clusters as a particular location condition implies the need for studies that specifically differentiate cluster aggregations from other degrees of concentration. This includes a need to consider the organizational characteristics of a cluster such as the relative participation of large and small firms, locally owned and foreign-owned firms. A heavy reliance on official statistics or other secondary data is typical of studies adopting a relative measure of clustering whereas more intensive studies, including original data collection, are needed to pin down the significance of clustering.

The final perspective of clusters as a research strategy has merit in its own right as an approach to revealing some of the interconnections between businesses in separate industries. As noted above, it does not start with a focus on learning the reasons for or consequences of clustering in the sense of a particular form of geographic concentration. The research focus is on locating linkages between activity in separate industries and on using these linkages as a template for comparing the profile of activity at different spatial scales (Chapter 4). The perspective of this book is that starting with a focus on clusters as a particular location condition will reveal whether the stress on interdependencies across industries is justified. As noted above, co-location implies some common dependencies between neighbouring enterprises but investigation of clusters is required to determine their significance. Priority to location rather than method may also be justified by the strong policy interest in understanding what benefits might be obtained from seeking to promote a cluster within a local economy. Moreover, the stress on clusters created through cross-sector independencies contrasts with the tendency for many identified clusters to be based on comparatively narrow specializations, largely confined with one or few similar industries.

Beyond viewing clusters as a particular location condition, this book does not seek to promote a particular definition of a cluster. Rather, precise definition should be seen as an outcome of further investigation of the extent of advantage for business by locating in close proximity to other businesses with the same specialization, buyer–supplier linkages or at least some common inputs. This simplifies the discussion of clusters to a specific proposition and differentiates it from assessments that assume a universal trend for business to form clusters exists and that see a uniformity of experience among clusters. As discussed in Chapter 2, among social scientists there has been a tendency to favour packaged explanations of change that assume all-embracing new models of organizational practice are taking hold (Wood 2002). This book favours an explanation of clusters that recognizes an individual context to their formation and significance. Similarly, this book uses cluster as a neutral term, denoting a spatial concentration in which firms have potential to gain from their mutual presence but that does not automatically denote advantage actually arises. A cluster may be a concentration of the weak, a legacy of some historic circumstance, a residual consequence of activity concentrating among fewer, larger establishments, a follow-the-leader concern not to miss out, or simply a common desire to locate near to facilities or markets.

This diversity is especially evident when looking at the experience of clusters in developing countries (Chapter 6).

Plan of the book

The next part of the book contrasts efforts to simplify explanations for clustering with evidence of the need to understand cluster experiences in the context of their particular industry, market and technological context. Chapter 2 commences this review by looking at evidence about the overall significance of business concentration, drawing on economy-wide data and case studies of a set of clusters in Sweden. It then considers three attributes that underlie most accounts that claim clustering is of increasing importance: trust, localized learning and externalization. Each of these attributes is linked to arguments that suggest a significant watershed in business behaviour has been crossed. That perspective is contrasted with the outline of a contingent perspective on clusters. Chapter 3 examines the role of agglomeration economies which lie at the heart of many accounts of business clusters. This discussion points out the difficulty of interpreting evidence of agglomeration economies but suggests most evidence points to the benefits of local economic diversity rather than specialization. Chapter 4 examines alternative ways that clusters may be identified and recommends input methods based on measures of a locality's economic concentration and specialization. Chapter 5 examines how new economic geography has approached the study of clusters and argues that its focus on regularities in economic location offer limited insight into the diversity of local experiences. Chapter 6 examines the case of clusters in developing countries where clusters often involve a more extreme form of geographical concentration than found in high-income economies. Chapter 7 considers the policy implications in the light of the appraisal offered in the book and by drawing on cluster-promotion experiences in New Zealand. The book concludes with a summary of three main responses that have been offered to the competing claims about clusters: clusters as chaos; clusters as art and science; and clusters as a contribution to diversity.

2 Approaching clusters

Recent decades have seen the increasing advocacy of prescriptive packages of managerial practices (Wood 2003). These packages are presented as all-embracing concepts that offer a fresh way of thinking in response to challenges that demand urgent action. The best-known packaged prescriptions have included world-class manufacturing (Schonberger 1986), 'lean production' (Womack *et al.* 1990), integrated manufacturing (Dean and Snell 1991) and 're-engineering' (Hammer and Champy 1993). More recently, following the Malcolm Baldrige National Quality Award, various models of 'business excellence' have become popular, modelled on the award's evaluation criteria (Dale 2002). Business clusters have become the local economic policy equivalent of such packaged solutions. For policy makers seeking to protect local economies, clusters defend against the ravages of globalization. They are presented as a mechanism for 'embedding' enterprise and reducing its inclination to pursue 'weak' competitive strategies based on the pursuit of the lowest input costs (Hudson 1999). For business managers, operating within a cluster facilitates 'rapid best practice improvement' and proliferates opportunities for 'distinctive competitive positions' (Porter 2000: 265). Indeed cluster advocates envisage the creation of seemingly perfect conditions for business growth:

> A concentration of visible rivals encourages the search for ways of competing that are not head on. Niche opportunities overlooked by others can reveal themselves. Ready access to suppliers and partners provides flexibility to configure the value chain in a variety of ways. A more positive-sum form of competition can result when customer choice is widened and different customers are served most efficiently.
>
> (Porter 2000: 265–6)

The tendency to view business as faced with stark choices is a common feature of the packages on offer. Firms can either be flexible or inflexible, a learning or a non-learning organization, quality or cost focused, locked into high- or low-road competition, part of the old economy or part of the new economy, but never, it seems, some blending of the extreme possibilities. Similarly, the relationships between firms are either high trust or low trust; suppliers or customers are either partners or engaged with at 'arm's length'. This form of presentation is encouraged by the perception of business challenged by economy-wide change. Thus much social-science attention on organizational change has sought to identify it as a shift away from Fordist, large-scale, hierarchical bureaucracies of mass production and mass service (see Amin 1994 for a summary of this view). Globalization has become another justification for exaggerating the need for organizational change (Hirst and Thompson 1996).

It is true that around the industrial world organizations have reacted to a similar set of changes in the economic, political and social environment in which they operate but this does not mean that business behaviour has coalesced around the globe (Whitley 1999). Pressures for change include reducing trade barriers between countries, the internationalization of economic activity, rapid technological change associated with the information revolution, the deregulation of markets, privatization and the ending of state monopolies, broadening conceptions of organizational stakeholders, demographic transitions such as ageing populations and changes in consumer demand (Holman and Wood 2003). These diverse pressures are experienced with varying degrees of intensity between countries, industries and businesses. Organizations are being pushed in various directions and only modestly towards increasing homogeneity in organizational practice and learning. The advance of globalization is resisted by national organizational styles that differ in their openness to change (Djelic 1998; Zeitlin and Herrigel 2000). Moreover, common organizational responses are encouraged by social pressures to conform to prevailing business fads (Burke 2002). The growth in mergers and acquisitions and the frequency of corporate downsizing and outsourcing does not necessarily reflect organizational strategies that are not later reversed by a change in fashion.

This chapter makes the case for examining clusters as a product of particular industry, technology and market conditions rather than being representative of a broad transition in business organization. It starts by examining trends in the level of business concentration within geographical clusters. That evidence shows no convincing trend towards clusters, although some limitations of the data and form of analysis do need to be noted. Claims about the importance of clustering tend to come more from case studies of individual clusters than empirical data relating to business location. A profile of clusters in Sweden is drawn upon to represent case-study insights. These case studies were prepared to illustrate clusters thought to be having an impact on business innovation. They have the further benefit of being prepared in the context of a single study, enabling comment on the extent to which they appear to respond to common influences. Three attributes often linked to arguments about the growing importance of clusters are then examined: trust, localized learning and externalization. Finally, the chapter discusses some of the ways that cluster opportunities are contingent upon industry, technology and market conditions.

How frequent are clusters?

A long view of regional specialization has been presented for the USA (Kim 1995). It finds a modest decline occurred from 1860 to 1890, then rose substantially and flattened out during the interwar years. Regional specialization then fell substantially and continuously from the 1930s to 1987. The net outcome was that regions were less specialized at the end of the twentieth century than they were in 1860. Alongside the increased diversity in regional economic structure, industries became more dispersed than originally. These trends were interpreted as showing that the geography of business activity is driven by patterns of resource usage and the pursuit of economies of scale. Typically resource availability has become less constraining on where industry locates, although it can still help explain the relative dispersion of individual industries. Average plant size (measured by employment) in most industries peaked in the 1930s or 1940s and subsequent falls have assisted the dispersion of activity.

Any advantage of being located near to like firms appears to be a minor influence on the distribution of activity. If important industry knowledge 'spills over' from one firm to its neighbour, it might be expected the activities most dependent on knowledge would have a greater propensity to concentrate than less knowledge-sensitive activities. This impact is not detected. Over time, most industries have seen an increase in their proportion of non-production workers and an increase in research and development expenditure. This has not been associated with more spatial concentration or regional specialization. Looking at contemporary industry, activity regarded as high tech tends to be more dispersed than low-tech activity.

The story presented by Kim (1995) is illustrated by changes in the distribution of structural materials used in manufacturing. At the outset of industrialization, the basic structural material was wood and this was available throughout the USA. As markets expanded and structural materials diversified to iron and steel, use close to the source of these manufactured inputs was encouraged as they were expensive to transport. As a consequence, industry activity tended to concentrate and regional specialization tended to increase. More recently, many substitutes for wood and steel have been developed including light metals, alloys, plastics, plywood and particle board. This has diversified the sources of supply and reduced the cost of transporting structural materials. Industrial activity became comparatively widely distributed and regional specialization tended to decline as a result of this.

This long view of industrial location may be seen as too generalized. It applies to the distribution of activity between states in the USA, many of which are larger than the economies of small nations, and considers broadly defined industries (two- and three-digit standard industrial classification level). It might further be argued that there have been significant developments in business location post-1980, partly through the greater diffusion of information and communication technology and the increased intensity of international competition. On the other hand, a similar study focused on the 1970s to early 1990s gives no greater impression of regional specialization accelerating, even with a detailed industry breakdown (four-digit SIC level) and when it compares results for the USA, Sweden and France (Braunerhjelm and Johansson 2003).

One overall finding is that industries tend to keep their same relative level of spatial concentration: activities that were most concentrated at the start are usually the most concentrated at the end of their study period. Typically, it is comparatively low-tech industries that have the highest levels of spatial concentration in the USA and Sweden. Knowledge-intensive activities are more frequently represented among the most spatially concentrated service industries, but services tend to be more dispersed than manufacturing activities. The most concentrated manufacturing industries have become more concentrated but this is linked to a decline in employment. Industries with a growth in employment are less likely to have experienced a strong increase in concentration than ones with declining employment. Comparison between the USA, Sweden and France suggests national conditions affect relative levels of regional specialization. Sweden tends to have the highest level of regional concentration and for its most concentrated industries to differ from those in the USA and France. This difference is put down to Sweden having the greatest share of large firms.

The macro-analysis suggests one possibility that may be of interest to the formation of business clusters. Increased spatial concentration of manufacturing activity is associated with declining employment. This implies mechanisms other than individual plant-level expansion are occurring. The entry of new firms or the relocation of established firms may be favouring a few locations (Braunerhjelm and Johansson 2003: 60).

Innovative clusters in Sweden

Case studies of individual clusters are a contrasting source of evidence to that from economic data analysis. A profile of 13 clusters in Sweden (Box 2.1) gives some opportunity to consider whether the statistical review of industrial location trends may be overlooking cluster formation. That might occur if clusters involve highly specialized activity or involve unusual cross-industry connections. The Swedish case studies have the further benefit of being selected by an expert group appointed to advise the Swedish Business Development Agency (NUTEK) on how to raise the effectiveness of cluster initiatives in regional growth programmes (Hallencreutz and Lundequist 2001). The case studies were selected to give representation to cluster projects in different parts of Sweden linked to traditional and new activities (Hallencreutz and Lundequist 2003: 537).

Box 2.1 Innovative clusters in Sweden

Automotive testing in inland Norrbotten: a cluster comprising members of the Swedish Proving Ground Association located in five settlements. The region's harsh winter climate has given it a role for testing the products of many of the world's leading car makers.

Umeå biotechnology: centred around research-based companies set up by former researchers working in the University of Umeå. Links between individual companies and the university remain stronger than those between companies.

Woodworking in Västerbotten: activity is distributed among smaller clusters centred on a lead firm. One such cluster comprises ten firms, some of whom specialize in components rather than complete products.

Crystal Valley (Dalarna): cluster participants include the Swedish LCD Centre, an industry research institute (www.lcdcenter.com). The largest company, Hörnell International, employs 200 employees and produces around a third of the world's auto-darkening welding lens. Other companies have different product applications of LCD technology.

TIME (Stockholm): a concentration of activities in the telecom, IT, media and entertainment industries creating new activities at the interface of these industries. The cluster has a formal organization involved in industry support initiatives. (www.time.stockholm.se)

IDEA Plant (Eskilstuna): centred around the Department of Information Design and Product Development of Mälardalen University and a formal network organization for sharing new product experience. There were 35 members in 2003. (www.ideaplant.se)

Rockcity (Hultsfred): developed from the town's annual music festival and the town's efforts to support music industry activity. The location of an Industrial Development Centre for the Swedish music industry in Hultsfred boosted the cluster. (www.rockcity.se)

Audiovisual cluster (Fyrbodal): centred on a film resource and production centre that seeks to attract and support film-industry activity in southwest Sweden. (www.filmivast.se)

The Polymer Centre and Cutting Technology Centre (Gnosjö): two clusters each based around industry research centres operating under local company ownership, although seeking to be national technology centres. (www.polymercentrum.se and www.skarteknikcentrum.nu)

The Kingdom of Aluminium (Småland-Blekinge): a membership organization for firms working in the aluminium industry that provides marketing and other services to members. Within the region, particular towns tend to have a particular activity focus but collectively make use of the Aluminium-riket brand. (www.aluminiumriket.com)

Telecomcity (Karlskrona): a cluster built through university and municipal government promotion of the locality's attractiveness to IT companies. The cluster has a membership organization giving ongoing support and developing projects to promote further development of the IT sector. (www.telecomcity.org)

Medicon Valley (Öresund region): a cross-border cluster initiative covering the Greater Copenhagen area and Skåne region in Sweden to promote the area as a centre for pharmaceutical and biotechnology industry. The Medicon Valley Academy provides a membership organization designed to encourage dialogue between hospital, university and industry representatives. (www.mediconvalley.com)

The expert group was established to help regional growth programmes make best use of cluster insight by drawing attention to the 'hallmarks of successful cluster strategies' (Hallencreutz and Lundequist 2001: 9). The selection of case studies was not guided by a specific cluster definition but it suggests that the Sweden's 'world-class' clusters share some common attributes (Box 2.1). Their review does not include statistical evidence about the size and significance of their chosen clusters but three observations are possible from descriptions of the projects, in the report and subsequently (Hallencreutz and Lundequist 2003).

Box 2.2 Features of Sweden's 'world-class' clusters

- Clusters are regionally based in the sense of activity being concentrated in one or more areas, with these local areas being an essential component of the cluster's competitiveness, including a history of association with the cluster activity. Participants are seen to cooperate to break down barriers.
- A cluster is conceptualized as a system of players who create added value by working together – 'a system in which 1 + 1 is 3'.
- A cluster perspective is a process-orientated way of working that aims to better utilize a region's development potential. It should clarify roles and the division of labour in development activity.
- A cluster encompasses multiple industries. Thinking and acting in clusters means encouraging 'dynamic interplay' between companies within a common strategic area of knowledge and between companies and other parties (educators, researchers, regional and municipal authorities).
- A cluster encourages a holistic approach to development promotion, encompassing: (i) a 'regional brand' to attract companies, expertise and capital; (ii) support to activity ancillary to the core businesses, such as providing attractive residential environments and offering work to spouses relocated to the area; (iii) adaptation of the local production environment to the specific focus of the cluster.
- Clusters with the greatest capacity for innovation are seen to possess: (i) companies stimulated by competition with each other and with a capacity for and willingness to invest in strategic business development; (ii) access to specialized labour skills, materials, components and services; (iii) demanding, loyal and trend-sensitive customers; (iv) close links to specialized suppliers, related industries, competent industry organizations and specialized education and research institutes.

Source: Hallencreutz and Per Lundequist (2001)

First, across the clusters a range of business processes appear to be in operation without any consistent drivers. A small cluster of automotive component-testing operations in northern Sweden, for example, exists because of its winter climate. A music-industry cluster came about from the location of a long-running annual music festival. Recognizing the benefits of the annual festival, the municipal government funded a permanent concert hall and office building and supported a number of other ventures to bring music-related activity to the town. In other cases, there can be a large dependence on publicly funded industry initiatives. European Union structural adjustment funds revived a project to promote film production in western Sweden. A separate cluster principally comprises the IDEA Plant that is an offshoot of a university information design and product development department. It aims to assist enterprise growth through its research and consulting activity in the broad area of 'information design'. Universities appear to play a central role in several of the clusters. A biotechnology cluster in Umeå, for example, principally comprises research-based companies started by former university research staff. Its origins are traced to the opening of a microbiology unit in the university during the 1960s. By 2001, the cluster comprised 13 companies of which eight had fewer than five staff. The Telecomcity cluster centred on the city of Karlskrona has been substantially influenced by a new regional university opening a campus in the city which has specialized in IT subjects. The Medicon Valley cluster of biotechnology, health, medical and pharmaceutical expertise was given added significance following the construction of the Öresund Bridge linking Copenhagen and southern Sweden.

Second, clusters can represent marketing projects more than a distinctive pattern of business organization. Medicon Valley, for example, is said to symbolize the ambition to distinguish the Öresund region as one of Europe's strongest and most attractive areas for the pharmaceutical industry (Hallencreutz and Lundequist 2001: 31). 'Copenhagen Capacity' is responsible for marketing the project with a particular focus on attracting foreign biotechnology companies (EU Expert Group on Enterprise Clusters and Networks 2003). Telecomcity has given rise to a membership organization in which the university, municipality and business members make different commitments for mutual advantage. Business members commit to: (i) strive for continued growth by initiating new business areas and identifying emerging markets; (ii) increase expertise and research and development efforts; (iii) support the university's efforts to become an international player in the area of IT and telecommunications. In return, the university commits to maintaining a focus on IT and telecommunications and to participating in the development of the business community. The municipal government commits, among other obligations, to 'offer community service and infrastructure with the right quality and at the right price' as part of its steps to promote an attractive business environment.

The emphasis on formalized membership organizations is another sign of the marketing role of cluster projects. At least eight of the 13 clusters have a cluster organization. Formalization does not need to indicate a high level of member commitment as fees can be modest and mainly significant in assisting the attraction of public funds.

Third, in the expert group's terminology, most of the clusters are not 'round' and this results in a need to draw on national resources for development and innovation. Moreover, some clusters classified as round are acknowledged to be best seen as part of a larger, more complete national concentration of activity. The 'Kingdom of Aluminium' cluster, for example, is included as a round cluster on the basis that most members are 'related in some way' to the aluminium industry. At the same time, the cluster gets 'rounder' when expanded to the larger Swedish steel and material cluster made up of mining, machine, steel and other metal industries (Hallencreutz and Lundequist 2001: 15). A woodworking cluster is said to be among the least round clusters. Members are subcontractors to an assembly plant supplying IKEA, the world's largest furniture retailer with stores in around 30 countries. IKEA's origins included a need to work with suppliers not contracted to other Swedish furniture retailers resulting in the early development of a supply chain stretching outside the Nordic countries (Maskell *et al.* 1998: 102–3).

Overall, the Swedish case studies perhaps say more about the flexibility of the cluster concept than the advantage of a particular mode of business behaviour. It offers a way of marketing new development projects and of giving recognition to well-established business communities.

Cluster theory

The theoretical approaches to the study of clusters are striking in their variety (Newlands 2003). A wide set of arguments are drawn upon to establish what advantages can arise to firms within a cluster, the extent to which these advantages rely on spatial concentration and to determine the balance between competition and cooperation that generates the advantages. Five main theoretical approaches are identified with acknowledgement that individual arguments can appear in more than one approach:

- *Agglomeration theory*: commencing with Marshall (1890; 1927), standard agglomeration theory explains that firms cluster to share a 'commons' of business services, a skilled labour pool and to enable individual specialization. Clusters are viewed as collections of atomistic businesses, connected through market relations rather than deliberate collaboration.
- *Transaction costs and the 'Californian School'*: the impetus to cluster formation starts from changes in market and technological conditions that increase the uncertainty faced by individual businesses and risk of becoming locked into redundant technologies. In response, produc-

tion chains have tended to 'disintegrate' among independent businesses connected through market transactions. Where tacit knowledge and trust are important, the cost of transactions can be minimized through the clustering of activity.

- *Flexible specialization*: unlike standard agglomeration theory, firms are expected to become interdependent through the flexibility of individual firm boundaries and the importance of trust in creating and sustaining collaboration within localized business communities. Firms within networks of trust benefit from the reciprocal exchange of information while being bound by mutual obligations that regulate behaviour. More than transaction-cost minimization, firms in a cluster gain from the transfer of industry intelligence outside formal transactions.
- *Innovative milieux and the GREMI research group*: clustering supports a collective learning process operating through skilled labour mobility, customer–supplier interaction and informal 'cafeteria effects'. Learning goes on through networks of mainly informal contacts in the context of casual and deliberate encounters. Institutions with a formal role in education and training and that influence the willingness to share knowledge can reinforce informal mechanisms.
- *Institutional and evolutionary economics*: technological development is path dependent, involving sequenced steps that give rise to irreversible choices being taken. A spatial dimension exists to these choices where business and institutional dependencies lock a particular business community into a common response. Contemporary clusters can thus be seen as 'accidents of history' arising from fortuitous decisions, although the appearance and ability of reinforcing institutions can give some influence to deliberate action.

Chapter 3 examines the contribution of agglomeration theory to the understanding of clusters. From the other approaches, three underlying processes can be identified that are present to some degree or other: trust, localized learning and externalization. Rather than debate the merits of individual theories, this section reviews the assumptions being made about these processes as a basis for arguing for the relevance of a contingent perspective on clusters.

Trust

An emphasis on non-market forms of interaction, including trust and non-traded interdependencies, distinguishes contemporary discussions of industrial clusters from previous rounds of interest in the possible advantage of keeping business transactions local (Harrison 1992). In essence, it is argued that proximity helps to build trust between businesses and that relations built upon trust are superior to relationships without trust. This is a problematic argument because there is little agreement as to what organizational arrangement makes most use of trust. Some research associates trust with small-firm activity and sees it as less relevant to large business organizations (Malecki and Tootle 1996). In contrast, the growth of big business has been taken as an indicator of higher levels of trust in a society. Only in societies with a prevalence of trust have large corporations with professional management emerged out of pre-existing small-scale family enterprise that otherwise remains stymied by the mistrust of non-kin (Fukuyama 1995).

These alternative viewpoints draw attention to the various ways that trust is produced. Historical perspectives identify a contrast between premodern and modern conditions of trust, reflected in the shift from trust arising from kinship, community and tradition to trust based on abstract systems, involving trust in money and systems of technical expertise (Giddens 1990: 110). Modernization sees an evolution from personal trust, founded on belief, to system trust founded on mutual self-interest and functional interdependence (Luhmann 1988); or from process-based trust, founded on past personal experience, to the development of institutions for professional accreditation and guardianship and the related means of enabling individuals and organizations to assess one another's standing (Shapiro 1987).

Claims about the contemporary importance of trust need to be associated with clear contextual boundaries rather than universal definitions (Rousseau *et al.* 1998). A comparative investigation of buyer–supplier relations in Japan and the UK thus produced a threefold categorization of trust (Sako 1992):

- *Competence trust*: this refers to the confidence that the trading partner will perform their obligations competently and that they have the skills and capacity claimed. High competence trust facilitates, for example, the minimization of goods inspection on delivery as required in the operation of just-in-time inventory systems.
- *Contractual trust*: this form of trust refers to the confidence that specific agreements will be adhered to. Different degrees of contractual trust may exist according to the willingness to accept oral agreements over written ones and the degree of written detail required. The lesser the detail expected in written documents the greater is the trust that both parties can be relied upon to uphold their promises with respect to issues such as delivery dates, product specifications, confidentiality and dispute-resolution procedures.
- *Goodwill trust*: this refers to mutual expectations that both parties have an open commitment to each other as reflected in the willingness to do more than that which has been immediately agreed. In effect this means that there is less emphasis on establishing explicit commitments or defining performance levels than on maintaining an ongoing relation in which both parties are prepared to take initiatives for mutual advantage whilst refraining from opportunistic behaviour.

   Two main questions arise from acknowledging the existence of different types of trust. First, are certain forms of trust superior to other forms as they affect business performance? Claims about the importance of business clusters tend to assume that personalized forms of trust between business are more effective than other ways of securing trust (see, for example, Lever–Tracy 1992; Malecki and Tootle 1996). An alternative viewpoint is that 'functional equivalence' can exist between different ways of securing trust (Box 2.3). Second, can trust be deliberately created such that a more desirable form of trust can be learnt or transferred between places and organizations? The scope for advocating clusters as a business-development strategy depends partly on the answer to this question.

Box 2.3 Functional equivalents for trust and Japanese work methods

If there are 'functional equivalents' to the trust that develops from reciprocal and personal relations the significance of trust is lowered. It implies the same outcome can be achieved in a variety of ways. The presence of functional equivalents has been used to explain the diffusion of Japanese manufacturing to Europe and North America without the transfer of the 'three pillars' of just-in-time manufacturing systems in Japan: lifetime employment, company welfare and seniority-based remuneration.

   Functional equivalents of the three pillars include the capacity of Japanese transplants to: (i) mobilize local political and community support in the context of high unemployment and regional competition for jobs; (ii) employ intensive selection procedures to identify compliant employees; (iii) benefit from political divisions amongst trade unions in an environment of declining union membership; (iv) introduce management-controlled participation techniques such as quality circles and team working as ways to enhance workforce commitment to enterprise goals.

   The extent to which trust can be substituted by instrumental ways of securing workforce commitment is debated (Elger and Smith 1994). The mix of functional equivalent attributes varies between locations where transplants are concentrated. Such variety suggests there is responsiveness to local opportunities rather than a calculated search for equivalence. In this manner, case-study evidence shows that employees in transplants identify traditional aspects of the employment relation such as wages and job security as influences on their commitment rather than any distinctive work environment created by careful design of 'functional equivalents'. Another doubt is that there may be no need for functional equivalents given the more restricted role of transplants than home-country establishments (Dedoussis and Littler 1994). According to this argument, transplants are established to carry out discrete operations and are peripheral to the organization as a whole. Without the same need for participatory and cooperative work relations, any deliberate pursuit of functional equivalent conditions does not mean the level of trust obtained matches that in the home country.

With respect to the superiority of one form of trust over another, there is a case for believing that goodwill trust has advantages. In contexts where trading parties are committed to assist each other, to share information and to avoid self-interested behaviour it would seem that the scope for improvement and innovation is maximized. It would, for example, act against a supplier withholding their knowledge about the performance of their component or of more effective ways it might be designed or used to assist the buyer's operation. The ability to consider long-term as well as immediate returns may further encourage performance that exceeds the minimum required, whether by early delivery, higher quality or some other means of assuring goodwill. The presence of goodwill trust also implies the absence of opportunistic behaviour, the suspicion that a trading partner may deceive or deliberately withhold information that might disadvantage their position in the immediate transaction. Such opportunism is minimized by contractual trust to the extent only that it is possible to specify and enforce preferred behaviours. Where goodwill trust prevails, the commitment to avoid opportunism is open ended (Sako 1992: 39). On the other hand, three considerations need to qualify any claimed superiority of goodwill trust.

First, the promise of goodwill trust is that it will encourage mutual learning and the sharing of expertise in ways that promote improvement and innovation. Obviously this requires that there is scope for such learning to take place. Where a buyer is obtaining a simple standard component or in situations where the buyer's technology is far superior to that of the supplier there may not be much scope or interest in the mutual sharing of information. Second, the gain obtained needs to be assessed against the cost of acquiring the advantage. Goodwill trust emerges through frequent and intensive communication, possibly implying experimentation with alternative candidates selected through exhaustive search processes. Third, the effectiveness of goodwill trust depends on their being a broad stability in the business environment such that there is little risk attached to entering comparatively exclusive forms of relationship. The danger of exclusivity is that the strong commitments to one set of partners forecloses or at least makes harder the option of breaking those links and forming others in response to superior or more appropriate alternatives arising. In brief, the case for goodwill trust requires that at least one of three conditions is satisfied:

- A long-term association can be maintained to pay back the high establishment costs, including stability in the key personnel in the respective organizations since individuals embody much of the trust.
- There is a large gap between the protection from opportunism provided by goodwill trust and the protection provided by other forms of trust.

- The underlying business environment is comparatively stable such that shifts in business partners are not a priority.

The second main question arising from the relative benefits of different kinds of trust concerns the mechanisms which create and sustain trust. While it has been suggested that time and effort will be needed to develop goodwill trust, there is a view that such investment would be ineffective because such trust cannot be manufactured. Rather, it is argued, open-ended trust arises as a product of 'higher' commitments and forms of association through shared familiarity, friendship, moral or religious values (Gambetta 1988). At the same time the attempt to build goodwill by cultivating friendship is stymied by the instrumental motive for the courtship (goodwill for the purposes of business advantage) undermining the attempt to build friendship (Sako 1992: 46). This leads to the conclusion that trust is often a scarce commodity being heavily dependent on the history of relationships in a particular place, the cultural disposition towards cooperation and the extent of commitment to higher goals in society. Such a view has had a strong influence amongst the proponents of business clusters, as seen in interpretations of Italy's industrial districts (Asheim 2000).

The perception of trust as a scarce commodity has helped in establishing a case for clusters as a distinct phenomenon but potentially leaves a problem with respect to the ability to reproduce organizational forms that rely on heightened degrees of trust. On the other hand, it has been claimed that under the right circumstances almost any set of common experiences can form the basis of a culture conducive to business co-operation (Zeitlin 1992: 286–7). Evidence of this has been claimed from the transformations observed in Italy's industrial districts. Whilst often described as localities with a long history of cooperation closer investigation has sometimes revealed intense conflicts (Sabel 1992; Amin 1994). In the case of Prato, for example, Sabel (1992: 228) notes how a modern-day visitor will be advised that trade unions and employers' associations work together, as they always have, but will not be told how 'for almost a decade after a wave of decentralization in the late 1940s, the unions and manufacturers were unable to sign a single collective agreement'. The preference amongst contemporary participants to see a long history of cooperation is indicative of the way present relations inform the interpretation of previous events. Instead of shared identities giving rise to social relations of trust, cooperative configurations are able to reshape identities to that which can be shared (Grabher and Stark 1997: 20).

The possibility of creating trusting business and personal relations in previously mistrusting environments has given rise to the idea of 'studied trust' (Sabel 1992). Where participants have an interest in developing cooperative business relations it is usually possible to obscure any recent history of conflict by reaching back to some prior period or form of cooperation that existed as a precedent for the existence of trust. Studied trust in this view is thus widely accessible. This accessibility is helped by the form of commitment that it is envisaged to give rise to. While partners are obligated to behave loyally in the present, it

> does not obligate them to refrain from asking – out loud – whether and under what conditions they should continue to do so in the future. Nor is it regarded as a breach of trust to make provisions – for example, by recourse to a second supplier – for the possibility that trust could be breached.
>
> (Sabel 1992: 224)

Similar ideas were developed from a study of subcontracting among small engineering firms in France, where trading partners have been judged to develop goodwill trust whilst remaining 'neither friends nor strangers' (Lorenz 1988). In the context of just-in-time delivery regimes various researchers have asked whether the cooperation arising can be characterized as reciprocal and of mutual development benefit or whether the relationship is based simply on the exercise of coercion (Sabel *et al.* 1989; Angel 1994; Sabel 1994; Phelps 1996). Contracting within the context of just-in-time production can mean greater mutual dependence between buyers and sellers. As this reorganization is generally at the initiative of large buyers, there is a possibility of suppliers losing control of their development and becoming dependent on a few dominant customers. In practice, reciprocity can exist even in the context of such asymmetrical inter-firm relations. This outcome has been found, for example in the relations between major retailers and their suppliers in the UK clothing and food sectors (Crewe and Davenport 1992; Foord *et al.* 1996) and in the UK automotive components sector (Panditharatna and Phelps 1995). It thus seems that suppliers can remain motivated to improve their performance even where buyers do not offer assistance or commitment in return. Suppliers presumably calculate that if they can help their customer to improve their market share their own business should benefit from the increased sales volume as well (Phelps 1996: 397).

Localized learning

A great deal of cluster advocacy is inspired by reference to Marshall's depiction of an industry's secrets existing in the 'air' (1890: 261). The implication frequently taken from this image is of cluster firms gaining from 'untraded dependencies' that promote information sharing and learning (Storper 1995). Technological trajectories are thus being traced to the development of localized pools of knowledge developed within clusters or, to use the terminology developed in relation to these claims, 'learning economies' (Lundvall and Johnson 1992) or 'learning regions'

(Morgan 1997). Whatever the transition to a globalized economy, it is argued that the key resources for competitiveness come from people and firms learning about new technology through sharing and exchanging information within localized business communities.

A case for the importance of localized learning has been made from investigation of Motor Sport Valley, a case that was introduced in Chapter 1. Since the motor-sport industry concentrated in a cluster, knowledge generation and dissemination have become more crucial to success in this business (Pinch and Henry 1999). It is claimed as well that through geographical concentration much knowledge circulates outside formal business transactions. Pinch and Henry (1999) identify six primary ways knowledge disseminates on this basis:

- *Staff turnover*: the transfer of personnel between companies provides a way of learning how issues are addressed in other teams. Many engineers and designers shift workplaces at the end of each racing season, partly because when a driver moves to a new team he takes some of his former support staff with him.
- *Shared suppliers*: component and service suppliers may have links to several teams. Confidentiality agreements are intended to control one team's secrets becoming known to other teams but the supplier is conflicted by the desire to give each client the best possible advice. Consequently, technical know-how gradually leaks throughout the industry.
- *Firm births and deaths*: as a high risk industry with wealthy patrons there is a high rate of firm creation and destruction. Each of these events is an opportunity for the mixing and diffusion of knowledge.
- *Informal collaboration*: teams are competitive with each other while being governed by detailed regulations set by the governing bodies of the various types of motor sport. Regulations give rise to working groups of team representatives for advice on rule changes as well as providing issues for informal discussion among people affiliated to different teams.
- *Industry gossip*: personal contacts between businesses are high, partly as a consequence of staff mobility and ongoing business connections. These networks are used for making recruitment checks, seeking engineering advice or other needs. However guarded such enquiries may be they inevitably give rise to speculation and gossip that spreads rapidly among industry participants who are intensely motivated to keep up with the competition.
- *Trackside observation*: the technology of racing cars is exposed at the race track where 'even the noise an engine makes can reveal a huge amount to the trained ear' (Pinch and Henry 1999: 825). The frequency of races, therefore, goes some way to explain why 'secrets' are rapidly discovered and new developments appear almost simultaneously on all competing cars.

These observations contrast with those made in the opto-electronics or photonics industry (Hendry *et al.* 2000). Opto-electronics combines computer, laser and optic-fibre technologies and can be viewed as one of the leading breakthrough high-tech industries with application in many product areas. At the end of the 1990s, the industry comprised in the order of 5,000 companies worldwide. Hendry *et al.* (1999, 2000) have studied firms in three countries (UK, USA and Germany) which with Japan account for much of world's industry. In their case study countries, opto-electronics firms are concentrated in regional clusters. This enables the investigation of the significance of clusters in this new industry.

Business networks were the focus of investigation rather than the contribution of untraded dependencies to shared learning. From interviews with company representatives it was nonetheless possible to make some evaluation of the interpretation of clusters as learning regions. This includes four observations that differ markedly from those in the motorsport industry:

- *Strong internal labour markets*: partly as there is a reliance on developing skills through in-house experience there is a high immobility of labour. Apart from periodic downturns and redundancies in related industries, there is virtually no mobility of scientists and engineers.
- *Market diversification*: the development of opto-electronics has been marked by a sequence of breakthroughs that have opened opportunities in new markets. To exploit new opportunities, firms cannot rely simply on the companies close to where they are located. Rather they need to seek out collaborations wherever the relevant expertise is located. Consequently, companies are frequently orientated more to customer industries outside their region than they are to developing a common technology with nearby firms.
- *Complex firms*: even relatively small firms in a high-tech industry engage in merger and acquisition activity, partly as it is necessary to assemble a range of expertise to develop a complete product or service. This can result in the activities of individual firms being dispersed over several locations. An example is given of a small company with separate locations for technology development, design, software development and manufacturing and distribution.
- *Hub and spoke networks*: business networks are largely controlled by the activities of large or otherwise powerful firms rather than through the collective action of small firms. Most firms interact with only a few firms in relationships that are typically controlled by one of the parties involved. The controlling firms are frequently multinationals whose networks connect independents in one location to its operations in other regions and perhaps other countries.

The immobility of spin-off firms is another indicator of low significance attached to localized learning. Most of the firms identified by Hendry *et al.* (2000) originated through an individual or group of individuals leaving a company or university to set up the enterprise. The tendency is to set up close to their former employer. This inertia typically reflects a personal preference rather than because of functional linkages to their parent organization, although the availability of relevant labour is given as a second reason for not moving far. Significantly, these responses are consistent wherever the firm is located. The implication is that clusters start by accident according to the presence of a focal organization and its propensity to incubate new enterprise. This propensity increases where large firms withdraw from activities and allow former employees to take over 'non-core' activities. This process also implies the breaking of ties given that the new firms lie outside the parent's main interests. Functional links might continue through purchasing fabrication, equipment, specialist engineering or business services but key technology and market connections need to be made elsewhere.

Assuming that both accounts are reliable, the propensity for localized learning depends on whether motor sport or opto-electronics is considered the more typical guide to business behaviour. As noted in Chapter 1, motor sport is not representative of contemporary industry. It is a highly regulated activity, is not cost sensitive and serves a single market that is unaffected by national differences in product design preferences or market channels. The need to conform to precise design specifications more than the sharing of knowledge explains the uniformity of understanding between competing teams. Moreover, where knowledge leaks out this can be despite strenuous efforts to control localized learning, as indicated by the following comment in a motor-sport trade magazine.

> On the technical side, a driver who has decided to leave will be stopped from doing any private testing. Indeed, teams will wait until the end of the season before testing anything new that is to appear on the car the following year. There is no question of the driver who is leaving knowing the least details of how anything works.
>
> (*En Route F1* cited in Combes and Duranton 2001: 8)

Opto-electronics also has attributes that account for its forms of business interaction: diversified end markets and the integration of complex technology in final products and international ownership (Hendry *et al.* 2000). These are at least a feature of other high-tech industries including computing and biotechnology (Swan *et al.* 1998) and, as seen in Chapter 1, among a segment of the visual-communications industry (Oakey *et al.* 2001). Given reasons for thinking that opto-electronics is not distinguished by unique attributes, and evidence about the break-down of localized learning in Italy's industrial districts (Chapters 4 and 7), motor sport can be considered the more unrepresentative experience. Hendry *et al.* (2000) observe that in the USA leading opto-electronics clusters are characterized by more localized trading than in the other clusters they studied and they speculate this might enhance localized learning. Whatever the potential gain from being located like motor sport, for the present at least business growth among firms in less sharing clusters has not been prevented.

Externalization

Externalization or outsourcing refers to the purchasing from external suppliers of goods and services that could be produced inside the firm. It is frequently linked to arguments about business clusters as a growth in outsourcing gives rise to more connections between businesses that might encourage activity to cluster. In practice, the significance of a decision to outsource varies according to the extent and sophistication of the transferred activity and the degree of control maintained by the outsourcing organization. Traditionally referred to as subcontracting, outsourcing has attained a new importance through both an overall increase in the proportion of inputs obtained externally and in the significance of the activities so obtained (Cunha 2002). Whereas subcontracting was typically regarded as being to the disadvantage of the subcontractor, improved outcomes for suppliers are widely claimed to be part of the outsourcing paradigm (Perry 1999). Organizations have been encouraged to shift more activity outside their own boundaries but to 'partner' their suppliers in more cooperative relationships than were maintained with subcontractors.

Partners to an outsourcing relationship are encouraged to recognize their interdependence and be willing to share information, cooperate with each other and customize their activity. In this form of relationship, performance is judged in terms of the voluntary willingness to improve the product or service supplied rather than simply in terms of fulfilling contractual obligations (Lamming 1993; Perry and Tan 2000). As well as the emphasis on relationships, outsourcing is linked to the idea that organizations should focus on their 'core competencies' (Hamel and Prahalad 1994). Core competencies are envisaged as the activities that give the organization its unique capabilities. To maximize the ability to exploit core competencies, it is recommended that organizations outsource other activities. This recommendation runs the risk of encouraging organizations to become too specialized. It is rarely the case that core competencies will not need to be frequently refreshed (Christensen 1997). Organizations need to maintain a wide-enough segment of their value chain to be able to test and protect new innovations and this implies a broad conception of their expertise (Miles and Snow 1992). In practice, many organizations have nominated general skills such as technology or their market position ('being number one or two in the industry') as their core competency (Micklethwait and Wooldridge 1997). At this level, clear competence-based rationalization of activity between internal and external production tends to be limited to services such as property management, transportation, selected human-resource functions, IT management and standardized component manufacture.

Even where the outsourcing of comparatively low-value services is involved, the idea of supply-chain partnering has become influential (Kerrin and Icasati-Johanson 2003). The essential proposition is that developing close, long-term working relationships with a limited number of suppliers reduces the risks associated with 'arm's length' contracting. It relies on both parties expecting a long-term relationship, developing complementary capabilities, sharing information and engaging in more joint planning than was customary. The commitment to a long-term relationship is the essential prerequisite. Cooperation is based on the expectation of reciprocal actions; for example, a supplier's willingness to share information on the true costs of production or invest in dedicated production capacity is based on the expectation that this will be rewarded with future work orders. In turn, for the purchaser to make a long-term commitment, it implies that their outsourcing is concentrated with a comparatively small number of suppliers.

As a guide to understanding how buyer–supplier relations may have been changing, the supply-chain partnership model is insufficient. Alongside interest in the nature of the relationship with individual suppliers, buyers have frequently given priority to standardizing the inputs that they buy (Phelps 1993; Perry 1999). This strategy widens the pool of suppliers that can be selected from and reduces the concern a buyer may have about their proprietary technology diffusing to competitors via subcontractors. Standardization works, therefore, in the opposite direction to supply partnering as it facilitates 'off the peg' sourcing rather than the need to rely on customized supply (Perry and Tan 2000: 46). This is a preferable outcome for many organizations. The continued, incremental customization of a supplier's processes, either voluntarily or at the core firm's insistence, can ultimately result in the inability of the supplier to compete in other markets and an obligation on the part of the core firm to use all of the supplier's output (Miles and Snow 1992). This risk became apparent in the computer sector in 2001 as organizations entered their first downturn in demand under their new supply arrangements (Martin 2001).

A contingent perspective on clusters

Whatever cluster theory is adhered to there tends to be a strong assumption of universal advantage. There has been relatively little consideration given to how particular industry, technology or market conditions affect the opportunity for clusters to upgrade business performance. This omission can make sense where industry is affected by some overriding challenge. As discussed at the outset of the chapter, much academic enquiry is motivated by the attempt to simplify changing economic conditions to a single uniform transition. There is, of course, much merit in seeking to identify the common forces behind economic and social change but equally there is a need to recognize that organizations will be affected by change with varying degrees of intensity. Equally, any new ways of organizing business are likely to be of varying assistance to firms of different type, in different industries and in different economic contexts.

At a broad level, for example, there is a need to reconcile the claimed significance of clusters with the formation of global value chains (Humphrey and Schmitz 2002). Claims about the importance of localized collaboration contrast with a reality that organizations with global reach control the production and distribution of many products. Cluster advocates and adherents to the importance of global value chains agree that interaction is central to the way that businesses enhance their competitiveness. They differ in the form of interaction that is believed to be most important and the certainty of business upgrading as a consequence of that interaction. Cluster perspectives argue that local interaction between firms and between firms and local institutions enhance prospects for business upgrading. In contrast, global value chains are recognized as typically involving unequal relationships that circumscribe the benefits obtained from interaction. These contrasting assessments overlap when applied to export-orientated clusters supplying global value chains. Such clusters are a feature of both developing countries (see cases studies in Chapter 6) and of those in high-income countries that supply consumer goods, such as shoe clusters among Italy's industrial districts (Nuti and Cainelli 1996). In this context, business upgrading in a cluster relies on special, contingent conditions (Box 2.4).

Box 2.4 Upgrading in clusters and value chains

Business upgrading can affect process, product, functional or inter-sectoral capacities or some combination of these:

- Process upgrading results in increased production efficiency arising from the use of new technology or the improved management of existing technology.
- Product upgrading occurs through moving into higher value products or services than previously supplied.
- Functional upgrading refers to the redistribution of activity in ways that the overall skill content of activities increases.
- Inter-sectoral upgrading occurs where firms apply the knowledge acquired in one area of activity to move into a separate activity, such as when skills acquired assembling television sets are applied to the assembly of computer equipment.

The organization of value chains typically takes the form of one of four characteristic governance structures:

- Arm's-length market relations that do not lead to the development of close ties between buyer and supplier.
- Networks involve firms interacting with each other and jointly determining the allocation of competencies between them. Network members develop relationships of reciprocal dependence.
- Quasi-hierarchy exists where one form exercises control over other firms in the chain, for example specifying the characteristics of the product to be produced and the processes to be followed.
- Hierarchy occurs where a lead firm takes direct ownership of some operations in the chain.

Upgrading prospects of clusters differ according to the type of value chain they connect to. Insertion in quasi-hierarchy offers favourable conditions for fast process and product upgrading but hinders functional upgrading. With arm's length market relations, process and product upgrading is slow but the route can open for functional upgrading. Networks offer the most ideal upgrading conditions but are least likely to exist for clusters in low-income countries.

Source: Humphrey and Schmitz (2002)

Transaction-cost economics is frequently turned to for guidance on how contingent influences affect the decision to make in-house or to outsource and the form that the outsourcing takes. It recognizes how business contexts vary in the degree of market uncertainty, technological complexity, exchange frequency, time pressure and product differentiation as well as other sources of difference. The transaction-cost approach holds that economizing on transaction costs is mainly responsible for the choice of one form of business structure over another. Transaction costs are incurred in establishing and maintaining a particular trading relationship or organizational structure plus 'the *ex post* costs of maladaption and adjustment that arise when contract execution is misaligned as a result of gaps, errors, omissions, and unanticipated disturbances' (Williamson 1994: 103). The total cost to the firm determines whether an activity is retained within the organization or obtained externally, either through independent or linked suppliers, with these decisions taken to enable the most effective specialization of each business unit.

Transaction-cost economists were amongst the first researchers to draw attention to the variety of transactions that cannot be categorized strictly as either markets or hierarchies (see Williamson 1975, 1979) but there are three sources of doubt about its interpretation of the 'third way':

- The organizational arrangements found in practice are too diverse to be reduced to the outcome of cost calculations. The original transaction cost ideas were worked out in the context of Anglo-Saxon business practice. This offered a limited range of transactional options compared with the inclusion of business practice in other cultures. The existence of place-specific institutional environments that influence organizational structure is suggested by the extent to which East Asian and European business structures and styles of interaction have varied from Anglo-Saxon practice. Transaction-cost economists now acknowledge that they were guilty of assuming that the institutional environment is everywhere the same. They suggest that treating it as a set of 'shift parameters', which induce changes in the comparative costs of governance, is a response to their previous simplification (Williamson 1991, 1994). For those who favour an 'embeddedness' perspective this proposed modification merely highlights the tendency for transaction-cost interpretations to rationalize particular economic structures without an explanation of why a particular range of options are under review (Sayer and Walker 1992). Moreover, the one-off adjustment implied by accepting the existence of distinct institutional environments is too static as cultural influences are continuously changing. Culture 'not only shapes its members but is also shaped by them, in part for their own strategic reasons' (Granovetter 1985: 486).
- Transaction-cost interpretations tend to be built around simplistic interpretations of the comparative risks and costs associated with internalization versus externalization. The comparison tends to emphasize cooperation and order within internal management hierarchies and risks of deception and opportunism in the use of market transactions (see, for example, comments on Williamson in Granovetter 1992: 72). Others doubt that the real world conforms to such simplistic dualism. They point, for example, to evidence (Macaulay 1963) of complex market transactions being unprotected by contractual obligation and reliant on little more than customary expectations of tolerable behaviour (Granovetter 1985). Compared with transaction-cost economists, therefore, the embeddedness perspective tends to be more positive about the effectiveness of market transactions and less persuaded of the effectiveness of internal hierarchies. The reason for this is that all business relations and transactions are seen to involve at least minimum levels of trust and mutual confidence, either through the way repeated interaction builds personal relations or through the reliance on personal knowledge and connections to initiate interaction. At the same time, the tendency for personal relations to modify internal decision-making structures can frustrate the smooth functioning of large organizations and is seen to be illustrative of the weakness of internal management solutions to business coordination (Granovetter 1992: 70–1).

- Transaction-cost analysis assumes that the most efficient organizational forms are the ones that survive. Adjustment to changing cost structures may be 'sticky', making transaction-cost minimizing easiest to observe in industries with ease of entry and strong competition but ultimately the fitter are selected whatever the industrial context (Williamson 1994: 87). Embeddedness interpretations are inclined to doubt that there is a necessary coalescence to efficient arrangements, or that exogenous pressures are the driver of organizational change. Industrial structure and organization are instead viewed as consequences, partly intended, partly unintended, of many processes of development and competition, encompassing organizational evolution and learning as well as responses to external pressures (Sayer and Walker 1992: 210).

Doubts about transaction-cost approaches are taken furthest by those who argue that economic activity is 'embedded' within a specific social context. It claims that economic 'actors do not behave or decide as atoms outside a social context, nor do they adhere slavishly to a script written for them by the particular intersection of social categories that they happen to occupy' (Granovetter 1985: 489). Rather, economic relations are seen to be a product of inherited patterns of behaviour, which may originate in pre-industrial times, as well as contemporary social structures and institutions that influence the conduct of economic affairs (Hamilton and Biggart 1988: S54). As social environments and historical experiences vary, business relations are expected to be highly variable and idiosyncratic, in contrast to the search for universal behaviours and institutional arrangements in transaction cost economics (Granovetter 1985; Hamilton and Biggart 1988; Williamson 1994). This can lead to an outcome as extreme as transaction-cost approaches, although this time in giving too little recognition to some degree of convergence in business practices around the industrial world (Djelic 1998; Zeitlin and Herrigel 2000).

Moreover, even within distinctive national contexts it is possible to find variations in the extent to which that distinctiveness is adhered to. In other words, national distinctiveness can be more apparent in some activities than others. This was shown in a study of contrasting levels of inter-firm cooperation within business clusters in Japan (Edgington 1997). Compared with the auto-assembly industry, industries such as ceramics, textiles, machine tools and office equipment had less development of the archetypal 'structured relationships' that were generally thought by outside observers to be the norm in Japan. The contrast in the development of inter-firm cooperation was explained by the use of fewer components in these other industries, often with less rigorous mechanical requirements and of standard design, and the existence of longer product cycles outside the auto sector. For instance, it was found that the office-equipment industry relied largely on 'off-the-shelf' electrical parts which were available nationwide, while in ceramic tiles and textiles, short production runs mitigated against the use of custom-designed parts and thus reduced the impetus to build formal relationships with suppliers (Edgington 1997). These findings are reflected in a case study of a ceramics cluster that started to fall apart as some of its members became suppliers of semiconductor components to the electronics industry (Box 2.5). That case is especially interesting as it shows how one type of organizational innovation (lean manufacturing) can be in opposition to another (clustering). Studies such as these indicate the need for sensitivity to the range of influences shaping business organization and the interactive nature of these influences. Another example comes from an examination of the origins of the particular contracting methods used in the electronics industry in Japan and Britain.

Box 2.5 The Seto ceramics cluster and lean production

The city of Seto (population 132,000 in 2003) is located 25 km north-east of Nagoya in the industrial belt linking Tokyo and Osaka. It claims to have been a 'ceramics capital' for over 1300 years. Despite some decline since the 1980s, ceramics, clay and stone industries have been the mainstay of Seto's industrial economy for over a century and accounted for almost 60 per cent of the manufacturing employment in 1990. Of the approximately 1,100 ceramic firms none had more than 300 employees, with a workforce of eight being the average, many specializing in manufacturing particular components used in the production of ceramics. A district ceramics association (Aichi Prefectural Ceramic Industrial Cooperation, APCIC) supports various cooperatives including the supply of porcelain clay.

Locally the phrase 'Seto Ltd' signifies that the ceramic industry operates as if it were a single firm. In practice, those making traditional ceramics (tableware and ornaments) or standardized industrial products (insulators) operate separately from firms making 'advanced ceramics' for use in electronic devices and as machine parts. Firms in both the old and new sectors are similar in terms of their local origins, preponderance of family ownership and generally small size but differ with respect to customer relations. The advanced ceramic firms have direct links to their customers whereas other Seto firms tend to sell to wholesalers and have no interaction with their end buyers.

In the mid-1960s, using support available under the 1963 Small and Medium Enterprise Modernization Promotion Law, APCIC proposed a cooperative venture be set up to jointly develop and manufacture electronic ceramics. The proposal did not succeed. Firms already working in the advanced ceramic sector were still in their technological infancy but were not inclined to join the cooperative. A group of four firms did set up a cooperative in 1970 and operated with limited success for 12 years. Without wider participation in advanced ceramics, Seto Ltd lost national industry share, declining by almost 75 per cent during the 1970s.

Individual firms acquired new technology through linkages to buyers outside Seto. These buyers tended to be large organizations with a supply network encompassing their own subsidiaries and component manufacturers. Some require confidentiality clauses that restrict their supplier's ability to cooperate with other suppliers. Further weakening of the cluster occurred as Seto's suppliers located new investment close to their customers.

Source: Izushi (1997)

To explain the greater use of 'obligational contracting' (supply-chain partnerships in today's language) among Japanese firms than among firms in Britain it was necessary to recognize the possibility for two-way causation (Sako 1992). On the one hand, organizational structures partly determine transaction costs and, on the other, transaction costs encourage certain organizational forms. Detailed comparative investigation revealed that universal rules were difficult to sustain and that the context in which transactions took place had an important bearing on the effectiveness of one form of contracting over another. The full understanding of organizational differences required reference to five influences: economic and technological variables; legal environments; financial-market structures; employment relations; the environment for small-firm entrepreneurship. In any one of these areas, Sako identified a range of issues as encouraging obligational contracting in Japan. The complexity can be illustrated through a summary of the influential economic and technological conditions in Japan:

- Industrial sectors vary in their suitability for obligational contracting. Japan had more of those sectors suited to obligational relations than had the UK.
- The use of external suppliers typically required the buyer to invest in assets specific to the transaction. This gave the buyer an incentive to cultivate a long-term association so as to avoid suppliers exploiting their sunk investment.
- Subcontracted inputs included some that relied on customized design input existing in the supplier firm.
- Buyer competitive strategies included product differentiation and diversification and accelerated product cycles.
- Transactions were conducted in the context of comparative market stability, both in respect of final sales and the buyer's preparedness to even out market swings for their suppliers (the latter willingness being influenced by the buyer's asset specificity and product-cycle strategy).
- Market growth made trust relatively inexpensive to acquire as it generates business confidence and a sense of shared success between the buyer and supplier.

This book approaches the study of clusters with the expectation that similar recognition of a range of facilitating and contingent conditions is required to explain how business clusters obtain an advantage. In Chapter 3, for example, reference is made to the conditions under which firms may gain in sharing a labour market with their competitors and the conditions that will favour operating in separate labour markets. In Chapter 4, attention is drawn to the changing characteristics of Italy's industrial districts as businesses in these clusters adapt to changing competitive environments. Chapter 6 includes discussion of the conditions that enabled business clusters in Indonesia to grow and in Chapter 7 the role of industry characteristics as a constraint on policy intervention is discussed.

Conclusion

Most explanations of clustering start with a list of advantages that firms can enjoy from a location among their industry peers and supporters. The presence of these advantages is simultaneously the explanation for clustering. Such an approach has three problems. First, it leaves a gap in explaining how the activity accumulated to the point where the advantages emerged. Presumably up to the time when an activity started to assume importance, future cluster members were small in number and part of a diversified economy. Second, the advantages ascribed to clusters are numerous and partly in competition with each other. A cluster that offers a gain through the sharing of tacit knowledge is unlikely to be simultaneously one that gains from the stimulus of intensified competition. If there is intensified competition it suggests a high degree of similarity between businesses and consequently not much new information to be gained from neighbours. Similarly, heightened competition is likely to reduce the likelihood of cluster firms benefiting from a shared labour market. As discussed in the next chapter, employers that 'hire and fire' their workers rather than invest in their human capital have less to gain and more to lose from employee turnover than firms which are differentiated from each other. Third, it suggests that all activity should be located in clusters. If clusters are simply about the pursuit of advantages, it would seem that organizations not availing themselves of them will fall behind those that do. For the present at least, clusters are a minority phenomenon and present evidence suggests this is likely to continue to be the case. Instead of the focus on advantages, it is helpful to consider the mechanisms through which clusters might be created and the contexts in which particular mechanisms are most likely to operate.

3   Agglomeration and clusters

Agglomeration economies are the cost savings to a firm that result from the concentration of production at a given location, either on the part of the individual firm or by firms in general (Parr 2002a: 718). They are at the heart of any claim that advantage lies in business clusters. This centrality is frequently traced to Alfred Marshall (1923, 1927). The advantages that he suggested firms can obtain from being part of a cluster continue to be cited frequently by advocates of clustering. In today's terms, Marshall's agglomeration advantages are the development of an industry-dedicated labour market, opportunities for business specialization and the ability to share technology knowledge and learning. Originally identified in the context of the steam engine and horse-drawn transportation, many continue to view these economies as equally relevant to biotechnology or 'dot.com' clusters. The classification of agglomeration has become more complex than offered by Marshall but his ideas remain influential, although less so in his explanation of why business clusters were more a feature of pre-industrial economies and the disadvantages they had for communities dependent on a narrow economic base.

It is desirable to distinguish between the relative influence of each type of agglomeration economy on particular clusters. In practice, it has proved difficult either empirically or theoretically to distinguish between the impacts of each potential source of agglomeration advantage. For example, one distinction is between agglomeration economies that are specific to members of the same industry (localization economies) and those that arise from being part of a concentration of unrelated enterprises (urbanization economies). Cities potentially contain a mix of activities, some as isolated representatives of their industry, others as part of an industry cluster. Much effort to determine whether specialized or diversified cities gain the greatest advantage has not yet resolved the matter. Distinguishing one source of localization economy from another has proved equally elusive although new ways to do so keep being tried. Particular attention has been given to measuring the role of technology spillovers. Their existence can seem more plausible than other possible advantages of concentration in a world where business organizations have grown in scale and complexity. They also appeal because of their association with innovative, leading-edge activities that are often claimed to thrive in clusters. In contrast, others advise that they should be ignored because 'Knowledge flows . . . are invisible; they leave no paper trail by which they may be measured and tracked, and there is nothing to prevent the theorist from assuming anything about them' (Krugman 1991a: 53).

Unless it is possible to demonstrate the influence of specific sources of agglomeration advantage it is hard to know what causes firms to concentrate. For example, it is plausible to say that the film industry is concentrated around Los Angeles because of location-specific externalities. Actors may be assumed to learn from each other and be inspired by each other's presence. Equally, it is plausible to believe that actors are inspired by the physical environment and that film producers are attracted by the climate. In which case, it can be argued that natural amenities explain the industry's affinity to Los Angeles (Hanson 2000). The possibility of alternative interpretations means that spatial agglomeration in itself is not evidence of the influence of agglomeration economies. Indeed, the experience of many older industrial economies in seeing economic growth concentrate in their 'sunbelt' has caused serious attempts to identify the influence of climate (Black and Henderson 1999) and urban amenities (Glaeser 1998) on city growth. Activity may simply share a common preference for the amenities of a location, although some may argue that this just means agglomeration gains are a secondary benefit rather than being absent (Parr 2002a).

This chapter commences with an overview of different sources of agglomeration economy explaining why the range of potential sources of agglomeration advantage has widened since Marshall's account. The three sources of localization advantage suggested by Marshall are then discussed in detail with a focus on identifying conditions where their influence may be greatest. The chapter then examines empirical evidence that tries to distinguish between the impacts of different explanations for agglomeration. This part of the chapter focuses on the debate about the relative performance of diversified versus specialized cities. The balance of this evidence suggests that neither type of city has an overwhelming advantage over the other. Consequently, it appears that there is a role for both large and diversified cities and smaller and more specialized cities. This argument is then supported with evidence from the footwear and biotechnology industries indicating that clusters survive through high rates of new form formation rather than from higher levels of performance among clustered enterprises.

Types of agglomeration economy

The sources of agglomeration economy identified by Marshall allow firms within the same industry to gain from their mutual presence close to each other. These benefits helped small firms located in clusters substitute for the internal scale advantages obtained by large businesses. Marshall recognized that other attributes were needed for individual clusters to survive (Box 3.1).

Reduced information transaction costs are the key feature of Marshall's economies (McCann 2001: 57). If firms are located together, it suggests that there is relatively easy access to representatives of other firms of interest. In contemporary terms, this is equated frequently with the sharing of tacit knowledge between organizations. These *information spillovers* may be realized through the ease of arranging formal, face-to-face meetings or through informal contact. The incentive for *specialist suppliers* to join the cluster is a separate benefit. Equivalent specialist support may take longer to emerge for a dispersed industry than a concentrated one, partly due to the effort in ascertaining demand or identifying the market opportunity. The original specialization advantage included *non-traded local inputs*, such as where a group of clustered firms invested in some form of testing or

---

Box 3.1 Threats to Marshall's clusters

Improved communication between places had an ambiguous outcome for the survival of localized industry (Marshall 1927: 273). Enhanced communication, whether created through improvements in transportation or the lowering of trade barriers, tended to increase long-distance trade. This outcome tended to assist the survival of localized industry. On the other hand, improved communication enabled people and skills to migrate between places and tended to disperse industrial activity.

Production of two types of good was considered most likely to remain in industrial districts: goods in general use that were 'not very changeful in character'; and goods that could be efficiently represented in illustrated catalogues or samples distributed to wholesale and retail dealers. These attributes were considered most likely to be 'within the grasp of a powerful firm' and 'once an industry has fallen for the greater part into the hands of producers on a very large scale, there is on the balance a tendency to a loosening of the ties that bound it to its old home' (Marshall 1923: 288).

Marshall (1923: 287) noted that a district may display leadership in an industry over many decades, surviving changes in production technology. Longevity was helped where technology changed gradually, as this meant there was 'no particular time at which strong incitement is offered to open up the industry elsewhere'. As well, activity dependent on manual skill was considered less easy to replicate in a new location than machine-based industry as such skill was perfected in 'a special industrial atmosphere'. A risk to the survival of all clusters was 'obstinacy and inertia' among its entrepreneurs. A failure to change could be exploited quickly by new sources of supply. The attraction of 'new shrewd energy to supplement that of native origin' was a characteristic of enduring districts.

certifying agency for their own, exclusive joint use. Labour-cost savings from the development of a *local skilled-labour pool* are a further potential economy. Greater use of the external labour market may be possible than for isolated employers. For example, it may be easier to lay off workers when business is slack: employees move willingly to better-performing employers in the cluster and employers have the assurance that skilled workers will remain in the locality. As well, on-the-job experience gained across several employers may reduce an employer's need to invest in training.

Marshall's economies envisage agglomeration as an industry phenomenon. A typology of agglomeration economies attributed to Ohlin (1933) and Hoover (1937, 1948) recognized that agglomeration benefits may accrue to firms, industries or cities. This tripartite classification has since been subdivided but the main types continue to be the basis of most discussions of agglomeration economies (Parr 2002a):

1   *Internal scale economies*: these arise from the expansion of a single establishment. In detail, they may be of three types: (i) economies of horizontal integration (the form usually thought of and arising from the fall in the unit cost of production with increased output); (ii) economies of lateral integration (or internal economies of scope and occurring when a firm's joint output of two or more products involves less cost than the same product range produced by single-product firms); (iii) economies of vertical integration (or internal economies of complexity and obtained by integrating steps in the production chain in a single operation). The ability to purchase in bulk, use specialized equipment, optimize the deployment of worker skills and equipment are all potential sources of internal economies. In many cases, organizations can realize these economies without consolidating activities on a single location (in which case these agglomeration advantages do not lead to geographical agglomeration). Recent literature on the agglomeration advantages of business clusters, at least that produced by non-economists, has tended to have a clear bias against recognizing the advantages of increased firm size because it challenges the importance of clustering (Box 3.2). For individual firms, any additional advantage from consolidation at a single location will be balanced by the loss of flexibility associated with multi-site operations.

2   *Localization economies*: these refer to the cost savings that accrue to a group of firms within the same or related industry, located in the same place. Strictly, localization advantages are those external economies that are immobile and are a function of the scale of the industry at a particular location (Parr 2002a: 719). Specific benefits are as identified by Marshall, although typically researchers single out one of the three sources of localization advantage. Collectively, they

are frequently identified as external economies because they are beyond the control of individual firms. Some degree of external economy is obtained from the scale of an industry to which the firm belongs, but their full realization is generally thought to arise where the industry or a significant part of it is spatially concentrated.

3   *Urbanization economies*: these economies arise where benefits are external to both individual establishments and the industry, being sometimes referred to as external economies of scope. Sharing of infrastructure and services among diverse firms are examples. Their magnitude is a function of the size and diversity of an urban concentration. Traditionally, it has been thought that small and new firms have obtained most benefit from urbanization economies, as with the so-called incubator hypothesis (Vernon and Hoover 1959), and evidence from the computer industry suggests that this continues to be the case (Beardsell and Henderson 1999). Activity-complex economies are a specific variety of urbanization economy. Mutual proximity of the members of a production-chain sequence can save transport costs and the need for inventory as well as improve the efficiency of material flows between stages of production.

Box 3.2 No gain from Swedish clusters

A test for the influence of internal-scale economies, urbanization economies and localization economies on the export performance of manufacturing firms in Sweden found localization economies had least influence. The localization effect was estimated to be between 40 and 80 times smaller than the urbanization economies effect, and between 50 and 100 times smaller than the effect of internal economies. These results indicated that actual importance was inversely proportional to recent scholarly interest in the different types of agglomeration effect.

The finding came from analysis of a database covering all Swedish manufacturing exporters in 1994. These 10,500 firms accounted for a quarter of all manufacturing firms and almost 90 per cent of manufacturing employment. The results were not sensitive to the territorial units or industry definitions utilized, although the influence of localization increases when industries are defined broadly.

The number of firms in the same or related industries located in the same territorial unit were used to measure localization. This was noted to exclude buyer–supplier relations across unrelated industries. Another gap may be that some manufacturers export through an intermediary in the non-manufacturing sector. On the other hand, the importance of localization economies was shown not to be affected by the presence of 'local leader firms', these being export firms with over 500 employees that potentially are linked to many small firms in multiple industries.

Overall, the localization of similar firms in small municipalities or labour-market areas was a small influence on export activity. Claims about the high importance of localization economies tend to be based predominantly on anecdotal case studies rather than comprehensive data.

Source: Malmberg *et al.* (2000)

New terminology distinguishes between the static and dynamic impacts of localization and urbanization economies. Static agglomeration economies permit firms to achieve production efficiencies, attract specialized infrastructure and support services and to develop a specialized labour pool. They may influence the allocation of activity to different locations and help explain why a variety of settlement types and sizes come into existence at any point in time. Static externalities alone do not necessarily guarantee continued innovation and productivity improvement. Dynamic externalities stimulate growth and are generally thought to be based on the accelerated flow of ideas across individuals, occupations and industries when activity agglomerates. If dynamic externalities are important, a high level of rigidity in industrial location patterns may be expected as once a cluster forms new locations will be unable to replicate the advantages of established locations (Box 3.3)

Box 3.3 Locating new industry employment

The existence of dynamic externalities suggests that the productivity of industry in a particular location is affected by the prior scale of the industry at that location. If dynamic externalities are strong, it suggests locations with little or no history of the industry will find it difficult to attract activity in that industry. The location constraint implied by static externalities is less. If new establishments set up in sufficient numbers, new locations can match the static externalities of existing clusters.

The computer industry in the USA from 1977 to 1992 shows little tendency to concentrate around initial centres of employment, even though this time coincides with the diffusion of personal computers. Among the eight cities with the largest concentrations of computer employment in 1977, four remain in the top eight in 1992. There are 13 big losers and 13 big gainers, measured by either at least a 50 per cent drop or gain on their 1977 employment. Seven cities entered and fell out of the top frame within the period examined ('flash-in-the-pans'). Employment changes are not the result of single large plant openings or closures: big employment gainers, for example, show much variation in their average plant size. Having a workforce with a high proportion of college-educated workers, being a large metropolitan economy and being relatively close to San Jose (Silicon Valley) increased the chances of gaining employment. Employment in associated electronic components, state taxes and diversity of the metropolitan economy were found to have no consistent relationship with the gain or loss of computer-industry employment.

The estimated productivity performance of a sample of computer firms in 1984–8 suggested that past employment had a large benefit for present productivity in the case of firms with computer activities at a single location. Single-site computer firms operating in a city with consistently double own industry employment compared with another city had 17 per cent greater output than if located in the other city. The same effect was not observed for plants affiliated to corporate groups. They appeared to be self-reliant and unaffected by externalities.

Source: Beardsell and Henderson (1999)

To distinguish between the static and dynamic effects, the terms localization and urbanization economies can be reserved for static economies. Dynamic localization economies are identified as Marshall–Arrow–Romer (MAR) externalities and dynamic urbanization economies as Jacobs externalities (Glaeser *et al.* 1992). These labels reflect linkage to particular growth theories. Romer (1986) made significant contributions to 'endogenous growth theory' by combining the existence of a competitive economy with technology, intellectual spillovers and human-capital externalities. Jacobs (1969) is credited with demonstrating that diversified urban economies have an advantage over specialized ones (Box 3.4).

Box 3.4 Urban diversity revisited

Jane Jacobs came to prominence as the author of *The Death and Life of Great American Cities* (1961). The book reflected rising popular resistance to large-scale urban-renewal schemes and the author's experience of being part of a campaign against the building of a highway across Manhattan. She questioned the value of urban renewal when it resulted in a loss of land-use diversity and 'street life'. Functional diversity was viewed as the basis of the community cohesion that Jacobs associated with traditional urban neighbourhoods, such as her own at the time of writing the book: West Greenwich Village in Lower Manhattan. Diversity brings people together who otherwise lead separate lives. Chance encounters foster relationships that are especially fruitful through the mixing of different backgrounds, experiences and aspirations.

The role of community diversity in sustaining urban economies was the theme of Jacobs' *The Economy of Cities* (1969). Cities are presented as the source of considerable innovation because they accommodate more diversity than smaller places. A theory is presented in which industrial variety promotes knowledge externalities and ultimately innovation and economic growth.

West Greenwich Village three decades after the writing of these books had survived urban renewal but the social community had changed from the images painted by Jacobs in the 1960s. The White Horse Tavern, where

Jacobs claimed to find dockers mingling with literary critics, had become a tourist trap. The neighbourhood store had been replaced by a gourmet delicatessen and in the street paraplegics might be found begging for small change:

> Set against the high rise condominium rabbit hutches east and west of Central Park, this is still an attractive area for certain types of people to live ... It offers low rent diversity, but Hudson Street was clearly never the soft focus idyll that Jacobs portrayed ... In the apartment buildings of Hudson Street, frail and incontinent widows die alone on urine-soaked beds, left forgotten for weeks before the super calls the police to tidy them away.
>
> (Sudjic 1992: 25)

Jacobs had been especially critical of Los Angeles as a planned city without urban diversity, lacking in street life and a conventional urban centre. Yet its economy proved more successful than New York's in the decades after Jacobs' writing.

Source: Sudjic (1992)

The distinction between static and dynamic externalities can become blurred. One assessment, examined at the end of the chapter (see case studies of the footwear and biotechnology industries), is that agglomeration economies have a dynamic effect on new firm formation but not on firm growth (Sorenson and Audia 2000; Stuart and Sorenson 2003). A long-term view holds that dynamic effects, of whatever form, ultimately have a limited life.

A life-cycle perspective on clusters suggests that they typically pass through four stages: critical mass, take-off, saturation and maturity (Swann 1998). By the third of these stages, it is expected that the costs of clustering start to outweigh the benefits as evidenced by declining rates of innovation and competition from businesses in lower cost locations. Driving the loss of agglomeration advantage are increased production costs and the tendency for cluster members to share a common set of business strategies and organizational structures that restrict adjustment to changing market opportunities. Such a process has been observed in the Manchester cotton industry (Box 3.5) and other late Victorian industrial clusters in England (Wilson and Popp 2003). As with other industry life-cycle models, there is no chronology predicted of the time between life-cycle stages. Evidence from Victorian England suggests that the time from formation to maturity might be as short as 20 years or over a century, although long-lived clusters tend to be extended by a slow decline.

Box 3.5 Manchester's relegation

Manchester's dominance of the cotton industry during the nineteenth century created perhaps the first modern industrial district of world significance. This north of England city and surrounding towns accounted for 40 per cent of the world's cotton manufacturing capacity in 1883 as well as being home to the merchants who dominated world trade in cotton. By 1938, British exports of cotton-piece goods were 80 per cent below those of 1913 and Manchester's cotton industry was in terminal decline.

Manchester's producers lost out as overseas countries expanded their own industries. Japan captured many markets while infant industry protection in India and elsewhere shut out Manchester. Some loss of market share was inevitable but the concentration of British production in the Manchester district deepened the collapse:

- Institutions central to the district such as the Royal Exchange and Manchester Chamber of Commerce were not suited to the discovery and exploration of unfamiliar opportunities.
- Division of activity among comparatively small undertakings encouraged over investment.
- The high indebtedness of individual mills, created by a mistaken impression that markets would recover in the 1920s, made downsizing harder to achieve than if the industry had been consolidated in fewer, large operations.

The predominant pattern had been for independently managed firms of similar specialization to be combined in holding companies. Within prevailing technology, individual mills achieved economies of scale so that there was no advantage in consolidating production in 'super mills'. Holding companies protected individual mills from intense competition and labour unrest while allowing independent management to survive. The control of holding companies fell to a small clique of directors who were driven more by financial speculation than industry innovation.

At the point of industry saturation, the district needed to diversify but the dominance of interests wedded to cotton's survival frustrated Manchester's move into new industries. In the 1920s, the Trafford Park industrial estate offered Manchester participation in the 'second industrial revolution'. It attracted electrical and motor-car manufacturers (including Ford's first assembly plant in Britain) but too much of the region's resources remained devoted to the defence of cotton. In 1931, Ford relocated its assembly plant near London. Contemporaries such as the economist J. M. Keynes judged that Manchester's entrepreneurs failed to recognize the need for change.

Sources: Wilson and Singleton (2003); Toms and Filatotchev (2003)

Reference to 'spillovers' is now frequent in discussions about agglomeration although this can overlook the fact that the term is reserved strictly for economies that are not transferred through direct transactions. This builds on a distinction, introduced earlier than the recent interest in clusters, between pure (technological) and pecuniary external economies (Scitovsky 1954):

- *Pure external economies:* these arise as an increase in industry-wide output alters the technological relationship between inputs and output for all firms. More activity, for example, means the possibility of more activity-specific knowledge and corresponding increases in firm efficiency through the industry-wide application of that knowledge. Spillovers are a public good as the use of a piece of information by one firm does not reduce the content of that information for other firms. Neither can any firm be excluded from gaining access to the information. For many economists, pure externalities or 'spillovers' are the preferred form of externality as they are compatible with an assumption of perfectly competitive markets.
- *Pecuniary externalities:* these are transmitted through price effects that may alter output decisions made by individual firms. For example, a large industry can support a market for specialized intermediate inputs and a pool of industry-specific labour. These bring benefits to the individual firm according to their purchasing decisions, such as their willingness to invest in complementary assets. Economists see them as encouraging imperfect competition and they play an important role in the models produced in new economic geography (Chapter 5).

Marshall was not aware of the distinction between pure and pecuniary externalities but economists now regard it as crucial to the form that agglomeration takes (Fujita and Thisse 2000: 11). His interpretation favoured pure externalities. Inter-firm relations were seen to be inherently transient with firms continually changing their relations with other firms and customers (McCann 2001: 64). The external benefits of clustering accrue to all firms simply by reason of their location in a cluster. Such an interpretation led Marshall to overlook the fact that deliberate collective action may be required to build effective market relations (Box 3.6). Indeed, deliberate collective action is seen as essential for unlocking cluster advantages in today's developing economies (Chapter 6).

Uncertainties with agglomeration economies

The debate about business clusters is mainly about localization economies but it is impossible to discuss one source of agglomeration without reference to other sources. Claims of the significance of agglomeration are most convincing when based on a specific source of advantage. One firm's internal scale economies may, for example, lead to another industry's

Box 3.6 Birmingham's jewellery cluster

From 1790, Birmingham became England's main centre of jewellery manufacture outside London. In the mid-nineteenth century, the Birmingham jewellery trade employed about 20,000 people concentrated in an area of around 100 acres where workshop owners and employees lived and worked.

Close proximity and high levels of interdependence between a multitude of small workshops did not control dishonesty. Fraud and high levels of theft by workers were endemic features of the cluster. Retailers and wholesalers frequently obtained goods on credit and sold at a loss for quick income. During the late 1880s, a price collapse led to the market being flooded with under-priced goods. Insolvent traders continued to obtain goods on credit and dispose of them at the best price on offer. Dishonest trading combined with Birmingham's reputation for shoddy, imitation jewellery brought the cluster to a crisis.

Collective action saved the cluster. In 1887, the Birmingham Jewellers and Silversmiths Association was established to regulate the conduct of the trade and improve product quality. It brought honesty to the cluster by providing members with a debt-recovery service, helped owners prosecute cases of theft and created a trading network of 'approved' businesses.

Marshall suggested that activity within business clusters could be coordinated without conscious effort. In Birmingham's case, market relations had not guaranteed honesty. The cluster survived largely through the efforts of two prominent entrepreneurs – Jacob Jacobs and Charles Green – who were both city councillors and affiliated individually to the two religious communities most widespread in the cluster. Trust had not come naturally partly because the ease of entry into the trade meant that social networks were constantly changing their configuration. In this context, the division of activity among many small specialists reduced the incentive for any individual producer to remain honest. The Birmingham Jewellery Association helped to give all participants an incentive to behave honestly. In the 1980s, close to half the precious jewellery assayed in Britain was recorded by the Birmingham assay office.

Source: Carnevali (2003)

localization economies. The production of electronic components, for example, is subject to strong internal scale economies that cause component production to be concentrated in a relatively few plants. As a consequence, users of components are more geographically concentrated than if component supply were highly dispersed. Similarly, the advantages of an urban area may be realized as localization or urbanization economies or both. The presence of a large number of employers potentially reduces employment insecurity for employees and aids labour recruitment. If the employers are in unconnected activities, the labour pool is experienced as an urbanization economy. If the employers are in related activities, it may be identified as a localization economy. The typical city combines localization and urbanization economies. How industries are defined partly determines which of these economies are most important. A broad industry definition makes it easier for a city to be identified as relatively specialized than when activities are examined in detail (Glaeser *et al.* 1992: 1148). Ambiguity in identification raises problems because clustering is often seen to rely on localization and urbanization economies being in opposition to each other (Henderson 1974, 1988).

The shifting boundaries of firms and industries are another barrier to identifying a specific source of agglomeration advantage (McCann 2001). A chemicals complex at Teesside in the United Kingdom, for example, shifted from generating internal scale economies to localization economies when the original owner (ICI) sold off parts of the complex to independent operators. In central Scotland, a cluster of firms affiliated to the electronics industry are thought to enjoy localization economies (Turok 1995; McCann 1997). They are mainly subsidiaries of multinationals from Japan and the USA. If the branches were affiliated to their specializations rather than parent companies, a cluster from disparate industries enjoying urbanization economies would be identified. Given today's frequency of ownership and sector changes through mergers and acquisitions, the distinction between different sources of agglomeration can be arbitrary.

As well as the ambiguity in distinguishing between sources of agglomeration advantage, the geographical scale over which they operate is a further source of uncertainty. When identified first, agglomeration economies were envisaged as arising through the close proximity of economic activity within urban concentrations. Today, location in an urban core can be associated with significant diseconomies due to congestion and property costs while the benefits generated within it are not nearly so circumscribed as formerly (Parr 2002a: 729). Similarly, the dissipation of agglomeration economies or at least a major extension of their spatial range has been claimed (Richardson 1995: 146). It has, therefore, been argued that agglomeration economies need to be redefined to fit a variety of geographical scales and spatial configurations rather than being constrained to spatially proximate activity (Moulaert and Djellal 1995). At the extreme are studies that claim agglomeration effects between countries or even across continents. It has, for example, been estimated that about half of the productivity growth in the United States can be attributed to technology improvements made in other countries (Eaton and Kortum 1996). Similar effects have been found in relation to the impact of foreign research and development activity on domestic productivity for a range of OECD countries (Coe and Helpman 1995).

Finally, the influence of agglomeration economies needs to be balanced by the existence of agglomeration diseconomies that encourage the dispersion of economic activity. The recognition that tightly confined agglomeration benefits are susceptible to erosion by congestion costs is one reason for seeking to extend the spatial influence of agglomeration. The sensitivity to the disadvantages of geographical concentration has arguably increased in recent decades, making it necessary to recognize attracting and repelling forces. Improvements in transport and communications, changes in the spatial organization of the firm and the growth of distributed (as compared with co-located) work have given at least some firms more location choice than formerly (Mogridge and Parr 1997).

When localization?

The literature about business clusters provides few specific rules about when industries gain most from localization economies rather than other sources of agglomeration advantage. A widespread perception has been that localization economies suit the needs of contemporary markets and capabilities of modern technologies to a degree that it is not reasonable to contemplate firms surviving without them. This is seen in the 'flexible specialization' thesis that links the significance of agglomeration to larger changes in economic organization. Increased market uncertainty and high rates of technological change are thought to have reduced the advantages of internal economies of scale and scope. The consequence, it is argued, has been increased horizontal and vertical disintegration of economic activity partly through the externalization of activity that was carried out internally (Scott 1988; Scott and Storper 1992). In place of internal capacity, firms are thus expected to be surrounded by a multiplicity of linkages to suppliers, supporting services and business partners as well as customers.

The flexible specialization account is now widely accepted as too sweeping and simplistic, partly because its assumption of a resurgence of near perfect competition is hard to sustain against a reality of continuing big-business dominance (Martin and Sunley 1996). Economic theory provides some guidance on when localization economies become important but the insight is limited by a dominant assumption that urbanization and localization economies are in conflict with each other. There is no undisputed empirical evidence to support this assumption (see 'Which economy counts' on page 67) but it has been the basis for most economic models that seek to identify when localization economies become important (Fujita, Krugman and Venables 1999: 19).

Henderson (1974, 1988) argues that agglomeration economies encourage urban specialization as it makes sense for industries with mutual spillovers to locate together and for activities that do not generate mutual benefits to avoid each other. So, for example, if film production and automobile assembly generate few mutual external economies, these activities are best located in different places to avoid generating congestion and high land rents for each other. A large city implies relatively high commuting costs and land rents. Specialization, therefore, enhances full exploitation of localization economies and ensures local land rent and congestion costs are minimized. Differences in city sizes are similarly explained by the variation in the scale of industry concentration needed to achieve the optimal agglomeration benefits. A film city may have little reason to accumulate more than a few film studios, whereas an automobile city might continue to gain advantages by attracting many assembly operations. Activities such as high-fashion apparel, high-value publishing and exportable services (finance, tourism, advertising, research and development) tend to be drawn to large metropolitan economies because of urbanization economies. Standardized manufacturing is influenced by localization economies and drawn to smaller specialized cities (Henderson 1997: 450).

Henderson's theory thus identified a number of circumstances in which clustering may be encouraged. It may be a reaction to increased urban diseconomies, facilitated by easier access to locations evading those diseconomies as well as from any changes in the importance of localization economies. Henderson's initial economic model that he built to test his theory predicted that all cities should eventually become fully specialized. This outcome contrasts with the continued growth of both relatively specialized and diversified cities (Duranton and Puga 2002). Subsequent versions of the theory have modified the assumptions, typically to substitute one form of agglomeration advantage for another or to allow for several sources of agglomeration advantage. For example, when pure externalities and cross-sector externalities are allowed to exist his model shows that specialized, diversified and mixed cities can be economically viable, although one assessment is that other outcomes of the models make the results no more realistic than those based on the original assumptions (Duranton and Puga 2002: 168).

New economic geography (see Chapter 5) has developed partly to understand how agglomeration influences the location of economic activity without prior assumptions of the relationship between different types of agglomeration economy. In its words, new economic geography prefers 'a story that places more emphasis on out-of-control invisible-hand processes' (Fujita, Krugman and Venables 1999: 21). To date, it has shown most interest in trying to explain the larger tendency for economic activity to concentrate in metropolitan-scale regions rather than in explaining localized business clusters. Metropolitan-scale agglomeration is thought to demand interpretation through externalities whose effectiveness does not decrease sharply with distance (Ottaviano and Puga 1997). Partly for this reason it has been biased in favour of pecuniary externalities. It has tended to discard the potential existence of spillovers as they are seen to rely on personal interactions. Consequently the treatment of agglomeration economies has tended to be partial producing results in which it seems that almost any settlement outcome is a plausible outcome (Duranton and Puga 2002: 177).

An open mind on how agglomeration economies influence location is still justified. To provide some guidance on when localization economies may matter, it is helpful to look in detail at the three sources of localization economy associated with Marshall. Although they may be seen as mutually reinforcing, most recent discussion tends to emphasize one source of advantage. Selectivity reflects different views about what is driving the formation of clusters. As well, the issue emphasized may reflect a wish to choose a form of economy compatible with a preferred competitive environment. Thus, those economists who prefer to assume perfect competition select spillovers as the drivers of agglomeration rather than specialization or labour-market pooling.

Spillovers

There has been a shift from emphasizing proximity-induced transaction efficiencies to the importance of technological and information spillovers as causes of agglomeration (Malmberg *et al.* 2000: 309). In particular, knowledge unique to specific agglomerations and localized 'collective learning' are referred to frequently as reasons for cluster formation and development (Chapter 2). The discussion of industrial districts especially has stressed the impact on firm competitiveness through enhanced learning and innovation (Asheim 2000). This enhancement comes, it is argued, from contact with early adopters of a new technology, rapid circulation of information about specific technologies and an added momentum to innovation through the density of firms experimenting with new technologies (Kelley and Helper 1999).

The dependence upon 'tacit knowledge' for innovation is seen to reinforce the importance of proximity to fellow industry affiliates (Leamer and Storper 2001). To make this case, tacit knowledge is contrasted with codified knowledge to stress the need for face-to-face interaction to gain access to technology spillovers. Tacit knowledge in the context of this argument refers to those aspects of understanding that defy codification or articulation in written and spoken words (Gertler 2003: 78). The person possessing tacit knowledge is not conscious of all the understanding they possess or is hampered by the absence of appropriate language to permit clear explanation to others or both. Consequently, observing, imitating and correcting others are the most effective means of the transferring tacit knowledge. The importance of shared language, values and culture among individuals or organizations wishing to share tacit knowledge is a further inducement to proximity. Moreover, tacit knowledge is held to be an essential complement to other forms of knowledge, reducing the ability to evade geographical clustering.

Two main arguments are used to justify an emphasis on tacit knowledge (Gertler 2003). First, is a perception that organizations no longer differ in their access to other forms of knowledge. Globalization and the spread of multinational corporations are prime forces seen to be homogenizing scientific, technological and marketing knowledge around the industrial world. Second, innovation is increasingly viewed as an outcome of interaction between economic entities rather than something that isolated businesses can perform successfully. Interaction between firms (customers, suppliers and competitors), research organizations (universities, public and private sector research institutions) and other public agencies is the basis for 'learning through interacting' (Lundvall and Johanson 1994). Close proximity between interacting parties increases the likelihood of tacit understanding being shared effectively. It facilitates formal and informal face-to-face interaction and provides a common social context for communication.

On the other hand, an equation that 'tacit equals local, codifiable equals global' is now accepted to be too simplistic, even by those who continue to believe that some form of knowledge agglomeration exists (Malmberg and Maskell 2002; Pinch *et al.* 2003). Much discussion tends to assume a willingness and interest in sharing business information in informal, out-of-work contexts that does not exist in practice (Box 3.7). Similarly, Gertler (2003) has questioned the ease of producing, finding, appropriating and sharing tacit knowledge. For example, recruiting people with tacit knowledge is not straightforward if, as commonly asserted, a new recruits' organizational context has to be imported along with the person. Neither is there agreement on how work is most effectively organized to encourage the flow of tacit knowledge between employees. There is much advocacy of the need for participative work cultures but there is no clear evidence to confirm which, if any, culture is most conducive to sharing tacit knowledge (Wright and Gardner 2003). Retention of tacit-knowledge holders is equally problematic and accentuated by their preference to work within 'thick labour markets' to maximize mobility between jobs.

Others are not convinced that there is substance to the argument that local-knowledge processes are shifting advantage to clusters, giving three reasons to be sceptical (Martin and Sunley 2003: 17):

1   Distinctions between different forms of knowledge are not as sharp as the emphasis on binary divisions (tacit versus codified, informal versus formal) implies.
2   The precise content of 'localized tacit knowledge' and how it acts as a source of competitive knowledge remains obscure. To influence competitive advantage, knowledge of whatever type must be utilized by businesses. In contrast, most accounts of tacit knowledge focus on 'territorial learning' and institutions other than businesses.
3   The role of tacit knowledge tends to be discussed in isolation of any account of how industries and innovation evolve. There is, for example, a need to explain how the advantages that are thought to

Box 3.7 Who talks about work?

A study of 70 small firms in the Sheffield metal-work cluster found that purchasing transactions with neighbouring firms were no more likely to bring face-to-face meetings ('embodied transactions') than were transactions with non-local firms. Buyers were reluctant to hold meetings with suppliers wherever they were located. The median frequency of face-to-face meetings with representatives of principal suppliers was three times a year. A fifth of respondents had no meetings in the previous 12 months with their principal suppliers. Two firms met their suppliers more frequently than once a week, contributing disproportionately to the total number of meetings.

Out of 765 recorded meetings, 60 took place on non-business premises and 14 were in a social setting, undertaken for social or recreational rather than business purposes. Informants advised that it was 'bad form' to discuss business issues when meeting socially. The regularity of meetings was not explained by the duration of trading relationships or whether the transaction involved standardized or customized inputs. At the same time, buyers generally had a personal contact in their supplier firms who they typically claimed to know well and rarely used formal contracts to manage their transactions.

Source: Watts *et al.* (2003)

draw firms together initially do not become sources of inertia and inflexibility. If tacit-knowledge sharing within a cluster encourages competitive strategies to coalesce there is a danger of failing to anticipate and react to strategies developed by firms outside the cluster.

One response to such criticisms is to search for alternative types of knowledge that can be demonstrated to cause agglomeration. For example, as discussed in Chapter 1, a theory of clustering based on 'architectural knowledge' has been proposed (Pinch *et al.* 2003). Others seeking to advance a knowledge-based theory of agglomeration acknowledge that for the present it remains difficult to identify the mechanisms that might explain why clusters form (Malmberg and Maskell 2002: 442). A widely cited source to support the existence of spillovers is a study of patent citations (Jaffe *et al.* 1993). This study warrants close inspection as the evidence it provides is not as clear-cut as often presumed.

Patent data have been attractive to researchers seeking to establish the importance of information spillovers as it is a type of knowledge flow that creates documentary evidence (Audretsch 1998). Both an individual patent's place of registration and that of other patents cited in the registration have been utilized to infer information spillovers. Against this usefulness, it is well known that patents are an imperfect indicator of knowledge generation. Not all innovations are patented, those that are may not be of economic significance and patents vary in the extent of innovation they record (Pakes and Griliches (1984: 378). Consequently, the use of patent data is perhaps best balanced with other indicators of innovative activity (Feldman and Audretsch 1999). When this is done, the significance of agglomeration differs from the evidence relying on patent information alone. First, the evidence from patents is summarized.

The locations cited in patent registrations show a few centres of innovation. In the USA, two cities (San José and Rochester) claimed over 645 patents per head of population 1988–92, with the next highest density being 350 (Albany) and 282 (Minneapolis) (Audretsch 1998). In absolute terms, 59 cities had an average of over 50 patent registrations a year of which 26 cities had over 400 per year.

The Jaffe *et al.* (1993) study exploited the need for new patents to cite any previous patents that relate to the innovation the new patent captures. It showed that patents cited other patents originating in the same city more frequently than did a control group selected randomly from patents issued at the same date and in the same industry as the city sample. The result held when patents released by different types of organization (universities, top corporations, other businesses) were examined separately and for comparisons at two points in time. Approximately 40 per cent of the sample citations were in different patent classes to the new patent. Further findings qualify the evidence in favour of any form of agglomeration advantage:

- The localization effect was statistically significant but a small source of variation.
- The effect was evident for the citation of patents up to 12 months' old but reduces for older patents. Established knowledge, therefore, shows less geographic concentration than new knowledge (as judged by the intellectual connections between patents).
- Citation patterns varied between industries. Industries including electronics, optics and nuclear technology had a tendency for high citation of other new patents but for patents to quickly cease to be cited (Jaffe and Trajtenberg 1996). Citation rates vary according to the organization registering the patent: university patents have higher citation than corporate patents and government patents the lowest citation of all.
- The average number of citations received by a patent declined in the late 1980s across all institutions and categories (Jaffe and Trajtenberg 1996).

The study suggested a general advantage in a location shared with other innovative activity rather than endorsing industry-specific spillovers. There is a localization effect but for new knowledge rather than enduring discoveries. Analysis of European patent data has similarly shown that clustering alone is not conducive to higher innovative performance (Box 3.8). Evidence from the semiconductor industry in the USA suggests that new knowledge sharing is linked to the migration of personnel into new ventures (Almeida and Kogut 1997). Whether this should be interpreted as an advantage of localization or a constraint on the location options of new entrants is considered in the biotechnology case study at the end of the chapter.

A database of new product introductions in the USA gives more support for the importance of urbanization rather than localization economies, providing that urban diversity encompasses complementary activity (Feldman and Audretsch 1999). The database allocated almost 4,000 new products to a source industry (four-digit SIC level) and specific location responsible for the work behind the innovation. These new products were introduced in one year (1982) and vary from modest to radical innovations. Cities dominate innovation with 96 per cent of the product innovations introduced by metropolitan-based establishments. To investigate whether pure city size, urban diversity or urban specialization drives

---

Box 3.8 Clusters can be good or bad for innovation

Patent-registration data for Italy and the UK were used as a guide to the location of innovative activity. Analysis preceded using two-digit SIC-level manufacturing industries (generating 15 sectors in the UK and 17 in Italy) and NUTS 3-level regions (65 counties in the UK and 95 provinces for Italy). The database assembled for the study comprised 26,055 firms in the UK (6 per cent with patents) and 37,724 firms in Italy (6.2 per cent with patents).

Patent activity was found to be unconnected to the level of all own industry employment in a 'cluster' (NUTS 3-level region) but was affected by the level of employment in own industry employment in firms with patents. This showed that clustering stimulates innovation only where the cluster is densely populated by innovative firms. No general advantage to belonging to a cluster is found. Indeed, a high concentration of own industry employment in non-innovative establishments appears to depress innovation. A strong presence in a cluster of innovative companies in other industries has a positive but insignificant impact on innovation.

The address attached to a patent registration may be the company headquarters rather than the site of actual innovative activity. Given the tendency for headquarters to be concentrated in a few locations, this may bias the results. The mechanisms causing innovation to cluster are still to be addressed. It remains unknown whether innovation diffuses through pecuniary externalities, such as through local markets for specialized services and inputs, or through knowledge spillovers originating in localized flows of skills and ideas.

Source: Beaudry and Breschi (2003)

innovation, industries are affiliated to a scientific base. This affiliation is based on separate survey data that asked research and development managers in individual business firms which areas of scientific research they took interest in. For each industry, the innovative output of a city is compared with an index of the city's industry specialization and with an index measuring diversity across industries sharing the same scientific base. Isolating the influence of city size, the extent of localized competition (identified by the number of firms per worker relative to the national ratio, industry by industry) and technological opportunity (recognizing that some industries are more innovation intensive than others) produced the following results:

- Innovative activity was lower in industries located in cities specialized in economic activity in that industry.
- The presence of complementary industries sharing a common science base was conducive to product innovation.
- High levels of localized competition promoted innovative activity (once the impact of city size is controlled for).
- Firms with activity across a range of science-based complementary activities had a higher innovation output than single activity enterprises.

Empirical evidence derived from patents and innovation activity, therefore, tends to suggest that if spillovers are important they are most effective in cities with diversified economies rather than clusters; a qualification being that diversity should bring together activities that have a common knowledge base, although from the study the commonality can be wide (for example, a joint dependence on 'chemistry' rather than a particular type of chemistry).

Labour-market pooling

A shared labour market may overlap with the existence of spillovers. Knowledge is embedded partly in workers. Flows of workers between firms can thus produce flows of knowledge. This is positive if viewed as a way of gaining access to the expertise and strategies of competitors. It is negative in implying strong competition for one of the most important assets of a firm. Thus firms that locate near to competitors face a trade-off between the benefits of labour-market pooling and the costs of labour-market poaching. The benefits of pooling rest with the opportunities for a firm to hire workers whose knowledge gained in other firms can be adapted to the profit of their own organization. The costs are that firms risk having their own knowledge workers poached or that they need to protect themselves from poaching by raising their wages relative to other firms.

Based on the analysis of an economic model in which reciprocal poaching among clustered firms is possible, Combes and Duranton (2001) argue that whether firms gain from sharing labour depends on the degree of product differentiation between firms and on market conditions. Their model assumes that as rivalry intensifies (with less product differentiation), the incentive to retain strategic workers leads firms to increase wages relative to competitors. Wage increases reduce the extent of poaching but lessen the benefits obtained from labour-market pooling (because wage increases are effective in reducing labour transfers). In these circumstances, it can be advantageous for firms to operate in separate labour markets. Their model contains two firms only. This may intensify the incentive to avoid poaching although the nature of the trade-off need not change. A reinterpretation of the comparison between Silicon Valley and Route 128 follows from the model as it stands, consistent with larger observations of the Silicon Valley labour market (Benner 2002).

The success of Silicon Valley and the relative decline of Route 128 during the late 1980s are attributed usually to cultural differences between these two parts of the USA (Saxenian 1994). Unconventional, open-minded managers in Silicon Valley let their employees move between employers with benefits for individual enterprises and the strength of the cluster as a whole. Around Boston, conservative mangers sought to retain employees and frowned on 'job hoppers'. Combes and Duranton (2001) reinterpret this case as the outcome of differences in business rivalry. Route 128 was focused on mainframe and mini-computers with little differentiation among firms. Software and Internet activities dominated Silicon Valley based on a diversity of firm activities and product designs. This difference, combined with the stronger market growth of Silicon Valley outputs, made it optimal for firms in Route 128 to prevent poaching and for firms in Silicon Valley not to prevent poaching. Combes and Duranton (2001) add that larger firms in Silicon Valley with local competitors sometimes acted to escape poaching. They cite the example of Intel as a company that in the 1980s located the production of new products away from Silicon Valley so as to reduce the risk of workers being lured away by competitors.

A similar point has been made from the perspective that high rates of inter-firm labour mobility may cause the strategies of enterprises in a cluster to converge (Stuart and Sorenson (2003: 235). They cite evidence, for example, that one firm's markets tend to diversify in line with the markets served by firms that any externally recruited managers are appointed from (see Boeker 1997; Rao and Drazin 2002). As a consequence of the heightened competition produced by such strategic convergence, sharing the same labour-market pool is more useful for new venture creation than it is for business growth (Stuart and Sorenson 2003).

Some additional attributes of the Silicon Valley labour market have been identified from empirical investigations that suggest further conditions favouring labour-market pooling. As above, the main significance of Silicon Valley is again seen to be its unusual conversion to market-based relationships between employers and employees in preference to long-term commitments (Cappelli 1999). This is reflected in the growth of temporary, contract-based employment. The reliance on the external labour market is made easier when that labour market is spatially concentrated for three main reasons:

- Recruitment constraints are minimized through a large labour pool that enables employees to move employer without moving home. This consideration is particularly significant in helping both members of a dual-income household maintain careers.
- Provision of training can be carried out by locally based institutions consistent with the needs of the labour market. With confidence of re-employment, employees are willing to invest in their own skill development.
- The commitment of employees is managed through the ability to check on the past performance of new recruits through the personal networks of the current workforce. Reputations are well known and create strong incentives for employees to perform at a high level.

Cappelli (1999) argues that combining market-based employment relationships with agglomeration in a shared labour market enables firms to rearrange their own capabilities quickly without increasing fixed operating costs. He further highlights how a market-based labour market shapes other ways that firms operate. Companies find it comparatively easy to start up where there is a pool of talent that can be hired away from competitors. Managing a high turnover of labour encourages firms to abandon vertical integration and make use of subcontractors and suppliers.

It is recognized that market-based relationships have not developed equally across industries or types of organization. Silicon Valley is an exemplar because the typical firm is always innovating and often breaking from the paradigms represented by its previous products, creating less need for continuity in experience and employment than might normally be found (Cappelli 1999: 177). Firms not working in this type of innovative context, or that are large and seeking to remain as vertically integrated organizations, risk being 'ripped apart' by the labour market. For employees, it tends to work best where there is a willingness to stay within a functional area of expertise rather than seeking to accumulate a diversified employment history that will assist movement up a management hierarchy. Such contingencies help explain why the labour-market advantages of agglomeration may not be open to employers with different market characteristics.

So far the potential benefits of a labour-market pool have related to situations where worker and knowledge flows overlap. Two advantages of labour-market pooling exist for employers of non-knowledge workers (Sorenson and Audia 2000: 432). First, when companies vary in the intensity of their labour demands, geographic concentration minimizes the risk of unemployment for individuals able to move between firms as demand dictates. In this case, workers may be encouraged to trade off employment security against lower wages. Second, the close proximity of employers sharing similar technologies and business strategies provides additional incentives for prospective employees to invest in industry-specific skills. Deepening skills will not result in an individual becoming dependent on a single employer and this may increase their willingness to invest in training. In this situation, the labour market of a cluster has been likened to the internal labour market of a large firm (Becattini 1990). In both, employees can move between jobs while making productive use of past experience.

A test of the latter possibility has been conducted in the context of Italy's industrial districts (Cingano 2003). It examined how employee wages were influenced by previous years of experience in another industrial district firm versus experience gained in a firm outside of any industrial district. The study matched the activity of past and current employers and focused on workers up to age 37. No evidence was found that experience in district firms was valued by district employers. Firm-specific experience had most impact on wage growth, leading the study to conclude that firms within industrial districts have a high degree of specialization despite the affiliation to the same industry. This outcome, therefore, might be viewed as consistent with the interpretation of Silicon Valley: clustered labour markets are optimal where firms are differentiated. For employees, the movement between employers can still lead to an erosion of their accumulated experience, at least in terms of the willingness or ability of employers to pay for it.

Finally, it is interesting to note that Marshall discussed how a disadvantage of localized industry could be a tendency to make extensive demands for one kind of labour. In some heavy-industry districts he noted, 'there are no textile or other factories to give employment to women and children, wages are high and the cost of labour dear to the employer, while the average money earnings of each family are low' (1927: 272). In a contemporary context, the growth of dual-career households has been identified as one reason for the continued economic expansion of cities (Buck *et al.* 1992). Within diverse city economies, both members of a household can pursue career aspirations whereas one may have to compromise in a small, specialized labour market.

Specialization

The third of Marshall's external economies is most frequently interpreted as the facilitation of an extended division of labour between firms in complementary activities and processes. When firms operating in the same industry locate near to each other, the ease of outsourcing certain production functions to other firms is thought to increase. If economies of scale exist in the activities that are subcontracted, and these exceed the scale of production that any individual firm can attain, then firms benefit from sharing suppliers. An increased pool of potential entrepreneurs is the direct driver of local specialization. Clusters provide individuals with opportunities to acquire knowledge of an industry, form networks and build confidence in the ability to open a new venture.

The process of locations becoming specialized as new firms spin out of existing establishments is known to vary with the organizational character-istics of incumbents. Small-firm environments, for example, have long been recognized as more productive in spinning out entrepreneurs than large organizations (Gudgin 1978). In the context of Silicon Valley, the impact of firm size was moderated by the tendency for even large organi-zations to adopt comparatively decentralized and flat organizational struc-tures. According to Saxenian (1994), this organizational preference provided employees with better opportunities to accumulate knowledge and build confidence to establish their own business than would have been obtained in high-tech companies with traditional management struc-tures. This interpretation may underestimate the significance of other influences promoting specialization in Silicon Valley.

The initial impetus to spatial concentration in Silicon Valley was encouraged by a number of features of semiconductor technology:

- The basic technology was invented at the birth of the industry, provid-ing a core technology which small firms could acquire at a reasonable price (Freeman 1982). Core technology was suitable for widespread modification into commercial products that could support large numbers of new firms (Oakey *et al.* 1990).
- In the early phases of the semiconductor industry, university basic research lagged behind the work done by industry (OTA 1984; Daly 1985). This was an inducement to concentration because university expertise tends to be highly dispersed whereas industry investment is comparatively mobile enabling it to concentrate around an initial centre of expertise (Sharp 1990).
- There was a short lead time between the conception of an idea to the successful first sale of products and services. New companies could exploit small 'time windows' created by the hesitation of former industry leaders in identifying market potential (Oakey *et al.* 1990). The ability to earn profits quickly allowed new companies to become established before incumbents were able to react.

Such attributes have been replicated in the Internet revolution that has provided a more recent wave of growth and new enterprise development for Silicon Valley (Benner 2002). High rates of new-firm formation in Silicon Valley are linked to its role as a 'breakthrough economy' (Florida and Kenney 1990). As long as technology keeps changing, there is opportunity for specialized enterprise. Once markets and technology stabilize, the balance of advantage can shift back to vertically integrated organizations (Perry 1999: Box 6.3).

Which economy counts?

Some cities remain persistently more specialized than others (Duranton and Puga 2002). This has been taken as an opportunity to examine the relative importance of localization and agglomeration economies. In a diversified city, it may be assumed that there is greater likelihood of ideas and resources from different industries being shared and for learning to take place across activities than in a specialized city. On this basis, localization economies can be taken as important if industries that give rise to a specialized city grow faster, or generate more new enterprise, when located in a specialized city rather than a diversified city. Of course, some limitations of such evidence need to be acknowledged.

Results are sensitive to the number of cities examined, how their boundaries are determined and how specialization is measured. A traditional view has been that city diversity is a function of size: large cities are more diversified than small cities (Parr 2002b). This can mean that differences in city performance are associated with size as well as the level of economic diversity. Data from the USA indicates that larger cities tend to be more diversified than smaller ones but, at least from the perspective of those who wish to investigate the consequences of diversity, the relationship is weak (Duranton and Puga 2002).

Places are classified as diversified or specialized according to the share of city employment in an industry compared with the industry's national share of employment. Cities may be specialized in an industry without this being a dominant part of the urban economy. Consequently, evidence based on specialized versus diversified cities is not capturing the position of clusters that involve a high degree of locality concentration on a single activity or set of related activities. Similarly, industries may be so broadly defined as to encompass a wide range of activities with little direct connection. Whatever the detail of the sample, agglomeration effects are inferred rather than observed directly (Hanson 2000).

On the other hand, two studies help to justify linkage between a city's economic structure and agglomeration type. Patterns of specialization and diversity have been identified as something other than the random allocation of activity to places, suggesting a role for agglomeration (Ellison and Glaeser 1997). The influence of resource advantages has also been ruled out, at least to the extent that 'local fixed effects' do not account for differences in city performance (Henderson 1997). Attempts to distinguish urbanization and localization effects have measured industry employment change and plant dynamics (as well as patent registration and innovation data as reviewed above).

Industry employment change

Looking at long-term employment change is potentially a way to test for the existence of dynamic externalities. A problem is that long-term studies require control over other influences on employment change and no study has yet done this in a sufficiently robust way (Henderson 1997; Hanson 2000). The two most cited studies disagree on whether localization (MAR externalities) or urbanization (Jacobs externalities) economies are most influential. Both these studies use employment data for industries in the USA for time periods of around 30 years.

The first of the two studies found that employment growth in a city industry is positively correlated with the initial diversity of industry employment in the city but not with initial own-industry employment in the city (Glaeser *et al.* 1992). In fact, the study finds that geographical specialization reduces growth ('specialization hurts') while city diversity helps employment growth. The main results held when mining industries were excluded, when services and manufacturing were examined separately and when manufacturing was divided between activities likely to serve local markets (ubiquitous industries such as fabricated metals) and export markets (specialized activities such as electrical equipment). As well, when industry performance was measured using a productivity indicator the results did not change the conclusions derived from the employment measure.

The story favoured by this study was illustrated by the example of the steel industry (Glaeser *et al.* 1992: 1140). Steel declined in the United States through the impact of foreign competition and through displacement by new construction materials. The steel industry located away from the specialized centres of the industry adapted best to the changing business environment. This may reflect the greater opportunity for ideas to cross-fertilize between industries in diversified cities than in specialized cities. The study does not confirm this but the story is consistent with ones told about heavy-industry districts in other countries (Checkland 1981; Grabher 1993).

Subsequent to Glaeser *et al.* (1992), others have argued that it is important to distinguish between sectors and give adequate representation to new and old industries. One study making such adjustments examined five 'traditional' industries (machinery, electrical machinery, primary metals, transportation and instruments) and three 'high-tech' industries (computers, electronic components and medical instruments) for the period 1970–87 (Henderson *et al.* 1995). The study sought to cover all cities where the industries are represented and encompassed 224 metropolitan areas to meet this objective. The conclusions present a different picture to the earlier study:

- A history of industrial diversity did not have a significant effect on any of the traditional industries, except for instruments. This was interpreted as indicating that Jacobs externalities are not important for mature industries.
- Employment growth in mature manufacturing industries was higher in cities with past employment concentrations in its own industry. This was taken as a sign that MAR externalities are important for mature industries.
- For high-tech industries, a distinction exists between cities that initially give rise to a new industry and cities that succeed in retaining the industry as it grows.
- High levels of past industrial diversity increased the probability that a city generates high-tech industries, suggesting an important role for Jacobs externalities in stimulating new activity. In contrast, retaining high-tech industry (as evidence by the distribution of high-tech industry at the end of the study period) was influenced by the prior concentration of linked industries. This was interpreted as indicating that MAR externalities had most influence on retaining high-tech industry.

An industry life-cycle story is, therefore, possible from the comparison of mature and high-tech industries. Firms in newer industries benefit from exposure to ideas drawn from many sources, while firms in industries with established production techniques benefit from proximity to firms in similar lines of activity. Glaeser (2000: 92) suggests that depending on how initial employment is measured, neither his own or the later study actually demonstrates that being in a specialized economy benefits the growth of the industry.

Plant dynamics

The rate at which firms open and close in diversified versus specialized cities is an alternative way to employment change of measuring agglomeration effects. This indicator was identified following evidence that a city's specialization can survive high levels of turnover in industry participation (Duranton and Puga 2002). A database covering all manufacturing establishments in the United States, for example, indicates that more than half of all manufacturing employees in 1992 worked in firms that did not exist in 1972 and that three-quarters of the plants existing in 1972 were closed by 1992 (Dumais *et al.* 1997). Such turnover is useful for the study of agglomeration effects. It indicates that industry concentration cannot be attributed solely to historical accidents at the time of geographical coalescence. Some forces appear to keep concentrations in place.

Using the database just referred to, Dumais *et al.* (1997) distinguish five categories of establishment change: births of new firms; the opening of new plants by existing firms; the expansion or contraction of existing plants; plant closures; and switches of plants between sectors. As with other establishment databases, real establishment closures may not be distinguished from changes in ownership. The database comprises five yearly observations during 1972–92 for 134 industries. The study examined how the prevalence of the different types of establishment change within industries were influenced by whether the industry activity was located in a specialized or diversified city. Key findings include the following:

• Geographical concentration of individual industries, measured by the Ellison and Glaeser index (see Chapter 4), remained largely unchanged. Textile industries are the main exception in showing increased geographical concentration. The behaviour of high-tech industries does not differ from the overall pattern.
• On average, areas where an industry was over-represented saw their 'excess' employment reduce by around 40 per cent over the study period.
• New plants were added disproportionately in locations with below-average specialization in the industry to which they were affiliated. Consequently, the distribution of new plants (and especially new firms) tends to reduce city specialization.
• Plants were less likely to close in locations that had a higher than expected share of employment in the plant's industry. The relatively low closure of plants in a specialized city was the sole component of change that was found to reinforce geographical concentration.
• Net expansions in employment of existing establishments tended to reduce geographical concentration.

Differences in establishment age and size influence these findings. Establishments in an existing industry concentration tend to be older and larger than the average establishment in an industry. In general, older and larger plants might be expected to grow more slowly and have a lower propensity to close down than new plants (Holmes and Stevens 2002). Once this influence is allowed for, the distribution of new establishments continues to reduce geographical concentration but by less than was calculated through the initial analysis. Similarly, the tendency for net employment expansion to be highest in diversified locations was less evident than in the analysis that was not adjusted for the age and size of plants. Even so, the researchers conclude that cities with a specialization tend to retain it by a disproportionately low closure rate while their comparatively low rate of new establishment openings prevents the specialization becoming stronger.

As discussed in the final part of the chapter, case studies of individual industries do not support the conclusion of Dumais *et al.* (1997). It has also been disputed in follow-up studies by Henderson (1999, 2001) using the same dataset with a slightly extended time frame (1963–92). The method differs in seeking to measure the influence of city specialization on a firm's productivity rather than through the impact on employment change or plant dynamics. The way productivity is measured introduces statistical assumptions into the analysis that have been assessed as making some results implausible or at least imprecise estimates of agglomeration effects (Hanson 2000: 23).

Studies in Europe provide similarly contradictory outcomes. Using data on the complete population of knitwear firms in Baden-Württemberg, Germany over the 30 years to 1998, location in a cluster increases the likelihood of plant closure (Staber 2001). In contrast, a study using data on establishments in France (Duranton and Puga 2002) has similar results to Dumais *et al.* (1997) although it is based on a short time period (1993–6). Of all new plants (numbering almost 255,000 in the database), 83.7 per cent arise in locations with comparatively diversified economies. The database separates relocations from new plant openings and finds that 29,358 establishments relocated. The direction of relocation is from comparatively diversified labour markets to comparatively specialized labour markets.

French evidence points to a complementary role for specialized and diversified cities. Firms learn about production processes that will boost their productivity in diversified cities, but then relocate to specialized cities to exploit such processes (Duranton and Puga 2002: 1456). This interpretation is best seen as a hypothesis. Out of the 18 sectors identified, five showed the tendency to relocate above average from diversified to specialized areas: research and development, pharmaceuticals and cosmetics, IT and consultancy services, business services, printing and publishing. These sectors suggest movement toward particular types of location: research and development to science parks; business and IT services to urban centres. In contrast, there were nine industries that had from less than half to a quarter of their relocations going from diversified to specialized locations, but these activities had comparatively low rates of relocation and low levels of geographical concentration.

Agglomeration and competition

The imprecise measure of clustering obtained by examining industries in relatively diversified versus specialized cities may explain why findings are inconsistent. Certainly a contrasting picture emerges when the local concentration of businesses is measured directly. Studies by Sorenson and Audia (2000) and Stuart and Sorenson (2003) compile databases for the USA indicating the location of each establishment relative to all other establishments in the footwear and biotechnology respectively and other details of each establishment. These databases have been used to test how the performance of plants is affected by the density of same industry plants around its location. The database shows annual establishment openings and closures allowing changes in industry geography to be linked to the density of establishments.

The two industry case studies find that establishments located among a high density of own industry establishments are more likely to close down than are relatively isolated establishments. In contrast, openings are most likely to occur in locations with an existing high density of establishments. These observations are used to propose an interpretation of agglomeration that views it as helpful for new entrants but as disadvantageous to incumbents. This interpretation is built upon three claims:

1   The current distribution of production determines the opportunity structure for new entrants. Dense clusters of like industry maximize the ability of individuals to accumulate the knowledge, social ties and confidence needed to form a new venture. Potential employees, investors, customers and collaborators assume greater risk in dealing with a new enterprise compared with an established enterprise with a known track record. Social capital helps would-be entrepreneurs overcome the advantage held by established organizations. It is built through personal relationships and tends to be concentrated among geographically localized contacts.
2   Organizations located among other industry affiliates face stronger competitive pressures than isolated organizations. The pressure is intensified by a tendency for the business strategies of clustered firms to converge. Increased similarity between enterprises is considered especially likely where there is a high level of labour migration between firms and where enterprises occupy structurally equivalent positions within buyer–supplier networks (meaning identical ties to identical actors).
3   The benefits to an individual enterprise of being in a cluster dissipate over time as managers' networks expand geographically. Market growth, participation in industry associations and industry-centred conferences facilitate the formation of ties among dispersed industry participants.

In brief, clusters arise as a consequence of the social structure of opportunity: agglomeration promotes new-firm formation but detracts from the performance of established organizations. The test of this proposition is that high founding rates rather than low failure rates sustain clusters. The footwear and biotechnology industries in the USA are both claimed to follow this pattern. A brief summary of each case study adds some additional insight into clustering processes.

Footwear

The footwear industry in the USA is located disproportionately in a few regions (Sorenson and Audia 2000). In 1989, four states (Maine, New Hampshire, Missouri and Massachusetts) had exceptionally high plant frequencies per million people. Within each of the four states, activity tended to further concentrate in and around a few main settlements with each settlement specializing in a particular type of footwear. Industry clustering survived despite substantially higher failure rates among plants in or near concentrations of activity than isolated plants. Location unevenness was highest in 1948. In that year, plants in dense locations had almost three times the failure rate of the most isolated plants (Sorenson and Audia 2000: 440). Location concentration persists because of the higher rate of new openings in locations with existing concentrations of shoe plants. The shoe industry would have dispersed evenly by 1964 had new ventures not disproportionately arisen in existing concentrations. Present trends indicate that it will take until 2047 for the industry to reach a stable location pattern (Sorenson and Audia 2000: 450).

Higher failure rates among clustered plants decreased with the age of plants but even long-established plants were found to have higher survival rates in isolated locations. Similarly, plants that belong to multi-establishment organizations, when located in densely concentrated areas, still exited at a higher rate than those in isolated locations. The location of tanneries, suppliers of a key resource of footwear manufacturing, had no influence on industry entry once the density of establishments was considered.

Biotechnology

The comparative significance of clustering on entry and survival in the biotechnology industry was studied with less complete information than the footwear industry but with similar results. Founding dates and locations were compiled for biotech companies that received venture capital from registered suppliers (Stuart and Sorenson 2003). The first sale of securities on the public equity market is taken as a key performance milestone for these enterprises. Incidence of these Initial Public Offerings (IPOs) is used to indicate the relative success of biotechnology ventures located among a high density of other biotechnology companies in the database versus those in isolated locations. The study is, therefore, based on a partial sampling of all biotechnology ventures but one that minimizes the potential diversity among all enterprises identified as biotechnology based. The assumption that all venture-capital-supported enterprises aspire to a public equity offering is arguably reasonable given that this is the main vehicle for venture-capital suppliers to realize profit.

Key results identify that locations most productive in new start-ups differ from locations best for new venture performance (Stuart and Sorenson 2003: 248). The two most fertile locations for new venture openings are north of Boston on Route 128 and Palo Alto in Silicon Valley. The location that performs best in terms of progress to IPO was found to be at the intersection of New Jersey, Pennsylvania and New York states. This high-performing location is a base for many large pharmaceutical companies but has a relatively low density of biotechnology companies. These results are not influenced by any rationing effect on the amount of venture capital received. The co-location of many new start-ups does not mean individual enterprises are less well funded than isolated ventures. A funding effect was observed in that closure rates were highest among ventures receiving comparatively small amounts of venture capital located in close proximity to the most highly funded ventures (Stuart and Sorenson 2003: 251). The ability of well-funded firms to recruit talented staff from poorly resourced ventures was the suggested reason for this outcome.

As before, the results are interpreted as showing that the influences promoting new venture formation differ from those that enhance the post-entry performance of early-stage companies. New ventures in geographically crowded areas benefit from proximity to established firms, providing a supply of potential entrepreneurs and new entrepreneurial ideas, and a source of skilled technical and managerial labour. On the downside, a location shared with other new entrants heightens competition. Firms recruiting from the same labour market tend to converge around a common set of technologies and strategies, especially with high labour mobility between competing firms. Proximity to a concentration of venture-capital suppliers can be a further disadvantage. It increases the likelihood of competitors being funded and adds to the competition for labour.

An extension of the analysis examined the relationship between local concentrations of universities and biotechnology enterprises. The results led to the suggestion that a comparatively high density of existing enterprises depresses the propensity for university staff to set up new ventures, a possible explanation being that the incentive to 'spin out' is reduced where there are opportunities to combine work as a consultant or scientific advisor to an existing enterprise with an academic position. Whatever the explanation, the finding adds to the doubt that agglomeration stimulates technology-based entrepreneurship. Rather, the spatial distribution of relationships and resources limits potential entrepreneurs' ability to create new organizations.

Conclusion

The tendency for economic activity to concentrate makes it likely that agglomeration economies have some influence on business location but demonstrating this in practice remains a challenge. Three complexities tend to be overlooked in enthusiastic endorsements of the importance of external economies. First, agglomeration economies offer a residual benefit after the cost of realizing them has been subtracted. There have been many claims that firms have become more influenced by agglomeration economies but typically without reference to the full costs involved in obtaining the benefits. Second, agglomeration economies can be realized internally through the growth of large organizations or externally through the concentration of independent establishments. The substitution is not perfect but frequently too little attention is given to the motives that firms have to capture agglomeration benefits internally. Third, the spatial extent of agglomeration benefits is unclear but it seems reasonable to assume that they are less confined than they were. These considerations have long been recognized but are frequently overlooked in the claims about cluster advantages. The current popularity of Marshall's explanation of the advantages obtained by business clusters overlooks the fact that he did not see these advantages as explaining why clusters existed and that he expected the pursuit of internal economies to reduce the prevalence of clustering as economies modernized.

Empirical studies based on the relative performance of specialized and diversified cities tend to show advantages and disadvantages exist with both settlement types. A diversified economic base appears to be important for generating new ideas and starting new industries. A specialized economic base appears to be important for maintaining the growth of established industries. These differential needs can explain why economies tend to show no overall tendency for cities to become more specialized or more diversified. A specialized city does not necessarily constitute a cluster but the evidence does question theories which give a high status to localization economies. When empirical evidence is based on the geographical density of establishments, to distinguish between concentrated and isolated activity, clustering appears to reflect the constraint that the current location of production places on the distribution of future entrepreneurs rather than agglomeration advantages. Clusters provide individuals with more opportunities to acquire knowledge of the business, form critical networks and build confidence in their ability to open a new venture. These influences increase the likelihood of employees leaving a current employer and starting their own venture. This process is most likely to involve movement within industries, or at least occupations. Working in a particular job both requires the individual to acquire knowledge about the business and allows the accumulation of personal contacts and industry skills. These forms of tacit knowledge significantly affect the willingness of individuals to enter business, even when the move is into 'ordinary' activities.

4   Counting clusters

Identification is the first step towards determining whether the occurrence of business clusters is changing and in evaluating the value of efforts to promote cluster formation. To date, no agreed method for identifying and mapping the distribution of clusters has been developed. Even strong advocates of the importance of clusters acknowledge that there are obstacles to any comprehensive and rigorous identification. It is noted frequently, for example, that cluster participants may not fit the categories identified in official statistics and that this risks even potentially large clusters being unrecognized. Such an instance has been claimed with a concentration of more than 400 medical-device companies, encompassing perhaps 40,000 jobs in Massachusetts (Porter 1998: 79). Official employment data allocated this activity among diverse industries. Once revealed, executives reportedly came together to work on issues of mutual interest, creating a strong cluster.

If cluster participants can be unaware of unrealized potential until others map this out, it appears that identification should be a priority. Equally, reflection on the Massachusetts experience might caution against racing to perfect a methodology. Clearly, to avoid misinforming executives about their cluster status, measurement needs to be accurate. Conceptual as well as technical challenges stand in the way of accuracy. Prior to its mapping, was the medical-device industry in Massachusetts merely an agglomeration of potentially linked businesses rather than a concentration to be counted as a cluster? Most definitions of clusters imply that they comprise a geographical concentration that changes business practice and performance. Clusters offering no special advantage to residents might remain uncounted on this basis. Such an approach would simplify definitional challenges. Cluster boundaries, for example, could be set according to the distance that cluster influence extends. This would avoid having to define a universal cluster size, as some researchers have attempted to set (May *et al.* 2001). On the other hand, a count of active clusters only can give a misleading impression of the significance of agglomeration. Excluding cases where there is no change in business outcomes from geographical concentration risks making geography appear more important than it is. Equally problematic, it raises a need to determine what types of business interaction constitute a cluster and how much change in business activity is needed to join.

This chapter favours geographical concentration as an indicator of clustering. It is typically calculated using official statistics and these enable representative surveys to be undertaken. A simple and objective measure of clustering has the further virtue of enabling evidence to be accumulated from individual studies with greater certainty than where idiosyncratic definitions are employed. Cluster identification has progressed beyond simple measures of geographical concentration but using more sophisticated approaches skews identification towards a particular interpretation and this has drawbacks. It risks exaggerating the significance of clusters by counting only those localities that demonstrate changes in business behaviour and performance. To avoid such a self-fulfilling proposition, the population of places with potential and actual clusters should be identified. Such information is needed to determine the attributes that promote clusters and the feasibility of building clusters where they currently do not exist. This is not to suggest that measuring industry concentration is straightforward, although there is experience to draw upon for guidance. The chapter examines alternative ways of measuring concentration and recommends that it is considered from both an industry and locality perspective.

Mapping without defining

How clusters are defined will influence the localities that get counted. A clear and precise definition of a cluster may, therefore, be viewed as a prerequisite for mapping their frequency. Unfortunately all definitions of clusters tend to be short on explicit guidelines. So, for example, stating that a cluster is a 'geographically proximate group of interconnected companies and associated institutions in a particular field, linked by commonalities and complementarities' (Porter 1998: 199) provides little guide on how to count them. There is no specification of the level of industrial aggregation at which the cluster is to be identified, the geographical distance providing proximity or the basis for recognizing an 'associated institution'. Further guidance is needed as well to measure commonalities and complementarities and to know how significant they need to be.

Relaxing the requirement for the cluster to comprise linked enterprises reduces identification problems. But even a simple definition such as 'a regional cluster is an industrial cluster in which member firms are in close proximity to each other' (Enright 1996: 191) is a poor guide to identification. Without specifying how much activity constitutes a cluster and how close the proximity must be, industry categories and geographical boundaries can be chosen either to maximize or minimize the number of clusters counted. Steiner (2001) provides an example of the malleability of cluster boundaries using different definitions applied to an Austrian province.

The problem, of course, is that a coherent definition and agreed understanding of clusters is unlikely to be produced without first studying clusters to identify their important attributes. To do this in a systematic fashion implies a need to identify their frequency or at least a sufficiently large sample to give a representative guide to their key attributes and influence on business behaviour. Consequently, while present efforts to identify clusters provide, at best, a shallow and indirect view of clusters (Martin and Sunley 2003: 21) this is not a reason for abandoning efforts to improve and standardize mapping efforts. Four starting points may be identified from the present range of mapping strategies.

One approach is to rely on the opinion of 'local experts', usually in the form of representatives of regional economic development agencies or academics with experience of investigating clusters (van den Berg *et al.* 2001). Martin and Sunley (2003: 21) point out the obvious dangers of this approach. What are claimed to be clusters often turn out to be no more than small and only loosely connected collections of similar or related firms. Expert opinions can be unduly influenced by local policy aspirations and from unwarranted optimism that all local economies are potential clusters provided that they are assisted to realize the opportunities. One possible illustration of this arose with one of the cluster-mapping projects reviewed below. Crouch and Farrell (2001) sought to draw on secondary information sources to confirm the existence of their statistically defined clusters but frequently public agencies reported on clusters that did not appear among their candidates. On the other hand, a role for expert identification may exist for cross-national research. The European Commission collected information on 34 'regional clusters' in 17 European countries based on the assessments of national 'experts' familiar with the individual clusters (Isaksen and Hauge 2002). This information can highlight whether prominent clusters in individual countries are thought to be experiencing similar trends. The limitations of expert identification increase the more that a representative list of clusters, identified according to a consistent set of criteria, is looked for.

The development of cluster typologies can be seen as a second approach to mapping. This strategy overcomes the problem of agreeing a single cluster definition by identifying a range of separate cluster types. As each cluster type is specified in some detail this should make identification easier than when working from a vague, all-encompassing definition. Unfortunately, the competition among typologies is only a small degree less than the competition among cluster definitions (Box 4.1). Robertson and Langlois (1995), for example, distinguish clusters according to their degree of ownership and coordination integration. In this typology, ownership integration relates to the degree of ownership separation between individual production units; coordination refers to the

---

Box 4.1 Hybrid clusters

The Vancouver film industry ranks as one of the most significant clusters of film-production talent to achieve international prominence during the 1980s and 1990s. Each year during the 1990s, Canada captured the production of at least two-thirds of the films that in the past would have been completed in Los Angeles. Vancouver built its film industry around these 'runaways'. With an estimated employment of around 25,000 in the late 1990s, it became one of the world's leading film-production centres.

An attempt to fit the Vancouver cluster within a fourfold typology developed by Markusen (1996) or an Asia-Pacific variant of that typology proposed by Park (1996) failed. Markusen's four categories comprised: (i) Marshallian industrial districts; (ii) hub and spoke districts; (iii) satellite platforms; (iv) state-anchored districts.

Shifting networks of small firms contributing to Vancouver's production activity gave some resemblance to a Marshallian industrial district. The dependence on finance from a small group of studios and media conglomerates in Los Angeles gave some of the features of a satellite platform. Although indigenous capacity was growing, making Vancouver more Marshallian and less satellite platform in character, it remained a hybrid. This outcome was considered unsurprising. Detailed investigations of individual agglomerations will inevitably cause broad-based categories to fragment and blur.

Source: Coe (2001)

---

cooperation between transacting parties, recognizing that common ownership can be associated with varying degrees of coordination. Their typology identifies three types of small-firm cluster (Marshallian industrial districts, Third Italian districts and venture-capital networks) as well as separate clusters with varying proportions of large firms.

Gordon and McCann (2000) share a Marshall-type cluster with the Robertson and Langlois typology but differ in their other two categories (see also McCann 2001):

- *Pure agglomeration*: there is no loyalty or particular relationship between firms. Buyer–supplier linkages, for example, continuously change according to immediate market needs and prices. The external benefits of clustering accrue to all firms located within its influence. The only entry cost is the relatively high price of land and property arising from the concentration of activity.
- *Industrial complex*: there are long-term and predictable relations between firms in the complex built around high levels of investment in equipment and infrastructure. Small firms participate mainly as suppliers to or buyers from large firms.

- *Social network*: strong local networks of inter-personal relations built on a common culture of mutual trust are the distinctive attributes of these clusters. Trust enables reciprocal relationships between firms and participation in joint activity but the key feature is an absence of opportunism. Individual firms need not fear reprisals after any reorganization of inter-firm relations. It is considered to capture the characteristics of Silicon Valley and Italian industrial districts whereas Robertson and Langlois see these as separate cluster experiences.

In practice, typologies such as these present ideal types that do match reality. The suggestion, for example, that Silicon Valley and Italian industrial districts are both exemplars of the social network overlooks the diversity of Italian districts (see below) and Silicon Valley's labour-market distinctiveness as its primary cluster characteristic (see Chapter 2). Indeed it has been doubted that a pure case of any of Gordon and McCann's clusters could be found (Martin and Sunley 2003: 16). Potentially helpful typologies are constructed from profiles of actual clusters. An example is given below in the case of Italy (Paniccia 2002). Of course, these typologies are specific to the clusters studied and are based on prior mapping of the total population of clusters.

A third possible approach to mapping focuses on the expected outcomes of clusters, such as innovation, export growth or new venture creation. The tendency for case studies of clusters to focus on success stories is perhaps the main use of an outcome focus. Given that successful examples are unlikely to be representative of typical experiences, reliance on case studies has been viewed as a source of weakness (Malmberg and Maskell 2002). Outcome indicators might be used to identify a larger population of clusters than covered with case studies, although this may not ensure a representative sample is obtained where clusters without expected outcomes can be overlooked.

Porter's (1990) interpretation of the origins of national competitiveness has been the source of the most systematic applications of an outcome approach. In this approach, clusters comprise national 'core' industries that directly participate in international trade and a set of supporting industries linked to the core as either suppliers or buyers. The core industries are identified by examining the share of world trade contributed by export activities. By examining national input–output tables, the supporting cluster can be identified. This approach was linked to Porter's 'diamond model' in which competitive advantage results from four determinants: domestic factor conditions, the nature of domestic demand conditions, the presence of related and supporting industries and firm strategy, structure and rivalry. This model has been subject to substantial criticism, particularly in the case of its relevance to small, open economies (Box 4.2). Similarly, Porter's methodology applied to Ireland was problematic because of the importance of foreign-owned companies in Irish exports and the dominance of food exports to the exclusion of clusters existing elsewhere in the economy (O'Malley and van Egeraat 2000). As a basis for identifying clusters it additionally suffered from its primary interest in the sources of national competitiveness. Clusters might be realized at any geographical scale, from a single city to a country as a whole or even a group of neighbouring countries (Porter 2000: 254), but there is no guidance on when a particular locality can be mapped as a cluster (Martin and Sunley 2003). In any case, Porter has since presented an alternative methodology for identifying clusters that shifts towards an input focus although still applied to national industry patterns. This is discussed below among the examples of mapping projects.

The final approach adopts an input focus and seeks to identify clusters through the attributes that are expected to change firm behaviour and

---

Box 4.2 Rough diamond

Porter's diamond model has been assessed as inappropriate for high-income resource-based economies such as New Zealand, Australia and Canada. It overlooked the fact that prominent exporters from these countries often sustained successful strategies of offshore production and value adding. This rendered domestic buyer–supplier relations less critical to national economic success than those built by the subsidiaries of domestic companies in their export markets. To allow for the inclusion of one or more other countries as potential sources of influence on a small economy's competitive advantage, a 'double-diamond' or 'multiple-diamond' model is appropriate. The single-diamond model is biased towards economies with businesses that export from a home base rather than investing overseas.

An ethnocentric United States view of the world was further reflected in the exclusion of foreign-owned multinational enterprises as sources of their host economies' competitive advantage. Foreign subsidiaries, it was argued, tended to lack key managerial and R&D functions, and this limited the opportunity for competitive advantages to be transferred. Cultural differences between the home and host economy were further seen as impeding the likelihood of significant information and technology transfer. The single diamond emphasizes indigenous home-based industry and assumes that competitively useful learning is country-bound.

As well as omitting important resource-based activity and multinational enterprise, the diamond does not deal adequately with how new successful firms emerge and what might be done to encourage their creation. The neatness of the diamond, apparently offering a generic solution for the problem all managers and governments would like to be able to solve – how to generate and keep strong firms that contribute to economic growth – does not mean the gaps can be overlooked.

Sources: Yetton *et al.* (1992); Dunning (1993)

performance. Given that uncertainty remains as to what the significant outcomes of clusters are, there is logic in adopting an input focus. Of course, this is not straightforward as there is not a checklist of agreed inputs. Two attributes are frequently attached to clusters: connectedness and concentration. Some degree of mutual interdependence is expected between participants in a cluster, although this might be anything from the stimulus of intense competitive rivalry, informal tacit knowledge sharing (or other non-traded dependencies) or buyer–supplier networks with varying degrees of loyalty between contracting parties. There is agreement that clustering implies a degree of activity concentration, although the spatial scale at which the concentration is to be measured is not specified. With two under-defined attributes there is a risk of compounding inaccuracy when both are used.

Connectedness has been searched for from input–output data (Box 4.3). This assumes that buyer–supplier interaction creates clusters or at least is part of the interdependence from which clusters are built. A top-down approach to cluster identification is implied by the use of input–output linkages. Without borders or customs administrations, regions are unable to collect detailed trade statistics either relating to trade with other regions or internally. Estimation techniques exist but the results are unreliable (McCann (2001: 162). In the absence of other information sources, nationally occurring linkages are used as a template for the connections that exist or can exist within local economies. The underlying rationale is that businesses will prefer to localize their links to suppliers and customers.

Box 4.3 Input output templates

Using detailed information on national inter-industry linkages, the United States manufacturing economy comprises 23 extended buyer–supplier chains. These chains comprise various major final market-producing sectors with their key first-, second- and third-tier supplier sectors. Close to 90 per cent of manufacturing was attached to the 23 national clusters in 1992. They vary in composition from 116 separate industries (defined at the three- or four-digit SIC level) in the case of metalworking to 4 in the case of tobacco. The linkages are revealed by principal components factor analysis applied to the 1987 United States input–output accounts. Interpretation of the results was guided by the objective to identify clusters based on industries with the tightest linkage to each other, allowing some cluster members to be linked to other clusters as well. At the same time, as far as possible it was aimed to produce mutually exclusive clusters to enable cross-cluster comparisons of size and growth rates. As well, statistical analysis sought to separate industries that are moderately or weakly related to several clusters and that potentially serve to link them.

The national clusters are used as templates for comparing broad patterns and proportions of sector representation present in states or regions. Input–output flows are regarded as the single best uniform means of identifying which firms and industries are most likely to interact, either in a formal or informal manner. Template clusters provide a means to identify potential specializations in the regional economy by revealing both relative strengths and absolute gaps in particular product chains.

Guidance from national templates is judged better than investigating actual input–output linkages in the locality of interest. Local data reveal existing connections. They do not suggest gaps in supplier chains that may point to development opportunities. Applied to North Carolina, industries that form part of the vehicle-manufacturing template cluster are discovered to account for 15 per cent of the state's employment. As the state did not currently have a vehicle-assembly industry, the presence of potentially linked activity is suggested to give grounds for expecting its attraction to the state. A profile of the state's vehicle-assembly industry reveals gaps in the existing range of activity compared with the national template. These gaps might represent specializations to be filled to help attract final assembly as well, although fuller investigation is needed to establish this.

Source: Feser and Bergman (2000)

Of course, the increased localization of trading relationships might be viewed as an outcome that is encouraged to varying degrees. Indeed there is much evidence to indicate that business linkages show little tendency to localize. For example, in the USA it has been shown that the location of the footwear industry is not influenced by the location of raw material or equipment supplies nor by the distribution of buyers (Sorenson and Audia 2000: 431). Even in the context of new 'greenfield' industries seeking 'just-in-time' supply relationships the impetus to concentrate appears to be low. A component industry was attracted to the so-called transplant corridor where most of the auto-assembly plants set up by Japanese companies in the USA located. One study showed that close to 40 per cent of suppliers were over 400 kilometres away from the assembly plant they supplied (Kenney and Florida 1993). Modern methods of communication permit long-distance supply-chain partnering even among organizations with exceptional dependencies on outside suppliers (Donaghu and Barff 1990; McGrath and Hoole 1992). As well as the capacity to manage long-distance exchanges and absorb transport charges (Chapter 5, Box 5.6), strategic concerns can lead organizations to favour dispersion of their supply relationships (Perry and Tan 1998). Such assessments might question whether connectedness can be considered an input approach to cluster identification. This approach carries a number of further implications as well:

- It implies that local economies can become miniature replicas of their national economy. If the chemical industry nationally exhibits connections with a range of suppliers and customers, for example, the assumption is that these connections have potential to exist wherever the chemical industry is located. Such potential overlooks the existence of economies of scale in production that limit the localization of supply networks. As discussed in Chapter 5, new economic geography has given attention to exploring such relationships and tends to see concentration in a single region as a more likely outcome than dispersed clusters of interdependent activity.

- It does not permit of business specialization within industries. Aggregate industry linkages revealed in a national template need to be reconciled with the reality that individual organizations vary in the range of activity undertaken. At the extreme, for example, food and drink production is conducted by organizations from boutique manufacturers targeting local markets to global multinationals. Linkages may be expected to vary with different scales and types of production.

- The spatial scale at which the national input–output template is applied is undetermined from the analysis. Proponents of the approach suggest a key advantage of the method is to identify latent opportunities in a local economy (Feser and Bergman 2000:4). These are taken to be indicated by gaps in the range of activity that the national template suggests can be present. The problem is that such gaps may just appear to exist because of the spatial scale to which the template is applied.

A need to conduct local investigations to verify that expected linkages exist between firms, either formally or informally, is acknowledged in research that has identified national input–output templates (Feser and Bergman 2000). The question, therefore, is not whether this approach provides the best identification of clusters but whether it offers the best guide as to where clusters might be searched for.

There are three main advantages of using industry concentration as a starting point. First, it permits of the possibility of negative cases: namely, clusters that have no effect on business performance. Mapping clusters on the basis of variables that require some observable change in business behaviour, such as the use and location of suppliers, risks reducing the issue to a self-confirming proposition. Clusters are identified by the change expected, ruling out the possibility of non-conforming cases. The expectation may be that clusters affect business performance but precisely how much and why need to be confirmed through studies of localities with varying attributes.

Second, typically concentration can be measured with a high degree of detail and reliability utilizing comparatively up-to-date official statistics. As well, some measure of ownership concentration can frequently be combined with that for activity concentration. This enables concentration arising from a single large undertaking to be identified, although the distinction is restricted often to 'establishments' rather than separate legal ownerships.

Third, it is selective in that only localities meeting specified criteria are identified as potential clusters. Using the input–output approach, the presence of activity that is part of the nationally identified cluster qualifies a locality as part of a cluster. As input–output linkages typically encompass multiple activity, few locations are going to be without connection to at least one cluster. In contrast, employment concentration enables discrimination between places, thus avoiding the risk of inflating cluster counts and providing the ability to focus detailed investigations.

It might be argued that since there is no agreed geographical level at which to measure clusters even the effort to map geographical concentration is futile. Labour-market catchment areas, as revealed through travel-to-work patterns, are arguably the most appropriate starting point (Box 4.4). Even so, comparative information from a variety of geographical scales may be mapped usefully to demonstrate how cluster counts are influenced by the selection of boundaries. In this regard, excluding cluster attributes other than concentration enables easy comparison of how different geographical scales affect cluster counts.

Box 4.4 Labour-market catchments and clusters

From any centre of population, travel-to-work time and cost constrain the spatial area over which residents commute to work. Travel-to-work areas (TTWAs) are thus a well-established basis for identifying local labour-market areas. As boundaries that capture a high proportion of the daily interaction among people and between businesses and local populations, they provide a relevant context in which to search for business clusters. This was recognized in Italy by Sforzi (1990) whose arguments for identifying industrial districts based on TTWAs were subsequently adopted by the Italian central statistical office (Paniccia 2002: 51). Local-government regions might comprise several distinct local economies with comparatively low levels of interaction and were thus discarded in favour of TTWAs.

Attention needs to be given to the statistical procedures and judgements that influence the identification of TTWAs. Boundaries do not emerge naturally from commuting patterns so much as being imposed upon them to simplify a more complex reality. For example, the number and shape of labour-market areas will vary according to the level of self-containment and the minimum population size set for the statistical analysis (Perry and Newell 2004). Judgements may also be imposed on the treatment of long-distance commuting and travel patterns outside normal work times. Similar specializations in neighbouring TTWAs might be seen as grounds for combining areas or as serendipitous outcomes. In Italy, amalgamation is allowed up to a maximum population only.

All boundaries are subject to change over time including TTWAs. Changes in transport infrastructure, commuting times and the distribution of population and employment potentially reconfigure local labour markets. Fortunately for the stability of TTWA boundaries, potential sources of change can cancel each other out (Perry and Newell 2004). Shifts in gender participation in work result in shifts in gender differences in commuting. Increased mobility is offset by increased congestion. Consequently, over one or two decades boundaries can be conserved. The extent of change also needs to be assessed against the instability of political boundaries linked to the organization of local government.

The risk of overlooking multi-industry connections is a frequent objection to the use of concentration. New industries, such as biotechnology and opto-electronics, are a case in point especially as industry life-cycle theories predict a tendency for these to concentrate (Dosi 1984). Groups such as these can be unrecognized in official statistics as new industries typically stay buried within large firms having other interests and in new start-ups with specializations yet to be recognized in standard industrial classifications. While there is a lag before new industries are reflected fully in the categories used in official statistics, trade publications and industry membership records may need to be relied upon. Of course, these may not always be available but caution is appropriate in assuming that emerging specializations justify mapping (Box 4.5). In the case of biotechnology,

---

Box 4.5 Shaky relations

Wellington (New Zealand) is home to a cluster of earthquake-engineering enterprises. Much of the expertise exists within multi-activity engineering and risk-assessment firms and research teams within university and government research institutes. They have formed a joint marketing identity to pursue work in overseas markets with support from national and local government cluster-assistance schemes. It is often presented as a group discovered by cluster promotion initiatives. In fact the 'cluster' had already existed, although organized as a professional association for individual earthquake experts. The business association set up with government cluster-assistance questions whether a significant Wellington specialization is overlooked by official statistics.

Initial membership split as it was discovered that the businesses had different specializations, with a separate natural hazards group formed. Members remaining in the earthquake cluster include solely Wellington-based businesses but often the Wellington office of a larger business with interests wider than earthquake technology. Some members have no base in the Wellington region. Public policy has helped give the earthquake-engineering cluster a profile but the activity is not on a scale to make it a specialization of the Wellington economy.

Source: Perry (2004a)

for example, constituent activity is typically more closely aligned to user sectors of its particular technology than to other sectors within the biotechnology industry (Prevezer 1998: 183). For this reason, standard industrial classifications still have their relevance.

The case of assembly or other activities that rely on inputs from multiple separate specializations may deserve attention. Thus boat building and marine engineering comprise both a final activity and a range of supplier inputs that are classified as part of other industries. Once again there is a risk of clusters being unrecognized although if there are important local linkages it implies the existence of a large local market and the ability to identify a concentration based on the core assembly activity, in which case, the risk is in underestimating the full extent of clusters rather than in their initial identification. On this basis, cross-industry connection may be pursued in the further investigation of all identified clusters rather than being an additional basis for inclusion in the initial population.

The perspective taken here is that mapping on the basis of industry concentration offers the best way of capturing the diversity among clusters. Equally, it is important to recognize that cluster maps are at best an approximate indicator of a phenomenon not captured simply by a high level of concentration. Present understanding means that embellishing initial identification criteria with additional attributes are likely to be based on particular interpretations of clusters. At the same time, it should not be overlooked that consideration needs to be given to the best way of measuring concentration.

Industry distribution and clusters

Clustering may be measured from the perspective of an industry or locality or both. An industry might be considered clustered if establishments within it tend to concentrate in a few locations rather than being comparatively evenly distributed among places. A locality that is the home of an industry concentration may then be counted as a cluster. It shows that activity of a particular type has accumulated in a particular locality to the relative exclusion of other localities, and most accounts of clustering see this as a basic requirement. On the other hand, the geographical distribution of an industry says nothing about a locality's dependence on the activity. An industry may be concentrated in a few places without it being a dominant or even important activity within the local economy where it has accumulated. Moreover, it is frequently the case that the majority of industries are concentrated at the same location (Brakman *et al.* 2001: 129). A degree of dependence between the locality and the industry is generally thought to be needed for a concentration to be a cluster. At the extreme, a locality dominated by a single activity is clearly of different significance to a concentration that is a small part of a large economy. The latter, for example, is unlikely to develop a specialized labour market, dedicated support industry or other components of the special 'industrial atmo-sphere' that are thought to stimulate the advantage of clusters.

At the same time, emphasizing the locality perspective raises the ques-tion of how to classify ubiquitous industries. For example, many small towns may have a high reliance on retailing, distribution and personal ser-vices and on this basis be classified as clusters but there are also reasons not to do so. Activities that are found in all local economies are unlikely to develop the same linkages to an individual locality as would an industry that is concentrated in a few places. This possibility would seem to be especially likely where, as is frequently the case, ubiquitous industries are dominated by national organizations.

The distinction between an industry and locality perspective is some-times referred to as a difference between 'concentration' and 'special-ization'. Some researchers may be interested in one dimension only. Brakman *et al.* (2001: 129) point out, for example, that concentration is the key issue for geographical economics (or 'new economic geography', Chapter 5). Indeed, they suggest that the interest of new economic geo-graphy is really focused on 'agglomeration' which they identify as the con-centration of all industry rather than specific industries. Much economic analysis potentially linked to the debate about clusters is, therefore, actu-ally investigating location concentration of a more prevalent form than clustering. This was seen in the discussion of the relative advantages of specialized versus diversified cities (Chapter 3) and is emphasized in the discussion of new economic geography (Chapter 5).

How far a combination of concentration and specialization is required to identify a cluster is a point of debate. One view, for example, is that both indicators are required to identify 'industrial districts' but not 'clus-ters' (Crouch and Farrell 2001: 163). In this assessment, clusters are a 'second-tier' concentration worthy of recognition as they indicate that some advantage exists in locating among similar activity. On the other hand, the evidence reviewed in Chapter 3 suggests that concentrated activ-ity may gain from urbanization economies as much as localization economies. It would, therefore, seem important to seek to distinguish cases where concentration is associated with some degree of local eco-nomic specialization as well. Requiring an activity to be concentrated within and a specialization of a locality increases the likelihood of activity being influenced by localization as well as urbanization economies. While the combination of concentration and specialization is recommended, it is helpful to discuss each measure separately.

Concentration

A cluster comprises a geographical concentration of similar activity, within a specific locality, that is expected to facilitate business advantage. Leaving aside the possible difficulty arising where the activity does not fit within the categories used in official statistics, geographical concentration can be examined from the perspective of the industry and the locality (see McCann (2001) for calculation procedures). An industry perspective provides an overall summary of the extent to which an industry's employment (or other measure of activity) is equally distributed among regions (or other geographical divisions). A locality perspective indicates how the proportion of a locality's activity in a particular industry compares with the national share of that industry and is assessed using some form of location quotient. To identify clusters in Germany, the overall concentration of industry employment was examined in conjunction with a measure of the industry's importance in individual localities (Box 4.6).

The Gini index has been the most frequently used way of assessing the degree to which the regional distribution of one variable (for example,

---

Box 4.6 Clusterless Germany

Applied to employment data, Gini coefficients express the degree to which employment in an industry is unequally dispersed over localities. The localization coefficient measures the degree of industry concentration in a particular locality relative to the average employment in the industry among all localities.

A locality with a high localization coefficient in an industry that has a high Gini coefficient, therefore, identifies a locality accommodating a particularly large concentration of an activity that is unequally dispersed and concentrated. These may be taken as more significant cases of clustering than where a high localization coefficient exists for an industry with a low Gini coefficient except that the effects of firm size also need to be considered. Industries that are dominated by large firms tend to show a high degree of spatial concentration as do industries which have specific resource requirements (for example, oil processing, iron and steel production, and shipbuilding).

In Germany, there are a few examples of industries dominated by small enterprises that have high rates of spatial concentration. Most numerous are industries where firms are small because of a dependency on proximity to clients (for example, car repairs, parts of the food industry and printing). Export-orientated and technology-intensive sectors are comparatively unconcentrated.

Claims that clusters are important tend to relate to specialized activities. These are difficult to verify in the absence of available statistics, especially as the scope of activities and the spatial limits of clusters tend not to be defined. Some claims appear to relate to activities where the presence of a few large firms in the area concerned can account for the concentration. The German economy is provided homogenously with collective competitive goods, implying that firms can expect no unique advantage from differences in institutions that would lead them to set up in one place rather than another.

Source: Glassmann and Voelzkow (2001)

employment in a particular industry) deviates from the regional distribution of a 'neutral' yardstick. The choice of the neutral comparison will influence the extent to which an individual activity is found to be distributed unevenly. The ideal comparison is with a distribution determined solely by 'random choice' and uninfluenced by agglomeration or decentralization forces. The most usual way is to compare an industry distribution with the distribution of all employment (or total manufacturing employment if a manufacturing industry is being examined). A complication is that this 'neutral' distribution contains some influence from forces promoting concentration and dispersion. Random choice can also lead to some firms selecting the same location. This has been discussed with the analogy of a map of the USA being used as a dartboard: if six darts are thrown at the map, two are likely to land in the same state (Ellison and Glaeser 1994). Any level of concentration above this random allocation has hence been argued to indicate spatial clustering even when the degree of spatial concentration is low (Brakman *et al.* 2001: 135).

No method to measure concentration establishes the industry or geographical divisions that should be used. There is probably general agreement that it is desirable to use a detailed industry classification (three- or four-digit SIC level) but more uncertainty about the appropriate geographical boundaries for identifying clusters. As discussed above, the use of labour-market catchments can be advantageous over regional boundaries as the latter can combine dispersed communities with little interconnection. Depending on which boundaries are selected, markedly different impressions of the level of concentration can be obtained. In the USA, using four-digit SIC-level industries, there is little concentration at the level of counties, more at the level of states but only among census divisions (dividing the USA into nine regions) is high concentration seen in more than a small minority of industries (Holmes and Stevens 2002).

A direct measure of concentration based on the physical distance between establishments avoids the need to prescribe geographic boundaries. As discussed in Chapter 3, this approach distinguishes activity occurring in high densities from isolated locations and has been applied to the footwear (Sorenson and Audia 2000) and biotechnology industries (Stuart and Sorenson 2003) in the USA. In these studies, a measure of localized density is obtained for each establishment. The calculation treats each establishment in turn as a focal plant and measures its distance from all other establishments. Each establishment is thus assigned a localized density score. Distances between establishments were based on latitude and longitude grid references. Outside the USA, where long distances can minimize differences between actual and geographical distances, measurement along transport networks might be required.

The relative degrees of isolation experienced by individual workplaces offers a useful insight but this differs from interest in the character of local economies. In another study based on geographical distances, the location of every registered company in England, Scotland and Wales was plotted (Bennett *et al.* 1999). It concluded that as most firms were concentrated in groups within 20 km distance of each other, there were unlikely to be problems arising from physical isolation.

Whatever the geographical scale at which clusters are identified, the relative importance of large and small establishments influences the degree of concentration observed. The Ellison–Glaeser index (Ellison and Glaeser 1997: 899) improves on a basic measure of activity concentration by recognizing that in industries consisting of a few relatively large plants, location concentration will be higher than in industries comprising many small operations. This adjustment was introduced to help judge whether industries were becoming more or less regionally concentrated in the USA and it produces markedly different results from an unadjusted index (Braunerhjelm and Johansson 2003). Similar difference was also obtained in an application to French data of the same two approaches (Maurel and Sedillot 1999). In the USA, of the ten most geographically concentrated industries measured by the Ellison–Glaeser index, four appear in a Gini coefficient top-ten ranking using the same 1993 data (Braunerhjelm and Johansson 2003: 53). Comparing each index over time, the Ellison–Glaeser index indicates greater instability in the industries that are identified as most concentrated in 1975 and 1993.

Small economies tend to be more specialized than large ones, especially if their openness to international trade is high (Maskell *et al.* 1998; Perry 2001). This immediately increases the likelihood of many activities being agglomerated because outside national specializations industries are small. In the early 1990s in Denmark, for example, none of the six most localized industries consisted of more than ten plants (Maskell *et al.* 1998: 61). Consequently, a high level of concentration does not have to mean that an industry comprises several spatially clustered groups of activity. Concentration levels can thus show a high level of sensitivity to shifts in the number of establishments. Among four Nordic countries covering periods from the 1970s to 1990s, 70 per cent of industries with an increasing Gini index (suggesting a more uneven spatial distribution of employment was developing) had a decline in the number of establishments (Maskell *et al.* 1998: 61). Thus even in small economies, examining spatial concentration without also considering establishment concentration can give a misleading impression of the trend towards clusters. It may result simply from the consolidation of activity in fewer, larger establishments.

On whatever basis the concentration measure is obtained there are three main options for analysing scores:

- Ranking: include all cases in the assessment, as an opportunity to correlate other attributes (for example, firm performance or employment growth) with the relative degree of concentration.
- Top cases: nominate a concentration level to mark a threshold

between concentrated industries. For example, localities with above the mean level of concentration might be taken as potential clusters. Such a threshold is likely to qualify a large number of areas as potential clusters. To reduce the list, the threshold can be raised or a number or proportion of cases that will be accepted as concentrated industries can be specified.

- Extreme cases: high frequencies of clusters are potentially in conflict with claims about the distinctiveness of clusters, making it desirable to select extreme cases only. Crouch and Farrell (2001: 163) suggest that using a threshold of 1.5 standard deviations above or below the mean is a way of identifying outliers or extreme cases when data is normally distributed and that this can serve as a guide to identifying clusters. Their data indicated that industry is not normally distributed across TTWAs, with most having zero employment in the range of industries they examined (defined at the four-digit level of the SIC). Consequently, they took three standard deviations above the mean as the threshold for identifying clusters. Unlike the previous methods, such an approach means that some industries may be without clusters.

Specialization

Specialization indicates that the local economy has a disproportionate presence of a particular activity. There has been a long history of studies concerned with the degree of local industrial specialization (or diversification). This has produced at least 11 different ways of measuring regional specialization (Dewhurst and McCann 2002). These methods can be separated between absolute measures that are based on employment for the locality in question and relative measures that involve comparisons of locality data with the distribution of employment between industries at a national level. These methods compare the proportion of activity in the local economy with its share of the national economy (or some other geographical aggregation of local economies). Results are sensitive to the measure employed to the extent that choice of measure can alter the conclusion as to whether specialization is increasing or decreasing over time (Dewhurst and McCann 2002: 550). Unfortunately, analysts are unable to recommend which way of measuring specialization is most relevant to an interest in clustering.

As with the level of concentration, the extent of specialization required to qualify as a cluster remains to be established. Experimentation is required with a range of thresholds to determine which is most effective in capturing clusters. One suggested starting point is to identify an absolute level of specialization that permits a particular branch of industry to influence the formal and informal institutions of a locality (Crouch and Farrell 2001). Levels of specialization existing among Italy's industrial districts were taken as a benchmark for this level of specialization. Such an approach assumed that Italy's industrial districts were characterized by institutional environments adapted to the interests of the dominant industry. As discussed in the case study of cluster mapping in Italy, similar levels of specialization have brought variable levels of institutional adaptation. A mechanistic relationship between the degree of specialization and the capacity for industry to influence the institutional environment cannot be assumed (Box 4.7). The history of the specialization, the extent of local ownership, the precise character of the institutional environment

---

Box 4.7 Leicester: when concentration does not help

A study of small textile firms in three textile towns – Como (Italy), Leicester (UK) and Lyons (France) – shows how similar business structures are associated with different impacts on business behaviour. Around half of the firms surveyed in each centre agreed with the statement 'because this locality has many firms in textiles and/or related activities, customers come from far and wide to find a suitable partner'. Nonetheless the three places were experiencing differences in economic vitality. In Como, 35 per cent of sample firms reported 'rapid growth' compared with 24 per cent and 11 per cent for Lyons and Leicester respectively.

Leicester had the highest proportion of young firms (30 per cent had started from 1980 to 1989, the year of the survey) but also had the highest share in decline (24 per cent), compared with under 10 per cent in the other communities. Compared with Como, the value of productive assets per employee were over eight times lower in Leicester and almost three times lower in Lyons. Como firms generated four times the sales per employee compared with Leicester.

In Como firms typically specialize in one or two processes within the textile or knitwear production chain. Lyons has a specialization in weaving while in Leicester knitwear firms tend to engage in all aspects of garment production and specialize according to product. In Leicester, 30 per cent of firms do not subcontract work or accept subcontracts, compared with less than 10 per cent of firms in the other two localities. If they do, typically it is for capacity reasons. Como has most evidence of strategic relationships based on specialization.

In Leicester, big retail chains tend to take responsibility for design. Firms in Como tend to be specialists. Specialization concentrates improvement effort and makes capital investment less daunting than where firms try to maintain multiple roles, as in Leicester.

Leicester is an industrial community: a place of industry specialization without the development of strategic linkages between firms (Lyons is similar except that networks may exist with strategic partners outside the region). Successful firms in the Leicester cluster develop a market niche and attain a size that enables specialist managers to be employed. This strategy supports the growth of some firms but even their sustainability is affected by the context of a locality in which many firms are declining or struggling to stay as they are.

Source: Bull *et al.* (1991)

and its capacity to be of assistance to industry all affect the relationship between specialization and institutional environments.

Given problems that may exist with nominating a specific level of specialization, it may be simpler to look at relative levels of specialization. As with concentration, once all localities have been ranked it is possible to take either a certain proportion of cases or extreme cases only. Crouch and Farrell (2001) found, for example, that it was necessary to adapt a uniform level of specialization to employment patterns in the United Kingdom. Here the average share of manufacturing employment in TTWAs was 10.58 per cent or less than half that in Italian districts. For individual manufacturing industries, they took 5 per cent as the minimum level of specialization to qualify 'industrial districts' when dealing with broadly defined industries and 2.5 per cent when dealing with sub-branches. They acknowledged that a local employment share of around 5 per cent was probably too low to yield the kind of influence they interpreted as existing in Italy. Their difficulty, as discussed below, was that no industrial districts would be identified using a significantly higher specialization level. On the other hand, omitting specialization from the eligibility criteria caused the number of 'clusters' to increase substantially.

Cluster mapping

Examining existing efforts to map clusters in a comprehensive fashion illustrates how the measurement of concentration and specialization is being applied. The experience of these projects can be used to ask whether expertise is accumulating in a way that gives greater certainty in the identification of clusters or, as Martin and Sunley (2003) argue, whether these exercises merely illustrate the lack of any coherent conception of clustering.

Harvard cluster-mapping project

The Harvard cluster-mapping project is associated with Michael Porter and forms the basis of a methodology that his affiliated consultancy firms are seeking to 'roll out' across Europe. The method has first been used to monitor the comparative performance of regional clusters and economies in the United States and is managed by researchers in the Institute for Strategy and Competitiveness, Harvard Business School. In summary, the method adopted to identify clusters comprises three main steps (Porter 2003):

1   *Identify 'traded industries'*: activities dependent on local resources or local markets are excluded from cluster membership. The rationale is that traded industries, being those that sell goods and services beyond their immediate locality, are most likely to make location decisions

based on the relative advantage of places. A combination of statistical analysis and qualitative judgement are used to distinguish traded from 'local' and 'resource-dependent activities'. Location quotients and Gini coefficients separate activities that fall outside the traded category. Widely dispersed employment is viewed as most probably indicating a high dependence on local markets; highly concentrated employment is an indicator of resource dependence. The final allocation of activities is then checked to ensure that the intent of the categorization is maintained. For example, employment data suggest retailing is a traded industry but 'judgement' results in it being allocated to the local group.

2   *Allocate cluster membership*: clusters are understood to comprise a range of activity from multiple industry groups rather than being limited to concentrations of similar activity. To identify linked activity, the location correlation between individual industries is calculated. Thus a high correlation between employment in computer hardware and employment in software is taken to indicate that the two activities are interdependent and that collectively they constitute a cluster, potentially including other activities as well. Cluster membership is built up through the pragmatic judgement of 'obviously related' activity and the correlation results. Where proposed clusters represented unlikely or unrecognized combinations, 'focused case studies' examined whether linkages could be present. This might include examination of national input–output tables, although buyer–supplier linkages are considered only one form of location interdependence.

3   *Establish cluster boundaries*: the average set of linked activities comprises activity from 29 industries out of the total of 638 traded industries mapped. There are 41 groupings indicating that many industries are present in multiple groups. The education and knowledge group, for example, shares with other groupings publishing and printing, financial services, medical devices, analytical instruments as well as other industries. Other groups, including footwear and forest products, are relatively independent of other industries. To reduce overlap, 'broad' and 'narrow' groups are distinguished. Narrow groups allocate each industry to the grouping with which it has the strongest location correlation to create mutually exclusive groups. 'Subclusters' are identified within broad and narrow clusters to identify industries more correlated with each other than the remainder of the group.

The above steps identify 'clusters' as groups of industries thought to gain from sharing a location with each other. In this approach, as with the input–output method discussed above, clustered industries are identified rather than the localities that accommodate clusters. Using location correlations rather than input–output data as the primary source of guidance reflects a wish to identify activity connections more fully than through trading relations alone.

At the level of local economies, the Harvard map identifies industries that the methodology implies are potentially linked, although researchers interested in particular locations would probably wish to confirm this in the context of the particular activity and locality. For example, a location dominated by branch manufacturing establishments may have fewer claims to be considered a cluster than a locality where the industry activity includes head offices and research activities that share the use of business services and that engage in activity generating significant knowledge spillovers. As pointed out, each region in the United States has some employment in almost every cluster but without the region having a mean-ingful competitive position in each cluster represented in its territory (Porter 2003: 568).

The Harvard approach to mapping clusters relies on attributes exist-ing in a geographically and economically large country that are unlikely to be found in smaller economies (Porter 2003). The key requirement is for a sufficient diversity of economic activity in a large number of dis-tinct locations. If too many locations have no or little representation in an industry, all other locations will be registered as having high concen-trations. Location correlations might then simply indicate a tendency for activity to favour a few locations rather than industry interdepen-dencies. Even in the United States, this problem arises. Industries with a major presence in large employment states like California and New York can register a high location correlation without any common interests actually existing between them. The Harvard project uses states as the base unit for computing location correlations to provide sufficiently large geographical aggregations to minimize the proportion of localities with zero or small employment in an industry. A disadvan-tage is that within large states, correlated industries may be separated geographically and have few mutual externalities. The researchers are aware of this problem and report that judgemental adjustments are made to the statistical results to try and minimize spurious location cor-relations.

Even after adjusting for doubtful location correlations, it is worth noting that the nine largest industry clusters (using the narrow cluster def-initions) encompass activities for which proximity to a large population, transport infrastructure and resource availability are potential influences on location (Table 4.1). Total cluster employment reduces by 60 per cent to around 18 per cent of all employment in the United States when these nine clusters are excluded. The tendency for most traded industries to belong to multiple broad clusters provides another source of doubt about the extent to which the Harvard method succeeds in separating linked activity. Activity that is simultaneously associated with many other activities suggests the operation of urbanization economies rather than localization

Table 4.1 Employment in the top nine of 41 'narrow' industry clusters in the Harvard Cluster Map, 2000

Cluster	Employment 2000	Share of all traded cluster employment (%)
Business services	4,667,320	13.3
Financial services	3,242,151	9.2
Hospitality and tourism	2,565,077	7.3
Education and knowledge creation	2,246,974	6.4
Distribution services	1,962,523	5.6
Heavy construction services	1,883,271	5.3
Transport and logistics	1,644,641	4.7
Metal manufacturing	1,412,368	4.0
Processed food	1,388,073	3.9
All traded clusters	35,028,441	

Source: Porter (2003).

economies, or that the level of analysis does not identify sufficient detail to separate clusters.

Cluster mapping in the United Kingdom

Two cluster-mapping projects conducted in the United Kingdom, published in the same year, share a stronger commitment to the conception of clusters as unique, local phenomena than the Harvard project's emphasis on national industry clusters (Crouch and Farrell 2001; Department of Trade and Industry 2001). Both include the use of location quotients but then differ in their efforts to go beyond this indicator alone. Direct comparison of the results is not possible. One study, for example, is based on regions, the other on TTWAs. If results are adjusted to a common basis, some comparison is possible. A summary below adjusts the findings to make a comparison, although ideally this would have reworked the original analysis rather than simply reclassify the published results.

The study conducted for the Department of Trade and Industry (hereafter referred to as the DTI study although actually completed by independent consultants) sought to identify 'geographically co-located activities whose interrelations reinforced their competitive advantage'. The analysis is based on regional concentrations of industries defined at the five-digit SIC level, excluding those outside the competitive economy (for example, higher education and hospitals) and activities judged to serve local markets only. Following Porter's interpretation of clusters, the study assumes clusters typically comprise linked activity from multiple industries. Much effort is, therefore, given to trying to establish connections between separate industries. The method comprised six main steps, although an iterative process is followed to allow ongoing refinement as information is accumulated:

1   *Regional 'highs'*: activities that are over-represented in a region are identified as an initial indicator of the presence of clusters. The 'highs' must have a minimum location quotient of 1.25 and account for over 0.2 per cent of the region's workforce.

2   *Highs grouped*: through a combination of 'judgement and interpretation' individual highs are grouped together into a single cluster of linked activity. This exercise makes use of known value chains. For example, because spinning, weaving and knitwear are known stages of garment production they are grouped as a cluster; similarly food and agricultural activities are taken as linked. Further guidance on the existence of industry connections comes from discussions with representatives of regionally based economic agencies. As well, Dun and Bradstreet business directories are used to examine the product profiles of larger companies to determine whether these suggest additional linkages. For example, a glass manufacturer is clustered with the food industry if the directory indicates some glass firms make food-storage containers.

3   *Unallocated activity reviewed*: Activities meeting either the location quotient or the regional employment-share criteria, but not both, are reviewed to determine whether they should be added to an existing group or form the core of a new group.

4   *Employment within regions*: employment patterns within local-authority areas (which may divide the typical region into 12 or more smaller areas) are examined. Concentrations at the local level may not be evident in regional data but justify inclusion as a cluster where they have a location quotient over five and total employment of more than 1,000 jobs or a share of national industry employment of 0.2 per cent or more. Concentrations in local-authority areas not accepted as regional clusters may be identified as 'less significant clusters'. At the same time, previously identified regional clusters may get excluded where local-authority data reveal that they are the result of one or a few large establishments.

5   *Cross-industry and cross-region clusters*: a combination of 'local knowledge' and business-activity profiles, obtained from the Dun and Bradstreet database, are used to identify clusters based on activity from multiple industry categories or adjacent regions (or both). Cross-industry groupings that are captured as clusters include biotechnology, opto-electronics, environmental services, research and development activity, and motor sport, of which opto-electronics and motor sport are examples of cross-regional clusters.

6   *Cluster profiles*: 'initial assessments' profile clusters according to their: (i) stage of development (embryonic, established and mature); (ii)

depth as judged by the extent of components (for example, a complete value chain) and supporting institutions; (iii) employment dynamics; (iv) significance, as judged by the sphere of economic influence from local to international, through regional and national levels.

The method followed is offered as a rough guide to the location of clusters acknowledging that 'some of the included industries may not be actually or potentially be part of the cluster' (Department of Trade and Industry, Volume 3 2001: 18). From the perspective of the researchers, the main information gap is the lack of certainty that activities allocated to a cluster are actually linked in a way that enhances or has potential to enhance firm competitiveness. For example, while the study is confident about the existence of an offshore oil and gas industry in Scotland, because of the extent of employment concentration in these activities, it expresses uncertainty whether engineering and distribution services form an additional part of this cluster.

As alluded to in the previous section, Crouch and Farrell (2001) approach the identification of clusters guided by interpretations of Italy's industrial districts rather than Porter's descriptions of clusters. One consequent difference to the DTI study is that less effort is given to combining separate industries within single clusters. Following methods used to identify industrial districts in Italy (see following case study), Crouch and Farrell base their study on TTWAs and limit examination to manufacturing activity. In addition to their category of industrial districts, different employment criteria are used to develop a fourfold classification of districts and clusters.

Industrial districts

Five criteria are used to distinguish industrial districts. The criteria vary according to whether a branch (two-digit SIC level) industry or sub-branch (three- or four-digit) industry is assessed. The working procedure is first to examine sub-branches and then consider whether additional TTWAs qualify using the higher level of industry aggregation:

1   A concentration of its employed population working in manufacturing industry that is above the national average.
2   An above average concentration of its employed population working in small manufacturing units (defined as having 200 or fewer employees).
3   An above average concentration of its employed population working in such small units within one or more industry sub-branch (failing that within one or more industry branch).
4   At least 5 per cent of its employed population working in that branch (or at least 2.5 per cent in the sub-branch).

5   More than 20 small employing units within the branch or sub-branch industry.

These localities, therefore, are required to display both a relative bias towards manufacturing and a specialization within the manufacturing sector built upon multiple separate establishments. Those localities with over 5 per cent of employment in a sub-branch are distinguished as the most concentrated districts. These cases are thought to have greatest potential to develop a supporting institutional environment dedicated to the interests of the cluster. Such customization of institutional orientation is expected to be the result of, and a further inducement to, high levels of industry concentration and locality specialization. The study itself does not provide evidence that this has or is likely to occur but it identifies a set of localities where the search for these relationships might be directed in the first instance.

Concentrated clusters

A concentrated cluster is counted where firms of a similar type locate together without them having a particularly important presence in the locality. This is expected to be the most usual instance of clustering. Firms in a concentrated cluster are believed to gain from their mutual proximity but local public institutions may be unconcerned about their presence, leaving further benefits unrealized (Crouch and Farrell 2001: 163). Strong and weak cases of concentrated clusters are distinguished. For the former, there are two selection criteria.

1   At least one industry sub-branch with an employment concentration at or above three standard deviations of the national mean TTWA concentration for that sub-branch.
2   More than 20 small employing units within the branch or sub-branch industry.

In the case of weak concentrated clusters, the 20 units may be attached to the industry branch from which the sub-branch with the employment concentration is drawn. A perception that establishments in the sub-branch may gain in some way from a wider community of not entirely dissimilar activities provides the rationale for the secondary forms of concentrated cluster.

Simple clusters

A TTWA that has more than 20 small establishments in a sub-branch is counted as a simple cluster. Although recognized to be a low threshold, it is claimed that establishments in a simple cluster will have a location advantage over isolated members of their activity. Consequently, even without an exceptional concentration of employment, there is believed to be justification for counting simple clusters (see the section 'Agglomeration and competition' in Chapter 3 for an alternative assessment). The low qualification requirements require three adjustments to earlier procedures so as to avoid excessive numbers of clusters being recorded:

1   TTWAs with large populations are more likely than sparsely populated TTWAs to reach the 20-unit threshold. TTWAs in the London region are excluded on this basis given their especially large populations.
2   Sub-branches which 'obviously' serve 'very local' markets are excluded, such as bakeries and suppliers of goods for the construction industry.
3   Residual activity groupings such as general printing or general engineering are excluded on the grounds that they do not constitute true specialist sub-branches.

Comparing cluster maps

Differences in the breadth of activity, geographical aggregation (regions versus TTWAs) and the DTI's efforts to include cross-industry clusters make it difficult to compare the cluster totals. Nonetheless, some overlap in the clusters identified clearly exists. In the case of Scotland, for example, Crouch and Farrell identify five industrial districts based respectively on fish processing, whisky, textiles (two) and clothing, with additional concentrated clusters based on fish, whisky and textiles. In addition, there is one concentrated cluster based on general mechanical engineering. Within the manufacturing sector, the DTI study identifies similar clusters as well as an ICT cluster (computer equipment and semiconductors), shipbuilding, and wood and paper products clusters. In the case of 'Silicon Glen', Crouch and Farrell (2001: 191) identified it as a cluster for Scotland as a whole but not for any of their labour-market areas. They suspected that the computer sector did not enter their cluster categories because of dominance by a few big operations that do not develop local supply chains.

To increase the comparability of the two maps, results are adjusted so that both are limited to manufacturing and regional boundaries (Table 4.2). Although caution is still needed in drawing conclusions, it appears that divergent perspectives on the frequency of clustering have been obtained The number of industrial districts and strong concentrated clusters identified by Crouch and Farrell suggest that concentrations of real significance are rare. In contrast, the DTI count suggests that clustering is a frequent phenomenon. This difference is partly an inevitable outcome

Table 4.2 A comparison of two UK cluster counts

Crouch and Farrell (2001)			DTI (2001)[1]	
Cluster significance	Unadjusted	Adjusted[2]	Unadjusted	Adjusted[3]
High	Industrial districts – 37 Concentrated clusters (strong cases) – 47	Industrial districts – 16 Concentrated clusters (strong cases) – 18	Clusters – 112	Clusters – 70
Low	Concentrated clusters (weak cases) – 60 Simple clusters – 488	Concentrated clusters (weak cases) – 18 Simple clusters – 67	Less developed clusters – 36	Less developed clusters – 19 (excludes London, Wales)

Sources: Crouch and Farrell (2001); DTI (2001).

Notes
1 All DTI counts exclude Northern Ireland.
2 Districts and clusters in the same sector are counted as one adjusted district/cluster; districts/clusters from the same sector and separate TTWAs within the same region are counted as one. See text for definitions of districts and concentrated clusters.
3 Service-sector clusters are omitted; London and Wales are excluded from the count of less developed clusters to be consistent with the regions covered by simple clusters.

of the different methodologies employed, although the methods are not entirely biased in a direction of either exaggerating or downplaying the frequency of clusters.

Crouch and Farrell have the potential to find many more clusters than the DTI study because of their use of TTWAs rather than regions. Concentration of a narrowly defined industry is easier to maintain in a small economy than a larger one. On the other hand, as seen in the example of Scotland, some concentrations that are counted at the regional level are not apparent for small areas. By including locality specialization as a criterion, and by requiring a minimum establishment population, Crouch and Farrell set entry requirements that exceed those required by the DTI. How the difference in emphasis on single-industry concentrations versus concentrations of industry groups affected outcomes is hard to judge without detailed insight into how the DTI clusters were compiled. A focus on single industries suggests potential for more clusters unless the grouping of activities qualifies activity that would not generate a cluster if single industries were examined.

The contrasting outcomes may be viewed as an indicator of the chaotic conception of clusters. In this vein, the classifications used by Crouch and Farrell have been judged as little more than a set of arbitrary judgements and the DTI study as without foundation in its assumption that regional employment concentrations say anything about the presence of clusters (Martin and Sunley 2003: 20–1). In the United Kingdom, regions are neither sufficiently self-contained or compactly settled to imply the sharing of infrastructure or labour (or generate any other potential cluster advantages). Such criticism would not necessarily be opposed by the proponents of either study as they both acknowledge their maps are indicative only and that further investigation is required to demonstrate any significance for business behaviour. Crouch and Farrell (2001: 175) thus describe the outcome of their statistical analysis as 'empirical clusters'. Concentration is taken as evidence of the advantage of being part of a crowd but a need to demonstrate the reality of this advantage is recognized. Interestingly, their own attempts to investigate individual cluster characteristics based on secondary sources are restricted by few of the identified industrial districts having been the subject of academic research, unlike some lesser concentrations that failed even to register as concentrated clusters.

One test for evaluating the studies is whether one or both provide the most appropriate guide as to where clusters might exist. Of course, the best information to make this test would be to contrast the results of further investigation of the nominated clusters. In the absence of this insight, four attributes give reason to favour the approach adopted by Crouch and Farrell:

- *Neutrality*: it does not involve assumptions about how business behaviour is affected by proximity and this means that potential outcomes of clustering are not used as defining inputs.
- *Transparency*: the method is based on statistical criteria applied to official statistics. This makes it straightforward to replicate, at different time periods and in different locations, facilitating comparison across studies.
- *Spatial fit*: the use of TTWAs provides a logical starting point for the search for localization economies.
- *Adjustable*: it is amenable to adjustment based on information obtained about the effectiveness of the cluster boundaries delineated with the first round of definitions.

Mapping Italy's industrial districts

Italy's industrial districts are generally taken as pronounced cases of business clustering with strong demarcations between the industrial specializations of districts. Such a view, as discussed above, led Crouch and Farrell (2001) to regard industrial districts as the most developed form of business clusters. In practice, one of the first attempts to map industrial districts showed that locality specialization was often less than frequently

Box 4.8 Italy's first cluster count

Based on an analysis of 1981 census data, Fabio Sforzi identified 61 'Marshallian industrial districts', which were mainly located in the three regions of Veneto, Emilia-Romagna and Tuscany. These localities were identified using three criteria: (i) a geographical cluster of small firms specializing in the different production phases of a single commodity; (ii) a social structure mainly comprising small entrepreneurs and extended families with high labour-force participation; (iii) close proximity between the workplace and residence of small-business operators. To be included, typically around half of total employment was in 'light' manufacturing with at least a quarter of this in the dominate industry. Out of the 61 districts, two-thirds were specialized in one of four sectors: clothing (16); wooden furniture (12); footwear (11); and textiles (5); with eight other sectors represented across the remaining 17 districts. District employment in these industry specializations accounted for around 4 per cent of Italy's total manufacturing employment. Of this employment share, around three-quarters was accounted for by the four sectors most frequently generating industrial districts. In terms of population significance, 4.3 per cent of Italy's resident population lived in the 61 districts.

The degree of specialization within individual districts varied. Overall, total employment in the dominate industries of almost 250,000 amounted to half of all manufacturing employment in the districts and 27 per cent of total employment across all sectors in the districts. The textile and clothing districts were the most specialized: close to 74 per cent of the manufacturing jobs in the five textile districts were in textiles, while the share was 64 per cent in the 11 footwear districts. Amongst the least specialized districts, the share dropped to 31 per cent in the case of musical instruments (over two districts) and 25 per cent in the case of electrical engineering (over three districts).

The industry on which an individual district is based can provide a significant share of secondary employment in the other districts. Of all employment in the 12 industries generating districts, 40 per cent existed outside the places where the sector was locally dominate. In the case of four sectors (metal goods, mechanical engineering, electrical engineering and leather goods) over two-thirds of total employment existed outside the places where the sector was locally dominate.

Source: Sforzi (1990)

presented (Box 4.8). Since then, an official count of industrial districts has been made by the *Istituto Nazionale di Statistica* (ISTAT) that incorporates indicators in that earlier assessment. An evaluation of a sample of the officially counted districts indicates that there continues to be much variety in their structure and economic significance.

The ISTAT analysis is based on TTWAs that have above national average manufacturing employment. Industrial districts must be specialized in at least one industrial sector that has an above average proportion of small and medium-sized enterprises (defined as firms with fewer than 250 employees). These criteria show that industrial districts account for a large share of Italy's employment. Around 50 per cent of total employment and 70 per cent of manufacturing employment are located in around 200 districts (Paniccia 2002: 50). This high importance is mainly an outcome of the regional concentration of manufacturing employment in Italy. Almost two thirds of national manufacturing employment is located in the North (ISTAT 2003). Most TTWAs with a location quotient above one are able to demonstrate that at least one of their manufacturing specializations has a disproportionate share of enterprises with fewer than 250 employees. In 1991, for example, 70 per cent of the manufacturing workforce was located in TTWAs with above average manufacturing employment: 60 per cent of these TTWAs were counted as industrial districts. Industries such as footwear and leather, on which many industrial districts are based, are even more regionally concentrated than manufacturing as a whole. Indeed, it is hard not to find a TTWA that does not qualify as an industrial district in certain regions (Paniccia 2002: 201).

The threefold requirements employed by ISTAT omit many of the features typically thought to be associated with the specialization of industrial districts, such as the importance of artisan enterprise, high levels of interfirm cooperation and an institutional environment dedicated to the support of district specializations. Paniccia (2002) selected a sample of 37 districts meeting ISTAT's criteria in 1991 to identify how widespread such additional attributes were among the officially counted districts. Her sample accounted for around a fifth of all manufacturing establishments and employment in the officially counted districts. The additional attributes searched for were grouped into three categories:

1   *Industry structure attributes*: these indicators went beyond the ISTAT qualifications to include measures of the degree of specialization in the leading industry, the presence of ancillary activity to the lead sector and the importance of artisan and micro-enterprise. Other indicators included were the production concentration among the five largest enterprises; the relative importance of subcontractors and independent manufacturers; the overall diversification of manufacturing employment; the presence of social and cultural services; and a rating of other infrastructure availability.

2   *Social capital*: the percentage of votes obtained by the largest political party or coalition was taken as an indicator of the degree of cultural homogeneity within a district. Workforce qualification rates, the frequency of extended families, union membership, rates of banking and financial service provision were assessed to capture other aspects of social and institutional environment.

3   *Labour-market inclusiveness*: female, youth and migrate employment
    rates were measured as aspects of a district's ability to provide employ-
    ment for a cross-section of society. Participation in clubs and local
    branches of national associations was taken as an indicator of social
    solidarity.

Factor analysis found two types of frequently occurring industrial district: craft-based districts (14 cases) and concentrated districts (12). The
remainder of the sample divided between peripheral districts (9) and
archetypal (or 'canonical') industrial districts (3). The two most numerous types of district differed greatly in character. The craft districts had a
preponderance of family enterprise among a high population of entrepreneurs and self-employed workers. In the concentrated districts, lead
industries had a high proportion of firms with over 50 employees and a
local support base of tool and machine suppliers. Sales, design and managerial activity within large organizations resulted in a higher proportion
of employment in service occupations than in the craft districts. Archetypal districts differed from craft and concentrated districts by their
degree of self-employment and presence of public- and private-sector
support agencies. The peripheral districts were located, with one exception, in southern Italy and had comparatively low levels of specialization
and high rates of local unemployment (suggesting less economic success
than other districts).

This diversity could be used to argue for a modification of the official
definition of industrial districts so as to capture a set of areas with less variation than seems to exist. In this regard, Paniccia (2002: 191) endorsed
the view that the diversity existing among districts was incompatible with
an overarching universal model of spatial agglomeration. At the same
time, refinement of the definition of industrial districts to a set of localities sharing identical characteristics was not proposed. Rather, caution was
recommended in assuming characteristics beyond those required by the
official definition. The term industrial district, she advises, should simply
denote agglomerations of small and medium-sized enterprises in a few or
complementary industries within limited areas (Paniccia 2002: 190).
Three justifications were made for retaining the diversity within the official count that results from such a definition.

First, all types of district tended to show higher economic performance
than other localities, suggesting that the simple definition was still effective in differentiating localities with advantage over other areas. Interestingly, in view of claims often made for industrial districts, export
performance from the early 1990s appeared to be the least distinctive
feature.

Second, many of the features thought to be present in industrial districts were typically absent and not required for high performance. In this
regard it is hard to determine which districts have the best case for

remaining and which do not. For example, one option might be to strengthen the requirement for a high participation of small and medium-sized enterprises in the specialized activities. If this option were taken, different localities potentially drop out depending on the choice of indicator. Craft-based districts have a high concentration of production in the top five enterprises, a comparatively low average firm size and a relatively high share of employees in micro-enterprises (Table 4.3). Consequently, whether craft-based districts survived as official districts would depend on whether average firm size or the employment share in establishments of less than ten employees was given priority.

Third, her further analysis showed that the organizational character-istics of districts evolve and understanding these trajectories is important to a full assessment of the significance of agglomeration. A broad defini-tion that allows organizational change to be monitored is useful for gaining this understanding. Such preference for an all-encompassing defi-nition is supported in investigations by other Italian researchers interested in that country's local production systems (Burroni and Trigilia 2001). The latter study examined how localities differed in their adjustment to changing competition, concluding that rather than one best model, differ-ent responses emerge in different contexts.

Conclusion

Mapping exercises are best designed as a two-stage process. First, localities that potentially accommodate clusters should be identified. Second, pro-files of the potential clusters should be conducted to confirm that they qualify for inclusion and to determine what use, if any, is made of the cluster by its prospective members. Such an approach is recommended to enable the frequency of expected cluster attributes to be judged against

Table 4.3 Alternative indicators of small firm importance in industrial districts

Measure of small-firm importance	Type of cluster			
	Craft-based	Concentrated	Peripheral	Archetypal
Average firm employment in the specialized industry	9.2	23.5	12.1	6.7
Production concentration in the five largest firms	22.5	29.7	19.2	8.0
Share (%) of employees in establishments of less than 10 employees in the specialized industry	29.8	10.4	18.3	39.7

Source: Paniccia (2002).

the frequency of opportunities for these attributes to develop. As well, given the many competing interpretations of the important attributes of clusters, it fits prevailing levels of agreement. A practical and further consideration is that a two-stage approach fits levels of data availability. Potential clusters can be revealed through official employment statistics whereas cluster profiles require original investigation, ideally based on a robust sampling frame. Questions do, of course, exist about whether it is possible to map potential clusters. It requires some judgement as to the appropriate geographical scale to conduct the search and on the levels of concentration and specialization deemed necessary. Experimentation with differing eligibility criteria may help determine those that are most effective in capturing localities that become accepted as clusters. To assist such experimentation, it is helpful if mapping projects follow methods that can be replicated based on transparent, quantitative indicators. Successful experimentation is nonetheless likely to leave potential clusters as a rough guide to where actual clusters might be found. As observed in Italy, cluster characteristics change as does the significance of location to individual industries.

5   New economic geography

A belief in the competitive advantage of business clusters can be attributed partly to their association with so-called new economic geography. This is not through the direct advocacy of clusters by those who practise new economic geography. A perceived tendency for economic activity to be highly agglomerated in a few metropolitan regions is more the spatial pattern that motivates new economic geography than localized clustering of the form of interest to this book. Even so, as new economic geography has raised interest in business location and because many may assume this includes an endorsement for clustering, it is relevant to consider its contribution.

A central goal of new economic geography is to explain why geographical space tends to divide between a core or central place containing most economic activity and a comparatively barren periphery. In this central-place pattern, places differ more in the range of activities conducted than in their industry specializations. As frequently observed, unearthing the origins of the central place settlement pattern is not a new question but there is scope to bring an explanation up to date with contemporary forms of industrial organization. So far, the subject remains dominated by the goal of building an economic model that can simulate the real world and show that a selected set of economic forces result in central-place formations. A model developed by Krugman (1991a) dominates investigation, sometimes referred to as the 'core model' of geographical economics (Brakman *et al.* 2001). New economic geographers stress that it is too soon to discuss the policy implications of their work and they have made no recommendation as to when one particular settlement arrangement may be superior to another. A desire to find policy conclusions is nonetheless strong among those who might apply the findings (Fujita, Krugman and Venables 1999: 349). Before doing so it is important to not to assume that more references to geography in rigorous economic analysis indicates endorsement for the advantages of business clusters. Economists are showing renewed interest in the clustering of economic activity but the clustering being thought of is frequently not specific in scale. Economists identify clusters at anything from the global level (dividing the world into seven regional clusters) through whole continents to sub-national agglomerations (see Brakman *et al.* 2001). Similarly, economic analysis sometimes refers to clustering as any form of location concentration including industrial parks, small towns or major cities (McCann 2001: 53). In this chapter, clustering will continue to refer to specialized local economies. Other forms of concentration will be referred to as agglomeration.

Krugman (1991a) cites examples of clusters in the USA that are consistent with the understanding of this book. One is the case of carpet manufacturing in and around Dalton (Georgia) and other cases are Silicon Valley and Route 128. In each of his brief accounts, the role of chance in creating the cluster is the main point of interest, as discussed in Chapter 1 in the case of Dalton. In Silicon Valley, the chance event was Fred Terman's presence in the Valley. These stories are important in providing a starting point for agglomeration. Model outcomes are sensitive to the initial distribution of activity given their tendency to predict that agglomeration reinforces itself. Forward and backward linkages mean that once an initial regional advantage is established it may be hard for alternative locations to grow, even if they might ultimately offer a superior economic outcome. Large manufacturing agglomerations attract more manufacturing and grow to absorb more of the entire sector. The key mechanism is the trade-off between external economies of scale and transport costs. In economically integrated territories with few transaction impediments (such as tariff or trade barriers, regulatory differences, cultural preferences or physical isolation) and high mobility of capital and labour, opportunities for individual locations to export to other parts of the region increase. In essence, trade allows regions to specialize and as trade expands, export industries gain external economies that reinforce the impetus to specialize.

This chapter summarizes the scope of new economic geography concentrating on its interpretations that are linked to the understanding of business clusters. The focus is on communicating to non-economic geographers the assumptions being made, the reasoning behind the core model and how the model has been extended to cover an explanation of regional specialization. Proponents of new economic geography stress that it is still early days in the development of its methods. Reflecting this, the purpose is to give an impression of the progress being made. One gauge of the progress is the outcome of tests proposed by the proponents themselves. Two such tests are reported: namely, demonstration of a 'home market effect' and increased convergence between the levels of regional specialization in Europe and the USA. The outcome of these tests, especially in the latter case, suggests the first generation of models produced by new economic geography need substantial revision. This result and the judgements of economists and geographers who have been doubtful of the progress being made provide the basis for evaluating how far new economic geography adds to the case for clustering.

The core model

In the narrowest use of the phrase, new economic geography can be traced to the contributions of Krugman (1991a, 1991b, 1993a), Fujita and Krugman (1995) and Fujita, Krugman and Mori (1999). This work has been subsequently summarized by these authors in a single publication (Fujita, Krugman and Venables 1999). The thrust of this work is to start with a real-world problem and then to build a model that seeks to capture the essence of that problem. The resulting model is specified mathematically and is kept as simple as possible so as to demonstrate the influence of key interactions. Underlying this approach is a belief that spatial unevenness is a product of economic forces that obey general rules. As in the case of Miss Evans and Dalton, historical accident can be important but it is part of a larger story dominated by systematic economic forces. Fujita, Krugman and Venables (1999: 285), for example, point to evidence that industry agglomeration in the USA is not the product of chance. This evidence comes from a study showing that levels of industry concentration, while frequently low, suggest that location decisions are not made as if 'the plants in the industry [had] chosen locations by throwing darts on a map' (Ellison and Glaeser 1997: 890).

The ultimate goal of new economic geography is to explain real-world regularities in settlement patterns (Brakman *et al.* 2001). This motivation raises the question as to whether any regularity exists in economic geography. As discussed later in the chapter, many geographers (as compared with economists) doubt that it does or at least not beyond a superficial level. For those willing to accept that regularity can be identified, one assessment suggests that there is reasonably consistent evidence about four generalizations obtaining to the characteristics of an urban system (Parr 2002b):

1 The urban system of a nation or region comprises two distinct components. One is based on economic activity whose location pattern is governed by the principles of centrality, the other involves specialized function activity whose location pattern results from diverse influences. The two components are present in all urban systems. The components interact in ways that reflect particular contexts and experiences.

2 There is a tendency for successive inclusion in the functions carried out by settlements of increasing size. A larger settlement carries out all of the functions of a smaller settlement but a smaller settlement carries out only some of the functions found in a larger settlement. This pattern is not perfect, especially among smaller settlements not built on central-place functions. At the bottom of the urban hierarchy, smaller settlements may differ in their specialization.

3 It is generally the case that the larger the urban centre, the higher is

the level of economic diversification. This pattern is especially strong when economic activity serving the local market is discounted and the focus is on export activities alone.

4   The size distribution of urban centres conforms to the rank-size distribution. In this distribution the population of the second largest city is expected to be half that of the largest city, the third largest city a third of the largest city, and so on down the urban hierarchy.

Beyond these regularities 'we would probably be speaking about a particular urban system or a particular subset of urban systems' (Parr 2002b: 79).

Central-place hierarchies and rank-size distributions were the regularities to which the attention of new economic geography was first drawn. Central-place patterns were first identified by two German scholars in the 1930s and 1940s and were once accepted widely as an accurate depiction of settlement patterns. The regularity of central-place hierarchies became an increasing source of doubt. Actual settlement patterns conformed rarely to the model (Box 5.1). Interest further waned from the want of any convincing explanation to account for central-place distributions. New economic geography has revived interest in the central-place pattern with the purpose of explaining how the spatial structure it describes is 'created or maintained by the actions of self-interested individuals' (Krugman 1998: 9).

Box 5.1   Central-place theory

The Christaller model of central places was based on observations of the spatial distributions of cities and towns in southern Germany in the 1920s. His model focuses on functions (services or manufactured goods) that are market-orientated rather than having a location influenced by proximity to energy sources, raw materials, manufactured inputs or labour. He sought to identify the minimum number of settlements that would be required to service a given population, evenly distributed on a homogenous plain. Each good supplied would require a minimum market area determined by the minimum volume of profitable production. Consumers sought to minimize their travel distance. The solution was based on two assumptions: (i) a settlement of particular size would conduct all the functions for which it provided the minimum market area and all the functions requiring a smaller market area than covered; (ii) market area would increase from the smallest size to the next by a constant factor. The outcome is a series of overlapping hexagonal-shaped market areas and a hierarchy of settlements, each located in the centre of the hexagonal area supplied.

The German economist Lösch specified demand and cost conditions facing a single producer located on a uniform plain, evenly populated with persons having identical preferences and with there being free entry into production. Consumers paid all costs of transport and, behaving rationally, sought supply from the nearest producer. In the case of a single industry, a

---

triangular spacing of producers was predicted with each located central to a hexagonal market area. In order to explain the outcome with a multiplicity of goods, the assumption of continuous population distribution was modified. The most efficient allocation of activity then turned into a central location where all goods were produced (the 'metropolis') from which ran six alternating settlement-rich and settlement-poor segments.

Settlement of an area of reclaimed land (1937–42) in the centre of the Netherlands was planned under the influence of central-place ideas. The land was flat and settled by farmers with fairly even land allocations. Planning envisaged one settlement of 10,000 population and ten of 2,000 each. By 1985, the total population in the settlements was over 28,000 with almost 19,000 in the 'central place' and most smaller settlements having fewer than 700 residents.

Central-place ideas originated at a time when it was generally thought that the location of urban concentrations was simply the outcome of local resources, such as raw-material deposits, transport nodes or particular labour skills. New economic geographers view Christaller and Lösch as having provided descriptive stories with plausible outcomes. In their assessment, the accounts fall down in not providing a decision-making theory that explains how individual decisions produce a settlement hierarchy.

Sources: Brakman *et al.* 2001; Parr 2002b

In essence, central-place patterns result in settlement concentrating in one or two cities that are generally to be found in the centre of the major populated regions of the country. For new economic geography, this justifies the claim that production gravitates to a few dominant cities and that large regional agglomerations seem to be more significant economic units than nation states. As graphically portrayed in satellite images of the world at night, large tracts of national space are left economically barren. This tendency to spatial inequality is in contrast to neoclassical expectations of counterbalancing centralizing and decentralizing processes. It invites interpretations of economic geography as a product of imperfect competition, externalities and cumulative causation that new economic geography has responded to.

Krugman's new economic geography was built on his earlier contribution to new trade theory (Box 5.2).

Krugman's core model is based on five main assumptions relating to: (1) the welfare effects associated with product variety; (2) the productivity of manufacturing; (3) homogenous firms; (4) the costs of transporting goods; (5) labour mobility.

1   *Welfare effects.* All consumers are assumed to have the same tastes including a preference for variety over consuming only one type of good. A given level of consumer expenditure will be distributed across

Box 5.2 New trade theory

Neoclassical trade theory was built on the idea of comparative advantage. Trade flowed between nations based on differences in technological capacity or factor endowments. New trade theory starts from the observation that a large share of international trade now takes place between countries with similar factor endowments. Contrary to the expectation of comparative advantage, inter-industry trade (exporting cereal in exchange for computers) is less important than intra-industry trade (exporting computers in exchange for computers).

New trade theory interprets intra-industry trade as specialization to take advantage of increasing returns to scale. If specialization and trade are driven by increasing returns and economies of scale rather than comparative advantage, the gains from trade arise because production costs fall as the scale of output increases.

Krugman (1980) developed a revised model of intra-industry trade that with three innovations links directly to the core model of new economic geography:

1   Increased market size causes more varieties to be made rather than for increased production by individual firms. Consumers are assumed to have a 'love of variety'.
2   Trade between nations incurs transport costs, making firms sensitive to the location of their production sites.
3   Market size varies between countries, not as an outcome of the model but as a given starting point. As firms are immobile, they minimize transport costs by concentrating on those varieties for which home-country demand is relatively high.

This model explained why there might be geographical concentration of a single industry but it also expected the overall distribution of activity to be even.

Krugman and Venables (1990) produce a two-country model that allows activity to agglomerate in one country. Each country comprises two sectors both producing tradeable goods, but one sector is perfectly competitive, and the other imperfectly competitive, and one country has more activity than the other. When there is a fall in transport costs, the country that starts with a larger volume of activity in the imperfectly competitive sector grows this sector. Exports cause the opposite intersector shift in the other country. As transport costs continue to fall, the distribution of activity goes back towards its starting position.

The prediction of agglomeration under intermediate transport costs mirrors the core model of new economic geography. The trade model differs in not giving a reason for the initial inequality in conditions.

Source: Brakman *et al.* (2001)

all available varieties rather than concentrated on one or a few varieties. Each producer of manufactured goods is assumed to make one unique variety of good. The availability of product variety is determined by the size of the total market for manufactured goods and the ability of producers to achieve a certain scale of production. At the same time, if the number of product varieties available increases, the fact that consumers value product variety means that the cost of attaining a given level of satisfaction falls.

2 *Manufacturing productivity.* Manufacturing is assumed to produce a variety of outputs under monopolistically competitive conditions with increasing returns to scale, meaning that the cost of each unit of production falls with increased output. For each firm, the labour required to produce any level of output comprises a fixed overhead component, that is independent of the level of output, and a variable component directly related to the level of output. Increasing returns to scale and the large number of potential manufactured goods means that each firm will focus on a single unique good (this is the state of monopolistic competition). The number of firms will, therefore, be the same as the number of products produced. The entry of new firms producing slightly different products eliminates monopoly profits and results in many little monopolists. Given scope for infinite differentiation, individual producers remain small enough not to exhaust their scale economies. Given sufficiently strong economies of scale, each manufacturer will prefer to serve the national market from a single location.

3 *Homogenous firms.* Consistent with the monopolistically competitive conditions, industries comprise similar firms producing differentiated products that are close but not perfect substitutes. No differences exist in the strategic choices made by firms.

4 *Distance costs.* Transport costs are modelled using the so-called 'iceberg assumption': a constant fraction of output is lost to the producer due to the consumer's need to pay a transport change. The iceberg analogy comes from the idea that the transport costs involved in towing an iceberg can be understood as causing an iceberg to melt away during the journey. It is a contemporary rendition of the original formulation, attributed to von Thünen in 1826, that the cost of grain transportation is mainly the grain consumed by the horses pulling the wagon (Fujita, Krugman and Venables 1999: 59). In whatever rendition, distance erodes a proportion of the good being shipped at a constant rate of loss for each unit of distance travelled. This means that the cost of distance is a function of the source price of the good (high-priced goods face a higher absolute distance charge than low-priced goods) and the distance travelled. To ensure that a given quantity of goods are delivered, the total quantity of goods purchased must increase compared with the required purchase volume at the source location.

5 *Labour mobility.* An assumption that labour moves freely between

locations according to differences in real wages (calculated as nominal wages deflated by the cost of living) is made in some versions of the model. The nominal wages paid to workers are higher the better is the access (determined by distance solely) of the firm to the market, the greater is the local-market income and the lower is the level of local-product competition. Large cities with a wide range of manufacturing activities producing a high variety of products are judged relatively inexpensive to live in, in real terms, because the high variety of goods locally available will allow any given level of utility to be achieved at lower real cost. Intense local competition means goods are produced at relatively low cost, allowing large market areas to be captured. Labour is, therefore, drawn to locations with large local demand. Consequently, firms do not need to consider labour-supply constraints as labour is available wherever businesses decide to locate. As discussed below, in more sophisticated applications of the model where manufacturing produces intermediate and final goods, labour is assumed to be immobile.

Krugman (1991a) illustrates these assumptions in a simple example to show how the core model is constructed. The example is based on a country comprising two locations, East and West. The economy is split into two sectors, one operating with increasing returns to scale (manufacturing) and one producing under constant returns (agriculture). Agriculture uses a location-specific factor (land). The level of employment in agriculture is determined by the area of land under production. Manufactured goods can be produced in either or both locations but transport costs must be incurred to supply the other market. The manufacturing labour force in each location is proportional to manufacturing production in that location. The demand for each manufactured good in each location is similarly proportional to that location's population. At the outset the following distributions are assumed:

- 60 per cent of each country's workforce are farmers, half in the East and half in the West.
- A typical manufactured good has a demand of ten units. Consequently, if manufacturing is concentrated in one region, local demand will take seven units (three from farmers and four from manufacturing workers). If manufacturing is evenly divided between East and West, each region will offer a local demand of five.
- Fixed costs of operating a plant are four and transport cost per unit is one.

These starting points give rise to three equally plausible outcomes.

- All manufacturing employment is concentrated in the East. A single firm contemplating where to locate will have a choice between a local demand of seven in the East or three in the West. Serving the national market from the East means a fixed cost of four and a transport cost of three; this is less than serving the national market from the West (fixed cost of four and a transport cost of seven) or of having two plants (fixed cost eight).

* All manufacturing employment is concentrated in the West. The same cost minimization is achieved if each firm concentrates its production in the East.
* Manufacturing employment is split between East and West. In this case each firm will be best advised to split their production. This option means a fixed cost of eight but no transport cost compared with a fixed cost of four and a transport cost of five if production is concentrated in one region.

This is a simple illustration but it draws attention to five distinctive characteristics of new economic geography that hold in more complex applications as well (Brakman *et al.* 2001: 62).

First, it indicates the importance of cumulative causation. If, for some reason, one location has attracted more firms than another, a new firm has an incentive to locate where the other firms are. Consequently, the impact of contemporary economic forces depends on the inherited settlement structure. For example, an initial high level of transport costs will cause the spreading of manufacturing activity. If they subsequently fall sufficiently, agglomeration will result. The critical value at which established agglomerations are no longer sustainable is referred to as the 'sustain point'. It differs from the 'break point' which identifies when a uniform spatial economy, without agglomerations, starts to concentrate ('symmetry breaking'). To break the agglomeration, transport costs would need to reverse beyond the level that previously sustained a dispersed distribution of manufacturing. So for the same level of transport cost, the outcome can depend on the order in which the level is reached. To use Krugman's expression, 'history matters', or in more formal economics language, there is path dependency. His emphasis on this point accords with long established claims that a given pattern of development, once established, tends to exhibit a high degree of inertia (Martin and Sunley 1996: 286).

Second, there exists potentially multiple equilibrium outcomes in which all firms have equal returns. Economic geography models tend to identify conditions under which agglomeration can arise rather than establishing that agglomeration must arise (Krugman 2000: 54). Self-sustaining concentration is one outcome but equally the models identify conditions under which dispersed activity arises. Determining when agglomeration occurs depends partly on the initial distribution of agricultural activity and the starting distribution of manufacturing activity. It is, therefore, hard to discern particular policy recommendations in favour of one particular settlement pattern over another. Drawing on the experience of Massachusetts at the end of the 1980s, for example, the ambivalent benefits of regional industrial specialization are stressed (Krugman 1993b). Specialization can be the basis of a high rate of export-led growth in one period and the source of prolonged localized economic depression if demand collapses or is captured by another local economy.

Third, an equilibrium outcome may be stable or unstable. A stable equilibrium exists where a decision by a single firm to relocate would not influence the location decisions of other firms. This is the case where, in the above illustration, all manufacturing employment is concentrated in either the East or West. Manufacturing employment evenly distributed between East and West is an unstable equilibrium in that if a single firm decides to relocate, the location selected will increase its attractiveness to all other firms. Consequently, in theory a single decision can trigger a snowball effect as all firms follow the pioneer. Moreover, sudden changes may be entirely unpredictable. Where industry starts from a position of being fairly evenly distributed, decisions made on the basis of pessimistic expectations for one location may become self-fulfilling expectations where the pessimism leads firms to migrate.

Fourth, an equilibrium may be non-optimal in the sense that it does not minimize total production costs for the economy. In the example, if all manufacturing takes place in one region there are transport costs of three compared with five when production is shared equally by both regions. If an uneven original distribution of agricultural activity were assumed, and manufacturing production was regionally concentrated, it would result in one region offering a lower-transport-cost solution than the other. In that case, a non-optimal stable equilibrium is possible where manufacturing concentrates in the region with the smaller share of agricultural employment. This potential outcome is consistent with the rejection of the neo-classical faith in the efficiency of markets on the grounds that the collective outcome of individual choices may be to lock in a bad result. When Krugman insists that all economic models should have a well-specified equilibrium, this does not accord with the neoclassical outcome of factors being rewarded equally (Martin and Sunley 1996: 275). The requirement is simply that models should specify how individuals behave and how outcomes emerge from the collective impact of these individual behaviours.

Fifth, the example illustrates the interaction of agglomeration and trade flows which is one of the key relationships for new economic geography. With complete agglomeration, all manufactured goods are produced in one region and results in trade between regions. It is produced from a so-called 'home-market' effect. Economies of scale and transport costs are responsible for the concentration of all mobile activity in a single location. The large region achieves the largest home market, enabling a high proportion of manufactured output to be produced without transport costs. Further, this region becomes the exporter of manufactured goods reflecting the more general proposition that large regions tend to become exporters of those goods for which they have a large local market.

The simple illustration of Krugman's economic geography shows some of the thinking behind the more complex economic models produced within new economic geography. Without getting into the algebraic complexity of these models, it is possible to give some further description of the core model and some of its extensions (Box 5.3). For example, the original two-location model has been applied to the so-called 'racetrack economy'. This depicts an economy of multiple locations, distributed evenly in a circle with transportation possible only along the rim of the circle. A racetrack may appear to be an unrealistic representation of urban geography but for economic model building it has the advantage of preserving the neutrality of space. Location outcomes are the result of the economic interactions among agents without influence from a pre-imposed geographical structure favouring economic activity in a particular location. When a starting point of many locations along the racetrack is assumed, with manufacturing activity randomly distributed among the locations at the outset, the model shows that a long-run equilibrium outcome can comprise three or fewer settlements. Each of the emerging concentrations has an equal share of manufacturing activity. Three parameter settings influence an outcome based on such high levels of agglomeration:

1   Low transport costs: where transport costs are high it encourages production close to markets and increases the number of locations.
2   Share of income on manufactured goods is high: if the share of income spent on manufactured items decreases, the immobile food sector becomes economically more important than otherwise. The tendency to diffusion is then encouraged given that manufacturing locations are influenced by the location of consumers.
3   There is low elasticity of substitution between manufactured goods: this condition describes a situation where consumers seek variety rather than preferring one manufactured good over another. Where variety is strongly preferred, the market power of firms increases and they can feasibly produce at a few locations only.

The above conditions relate to the generation of agglomeration. When Fujita, Krugman and Venables (1999) address what they refer to as industrial clustering, their model considers the allocation of manufacturing industries between countries. Clearly, this analysis is still geared towards explaining agglomeration at the grand scale. In this case, the central issue is why one country might attract more industries than another. As economic forces are expected to encourage the national specialization to be specially concentrated within its national boundaries, the model has some relevance to the debate about localized clusters. It is thus presented by Fujita, Krugman and Venables (1999: 284) as a model leading to explanations of the emergence of Silicon Valley, Hollywood, the world's financial districts and other like clusters.

Box 5.3 The core model of new economic geography and its extensions

The core model is set within one-dimensional space and based on simple assumptions regarding the costs of distance, the utility of consumers and the productivity of manufacturing and agriculture. Further assumptions exist in relation to welfare effects, manufacturing productivity and transport costs:

1   *Welfare effects*: consumers have identical preferences; there are a variety of manufactured goods and a single agricultural good. The proportion of expenditure on manufactured goods determines the share on agricultural goods. The strength of the consumer preference for variety can vary according to the willingness to substitute one variety for another. The minimum cost of purchasing a single unit of the composite manufactured good falls as the number of varieties increases. The fall in the cost of living with increased variety is greatest where the consumer willingness to substitute varieties is lowest.

2   *Manufacturing productivity*: labour is the sole input to manufacturing. Production uses a fixed overhead component and a variable component. With increasing returns to scale and consumer preference for variety, each firm concentrates on a unique variety. In a monopolistically competitive environment, producers have an elasticity of demand determined by the consumer preference for variety. With freedom of entry into manufacturing, producers operate at the level where price equals marginal labour cost. The number of workers in a region and the consumer elasticity of demand become the key determinants of the number of firms (manufactured goods) in a region.

3   *Transport costs*: all goods shipped are affected by a constant rate of decay determined by the distance transported. To ensure that a given quantity of goods is actually delivered, the total quantity of goods purchased at the source must increase to offset the in-transit erosion.

Brakman *et al.* (2001) identify three extensions of the core model that have been made by followers of new economic geography. Type I extensions incorporate 'non-neutral' space such as the variation in transport costs arising from physical features (mountain divides, coastal locations and transport nodes) and the type of commodity transported. Type II extensions vary the production aspects of the model to, in different versions, incorporate multiple factors of production (in addition to labour), intermediate and final goods production, horizontal and vertical integration. Type III extensions incorporate the role of expectations, migrant behaviour and influential decision takers (such as land developers).

Source: Brakman *et al.* (2001: 167–8)

In the simplest case, the model comprises two countries, two manufacturing industries, no agriculture and a single factor of production (labour). Each country is endowed with one unit of labour that is assumed to be internationally immobile and that may be employed in either manufacturing sector. Industries are similar in other aspects and each takes half of consumers' total expenditure. This model divides manufacturing output between the production of intermediate outputs (used by other manufacturers) and final goods. This introduces a real-world reality into the model although for the purpose of the model a symmetrical transactions matrix is assumed: each firm produces output that is both a final good sold to consumers and an intermediate input to all other producers in the same industry. The central idea is that upstream (final goods) and downstream (intermediate goods) firms can benefit from each other. As the upstream industry has increasing returns to scale, an increased demand for its product induces firms to produce at a more efficient level of production. In turn, this raises the efficiency of the downstream industry to which it is linked. As labour is now assumed to be immobile, expansion of a single activity requires that workers are pulled away from other sectors of production within the same region. Immobility introduces wage levels into the model. In earlier models, labour mobility was assumed to equalize wages between locations but now wage levels vary with the change in demand for labour.

The model gives an outcome that depends on transport costs. At high transport costs, both industries operate in both economies. As transport costs are lowered, concentration becomes first possible and then necessary. This means that even though the two economies have the same wages and income levels, they can come to specialize in different industries. This outcome is, of course, influenced by the symmetry built into the assumptions and the absence of any differences in technology, preferences or endowments. Even so, Fujita, Krugman and Venables (1999: 290) suggest the result may give the reason why the industrial geographies of the USA and Europe differ. These regional economies are of similar size and technological development but differ in their propensity to produce industrial concentration. In the USA, industries are claimed to be typically monocentric with concentrations in or around a Silicon Valley, Detroit or Wall Street. In Europe, the same industries tend to have three or four major centres. The reason for the difference, it is speculated, are higher transport costs in Europe as a consequence of national boundaries blocking continental-scale industrial clustering. Consequently, in one of the few definite policy recommendations arising from applications of the core model, the benefits of regional integration are endorsed. A note of caution follows the endorsement in the extent of labour-market adjustment required to support industry agglomeration. Others have pointed out that the assumed capacity for labour mobility (which is higher in the USA than Europe) is an aspect of new economic geography's American bias (Martin and Sunley 1996: 286).

In a situation of multiple industries, the outcome may not be an equal distribution of activity creating the potential for countries to have an incentive to try and attract industries from the competing location (Fujita, Krugman and Venables 1999: 299). The modelling in the multiple-industry case indicates that at high levels of transport cost, no agglomeration is possible. At low-transport-cost levels, the number of industries in each country is expected to be the same with each developing specializations. In the intermediary range of transport costs, the range of outcomes is wide according to the assumed level of intra-industry linkages (as measured by the share one industry's output being an input for the same industry). Where intra-industry linkages are high, the number of industries attracted by one country may be more than three times that of the other country.

Evaluation of new economic geography

Assessing the progress made by new economic geography, Krugman (2000: 59) stresses that the models are too simple and too stylized to reproduce real economic geography. As he says, they tend to be limited by a focus on what it is easiest to model than on what ideally would be included. Thus in reference to Marshall's three reasons for agglomeration – backward and forward linkages, specialized labour markets and technological spillovers – linkages are incorporated in his models although it is acknowledged they may well be the least significant source of agglomeration advantage. This selection has also been influenced by a perception that technological spillovers are most relevant to new technology sectors whereas the spatial concentration of low technology industries is more evident in the USA (Krugman 1991a: 59). Similarly, of three potential inducements for economic activity to disperse that Krugman recognizes exist – immobile factors of production, land rents and external diseconomies – immobile factors only are considered (Krugman 1998).

Krugman's self-assessment is that new economic geography is significant in showing economists some ways that spatial considerations can be incorporated within economic models. A different evaluation comes from other economists and from geographers who study economic geography. The former tend to be sympathetic to the purpose of economic modelling and identify design gaps that need to be filled before the work can be regarded as having created a new field of enquiry. Geographers, on the other hand, tend to doubt that building economic models generates useful insight. A short summary of both viewpoints is given before looking at the match between new economic geography and empirical evidence.

Limitations of new economic geography

New economic geography follows in a tradition of focusing on a single cause of trade and location (Neary 2001). With new economic geography the essential cause is monopolistic competition. Previous monocausal interpretations have variously been built on technology (Ricardo), factor endowments (Heckscher-Ohlin) and oligopolistic competition (Brander). Neary (2001) argues that while such explanations serve an important role in illuminating the influence of interest, and are essential for understanding the world, they cannot capture the complexities of economic development. In particular, with new economic geography there are shortcomings in the treatment of: (i) increasing returns; (ii) firm strategies; (iii) transport costs; (iv) space.

1   *Increasing returns*: the ultimate driving force for agglomeration and trade is the existence of increasing returns to scale. The modelling of increasing returns is based on assumptions about their relationship with the substitutability of the good being produced. An inverse relationship is assumed between the ratio of variable to fixed costs and the substitutability of goods. Firms that produce goods with high substitutability have a high ratio of variable to fixed costs, firms that have low substitutability have a lower ratio of variable to fixed costs. Neary suggests that this claim is not necessarily based on technology differences between producers with high and low substitutability. Some firms may have potential for increasing returns but are prevented from realizing them because of high substitutability with other goods. Strictly, all that can be claimed is that the pattern of demand is determining whether returns to scale are being more or less exploited. For the present, models are unable to distinguish the effects of greater substitutability in demand from the effects of a higher ratio of variable to fixed costs. Neary (2001: 548), therefore, argues that the theory of the firm embodied in Krugman's models is not as rich as might be supposed.

2   *Firm strategies*: the models have little to say about individual firms. Apart from the existence of increasing returns, firms in new economic geography are simple organizations. An assumption of free entry leaves almost no role for strategic interactions between firms. For example, the distinction between fixed and variable costs does not continue into the recognition of the presence of sunk costs that may constrain location choice. Similarly, firms do not engage in the kinds of activities that are at the heart of contemporary business practice. They cannot make strategic commitments to create artificial barriers to entry, nor vertically integrate to internalize the externalities arising from the combination of intermediate inputs with increasing returns. Outsourcing, mergers and alliances do not feature.

3   *Transport costs*: the model makes important connections between transport costs and location outcomes. If transport costs are low enough, there are no barriers to agglomeration: if they are high enough, there is no alternative to dispersion. In the basic model, this

centrality is demonstrated with the assumption that manufactured goods only are transported at a cost and that agricultural goods are transported without charge. In practice, of course, agricultural commodities can face transport costs that are at least as high as manufactured goods. In Fujita, Krugman and Venables (1999: Chapter 7) agricultural transport costs are included. Depending on the other model conditions, agglomeration forces are either neutralized or enhanced. Whichever the sectors applied to, there is no testing of a variety of transport cost structures although in the real world the ratio of fixed and variable costs varies between individual transport modes. Nor have models recognized the existence of a transport industry with costs that are influenced by the scale of demand for individual services.

4   *Space:* the uniform surface over which economic activity is distributed contrasts with the unevenness of actual space created by transport networks, topography and economic history. Another simplification relates to how models dealing with the allocation of activity within countries are differentiated from those allocating activity across countries. In the former, labour is assumed to be mobile and intermediate inputs are the trigger for agglomeration. In the multinational model, labour is assumed to be immobile and intermediate inputs are not included. Although labour mobility is generally less across countries than within, international labour migration can be of considerable significance to small countries. Neary (2001) refers to the case of the high labour mobility from some small to large European countries. Equally, the focus on intermediate inputs as a source of country rather than within country specialization does not fit with the origins of many clusters. As Neary notes, Silicon Valley is not explained through the migration-induced final demand for computer hardware and software.

Consequently, while not opposed to the need for simplifying assumptions to illustrate economic possibilities, one assessment is that some of the assumptions made by new economic geography are too limiting. From the perspective of trying to progress new economic geography, others have pointed out that the core model predicts unrealistic levels and forms of agglomeration (Brakman *et al.* 2001: 123). Referring to the racetrack-economy application, activity is shown to concentrate in a single location from a starting point of dispersion among multiple locations under many of the scenarios tested. Where an outcome of two or three settlements is obtained, each settlement is of equal size and evenly distributed around the racetrack. In brief, compared with actual experience, the models tend to produce too few settlements that are too evenly spaced (Box 5.4). This is a consequence, according to Brakman *et al.* (2001), of the failure to consider the impact of congestion costs. When they do this and apply their

---

Box 5.4 Too few settlements

The core model has been applied to non-neutral space using a geographical grid. Space is represented in the model as a finite square grid subdivided into equal-sized squares. The corner of each square has a distance of one to its four direct horizontal and vertical neighbours and a distance to a diagonal neighbour equal to the square root of two.

Non-neutral space is introduced by making holes in the grid to approximate for physical impediments to transport. The ability to approximate real geographical space increases using a fine-grained grid. The model starts with a flat initial distribution in which all locations on the grid are of equal size. The task is then to calculate the optimal distribution of economic activity using assumptions derived from the core model.

A grid of western Europe starting with 2,542 locations and using a variety of model parameters produces an equilibrium outcome of from 94 to 60 cities. Taking the outcome with 94 cities, the model produces an optimal city distribution that is more evenly spread than in reality. There are too few cities predicted in the north (UK, Netherlands, Belgium) and too many in the south (Spain). The largest real agglomerations – Paris, London, Madrid and Rome – are not identified. Germany, on the other hand, is suggested to be well simulated.

The technique was intended to show how the core model can produce an urban hierarchy. A close match to reality implies the triumph of economics over all influences on city formation. Such an outcome was not expected although it is claimed that the approach can be refined to get closer to the actual geography of economic activity.

Source: Stelder (2002)

---

method to the racetrack economy, it is shown that many centres of economic activity of variable size can be a long-run equilibrium outcome. As they admit, this result shows merely that the inclusion of an addition spreading force encourages economic activity to spread. A modified model that includes congestion balanced with additional forces of agglomeration has yet to be produced. Krugman (1998) indicates that the restricted present scope is partly to avoid something that looks too much like asserting agglomeration takes place because of agglomeration economies. For the present, this concern also means that new economic geography gives a partial assessment of the diseconomies of large concentrations.

Old versus new economic geography

Geographers represent old economic geography in the sense that, unlike economists, they have always had an interest in understanding settlement patterns and the distribution of economic activity. A range of methodological preferences exist among geographers but generally there is now a rejection of the approaches reflected in new economic geography. The search for regularities in settlement patterns, as represented by central-place theories and rank-size city distributions, was once central to the work of geographers (for example, see Lloyd and Dicken 1977). Even with the revival of these ideas by new economic geographers, contemporary textbooks for teaching economic geography to geographies give little or no space to the search for regularity in settlement patterns (for example, see Hayter 1997; Dicken 1998). In this sense, most geographers would agree that new economic geography is neither new nor geography (Martin 1999). A stress on the mathematical modelling of economic forces, it is argued, leads to a neglect of the diversity existing in the real world.

From the perspective of evaluating the contribution of new economic geography, it is useful to identify three reasons geographers had for abandoning interest in a search for economic explanations of geographic unevenness. These reasons do not account for all of the evolution in geographical thinking but are focused on here as sources of difference with Krugman's approach to economic geography.

First, it became accepted among geographers that some of the economic forces that had been assumed to explain settlement patterns had lost their significance. This was particularly the case with transport costs. Going back to models of industrial location first proposed at the beginning of the last century, transport costs had been assumed to have a significant influence on where economic activity located, and, further, that transport costs exerted a systematic influence on location because the extent of transport costs incurred was directly related to the distance goods were transported. By the 1970s, these assumptions were challenged by economic evidence that transport charges were rarely above 2–3 per cent of the business costs in most industries. The conclusion that transport costs had lost their significance was reinforced by investigation of transport charges. Transport providers frequently did not impose a distance-related charge or at least not in a way that was as sensitive to distance as economic models assumed. As well, the possibility of switching between transport modes helped to minimize distance costs. These assessments were reinforced by observations of the increasing distance over which economic transactions were conducted and the declining importance of bulky, low-value items in modern economies. In contrast, new economic geography has reasserted the importance of transport costs (Box 5.5).

Second, the willingness among geographers to accept the existence of regularities in geographical unevenness reduced. Empirical reality became too inconsistent with geometric representations. Geographers' increasing unwillingness to accept the rank-size rule as a useful summary of the distribution of city sizes is an example of this. Rather than the existence of regularity, emphasis shifted to identifying how context and

---

Box 5.5 Transport costs

In the 1980s, transport costs comprised 2–3 per cent of the total costs faced by most manufacturing industries in the UK compared with typical labour costs of 40–50 per cent (Tyler and Kitson 1987). This empirical evidence is matched by the advent of new technologies such as containerization, fuel-efficient long-haul aircraft and reduced port-handling costs. Recycling of basic materials has reduced the need to transport low-value commodities for processing and many physical goods have reduced in bulk through modern electronic technologies. The growth of world trade has provided economies in transport, as through the development of port hubs that service continuous round-the-world shipping services (Rimmer 2003).

To maintain that distance-related charges are important, it is argued total logistics costs should be examined (McCann 1998). Logistics costs comprise transport costs plus the cost to hold, store and handle inventory. These costs have been affected by increasing demands for more frequent deliveries of comparatively low volumes, as required to fit within just-in-time production systems. This trend has reduced the total value of inventory held at any point in time but increased the need for reliable and timely delivery.

The impact of just-in-time production methods in the consumer-electronics industry shows two opposing outcomes (Perry 1999). On the one hand, component supply is being concentrated among fewer, strategically located supplies that may be geographically distant from user locations. On the other hand, final assembly close to the end customer is occurring to maximize demand responsiveness.

---

scale were critical influences on the distribution of urban population. In contrast, new economic geography has caused a revival of attempts to claim that the rank-size rule is a close approximation to reality (Box 5.6).

Third, a desire emerged to move further down the chain of causation than a focus on immediate economic forces. For new economic geography, the location forces that explain how clusters are encouraged today are the same forces that shaped the emergence of clusters in the nineteenth century. Both are the product of increasing returns to scale, monopolistic competition and agglomeration costs and benefits. Changes in the distribution of activity are explained by the interaction of these economic forces with inherited settlement structures. To fully explain why outcomes change, geographers emphasize the need to explain the shifts in the relative importance of the individual economic forces. Underlying this search for deeper causes is a perception that patterns of spatial unevenness are subject to frequent change and that at any point in time there is great variety in the responses to the same economic forces. In contrast, new economic geography's concern with regularity in settlement patterns stresses continuity rather than instability and uniformity rather than

---

Box 5.6 Rank size rule

The search for regularity in settlement patterns has an extreme expression in Zipf's Law. This law states that the largest city is twice as large as the second largest city, three times as large as the third largest city and so on. It is a special case of the rank-size distribution which states that there is a tendency for the population size of a city to be equivalent to the population of the largest city divided by the rank of the smaller city. If Zipf's Law holds, the coefficient of the relationship between city rank and size $(q) = 1$, the largest city is precisely k times as large as the kth largest city. If all cities are the same size, $q = 0$. The ability to emulate Zipf's Law is often seen as a way of judging the success of an economic model of city distributions.

New economic geography has encouraged investigation of empirical data to confirm the accuracy of Zipf's Law. The results are not straightforward as differences in city definitions, sample sizes and time frames give different results. The closest approximations to Zipf's Law are obtained when: (i) the smallest cities are ignored; (ii) cities are defined by the agglomeration in and around the legally defined city rather than being limited to the population within the city's political boundaries; (iii) low-income countries with large primate cities are excluded. In high-income economies, cities at the time of early industrialization tend to be closer to Zipf's Law than the contemporary distribution of urban population. The latter are affected by the shift from manufacturing to service-sector employment.

A study of 42 countries measuring contemporary city populations relating to legal boundaries found five with a q value close to 1: Belarus, Bulgaria, Iran, Turkey and Vietnam. The 42 countries covered countries with at least ten cities of over 100,000 inhabitants. Among the sample, the value of q varied from 0.49 (UK) to 1.54 (Australia).

Source: Brakman *et al.* (2001)

---

diversity. The interest most geographers have in the 'regulation' of economic activity (Peck 2000) and its 'embeddedness' in particular social contexts (Dicken 2000) illustrate how they differ from new economic geographers.

Testing new economic geography

Measuring the existence of a 'home-market effect' has been proposed as possibly the closest thing to a direct test of new economic geography (Krugman 1998: 15). This test would observe whether a larger demand for the products of an industry in any given industry will lead, other things being the same, to a more than one-for-one increase in the regional production of that industry. Work to this end has been completed, although others have questioned the significance of the test (Box 5.7). For another test, Krugman (for example, see 1993b) has proposed examining

---

Box 5.7 Home-market test

The core model assumes a home-market effect in which the larger demand for the products of an industry in any given region is expected to lead to a more than proportional increase in the regional production of that industry.

Davis and Weinstein (1996, 1998) found little evidence for home-market effects in a sample of 22 OECD countries and 26 industries: in nine industries only above-average home demand was associated with a disproportional growth of local production above world demand. A subsequent analysis modified the investigation by: (i) allowing demand from neighbouring countries (or regions for a study within a single country) to be taken into account; (ii) the examination was confined to a single country (Japan) without the inclusion of transport costs. This time there is evidence of a home-market effect in eight of 19 sectors examined with the inclusion of an allowance for regional factor endowments (Davis and Weinstein 1999). The inclusion of factor endowments reflects the intention to determine whether comparative advantage or Krugman's (1980) model of international trade based on increasing returns best explains trade. Brakman *et al.* (2001: 144) argue that second version of the test applies more to Krugman's new trade theory than his new economic geography.

---

whether the distribution of economic activity within Europe (more specifically, among members of the European Union) is becoming more like that in the USA. This test will be discussed as it has generated more investigation than the home-market effect and because it directly links to evidence about business clustering.

As noted above, in proposing the trans-Atlantic comparison, Fujita, Krugman and Venables (1999) start from the claim that regions in the USA are more specialized economically than are comparable regions in Europe. The test proposed is to examine whether market and monetary integration within Europe is associated with increased regional specialization. New economic geography predicts this specialization will occur. Reduced restrictions on trade within Europe is expected to lower transport costs and enable external economies to be more fully exploited than before, leading to the geographical clustering of industries.

Issues in comparison

This test is indicative of the scale of agglomeration addressed in new economic geography. When the test was first conducted, Krugman (1991a) divided the USA into four regions for comparison with each of Europe's four largest economies (Italy, France, Germany and the UK). This scale of analysis is problematic given the internal variation in economic structure within countries and mega-regions. Depending on the geo-graphical scale used, it is conceivable that the level of regional special-ization varies (Martin and Sunley 1996: 278). Investigations made subsequent to Krugman's original test have added further geographical subdivisions but the discussion remains focused on specialization at the level of large territories rather than clustering at the level of individual settlements and districts. A further problem is that the use of political boundaries to differentiate regions may not fit well with actual labour-market boundaries. Similarly the industrial specialization is envisaged in terms of broad industries (textiles, apparel, transport equipment, machinery and so on) rather than specializations that define individual businesses. In the discussion below, priority is given to those studies that seem to be based on the most detailed levels of analysis. Prior to present-ing evidence on the results of the test, other difficulties in making the comparison are necessary to note.

In proposing the test, the degree of similarity required to confirm the expectation that trade promotes specialization is not specified. As well as the lack of clarity about the appropriate geographical and activity detail at which to conduct the investigation, there is no precise guide as to the pace of adjustment between market integration and regional special-ization. Within Europe, a common market was enacted in 1992 but it is generally agreed that other barriers to trade (national currencies, lan-guage and cultural ties) mean that it does not match the economic integration of the USA. It has, for example, been doubted that labour mobility will ever reach the levels achieved in the USA (Casella 1993: 264; Martin and Tyler 2000: 605). Another force for difference is the propor-tion of the USA's land mass that is inhospitable for economic activity due to its physical environment.

Two further uncertainties make it difficult to know what degree of increased similarity between the economic geography of Europe and the USA provides evidence of agglomeration forces at work:

1   There is no specification of the most appropriate economic indicators to be used. Potential measures that have been used include GDP per head, employment and value added and it appears that results are sensitive to which indicator is used (Martin and Tyler 2000; Aiginger and Leitner 2002).

2   Alternative interpretations exist for any coalescence between the eco-nomic geography of the two regions. For example, a study of levels of industry concentration in the USA has concluded that both neoclassi-cal theories and new economic geography are consistent with the pat-terns observed (Ellison and Glaeser 1997). The main focus of analysis is the period of increased European integration post-1990. Such short-term change is especially subject to random outcomes and temporary adjustments as well as systematic forces.

Comparing regional specialization

Higher levels of regional specialization in the USA than Europe have typically been taken as given, causing studies to focus on the European evidence. A more questioning starting point than usually encountered has noted that the 'common knowledge' of differences in regional specialization is based on surprisingly sketchy evidence (Aiginger and Leitner 2002). This study may also be preferred for its comparatively detailed analysis. It is based on 49 regions in the USA (comprising 48 states and the District of Columbia) and 70 NUTS [Nomenclature of Territorial Statistical Units]-1 regions for the European Union. The data are disaggregated into ten manufacturing industries and cover the period 1987–95 for the European Union and 1987–95 for the USA. This activity division and time period is less than ideal but the measurement of industry value added and employment strengthens the dataset. Productivity differences are overlooked when employment alone is examined. As well, recent industry employment trends are confused by the growth of part-time work and outsourcing. These complications add to the advantage of using value-added data to measure specialization.

Aiginger and Leitner (2002) use four different measures of geographical concentration to measure how far an industry is concentrated in a few regions (Box 5.8). The following results are obtained when value added is examined:

1   Overall, regional concentration of industries is significantly higher in the USA than Europe.
2   The degree of higher concentration in the USA varies between industries. Minerals, transport, food and textiles have the greatest tendency to be more concentrated in the USA than in Europe.
3   Different results can be obtained depending on which measure of concentration is used. Comparing 10 per cent of the regions with the highest concentration of each industry, electronics, machinery, paper and miscellaneous manufacturing are more concentrated in Europe than in the USA. The same indicator is highest overall for concentration in Europe.
4   Regional concentration is declining in the USA and Europe. This finding is consistent against all four concentration indicators, for the majority of industries and for manufacturing as a whole. In Europe, the decline in concentration accelerated post-1992 and formation of a single common market.
5   Industries with the steepest declines in concentration are metals, machinery and electronics. These are high-growth sectors compared with those experiencing increased concentration: textiles in the USA and textiles and food in Europe.

Box 5.8 Comparing concentration in Europe and the USA

The degree to which an industry is concentrated in one or a few regions can be measured using concentration rates, the coefficient of variation and the Gini coefficient:

1   *Concentration rates*: this measure shows the share of an industry located in each region of interest. To aid comparability between samples that may contain different numbers of regions and volumes of economic activity, the concentration in specified deciles may be used. For example, the top decile shows the concentration in the 10 per cent of regions with the largest concentration.
2   *Coefficient of variation*: this is based on the standard deviation of the shares of individual regions as an indicator of concentration. If all regions have the same share of a sector, the standard deviation is zero; the maximum score is attained when one region attracts all activity. The coefficient of variation adjusts the standard deviation for the number of regions examined.
3   *Gini coefficient*: this coefficient compares the actual distribution of activities with an even distribution of the activity. It requires that the location quotients of each of a region's industries are ranked in descending order. These are calculated as the ratio of the regional proportion of activity in a given sector relative to the national proportion of activity in the same sector. The coefficient is derived from the cumulative sum of the numerator and denominator terms in the location quotients. It ranges from 0 to 1, with 0 indicating no specialization.

Using the same data, different impressions of regional specialization in Europe and the USA are obtained (Table B5.1). Most assessments have used a combination of activity variable (employment) and concentration indicator (the Gini coefficient) that indicates the largest difference between Europe and the USA. Relative insensitivity to differences between the samples under comparison is a justification for using the Gini coefficient.

Table B5.1 Average concentration in Europe and the USA (1987–95)

	Concentration rate top decile	Coefficient of variance	Gini coefficient
Value added – European Union	35.32	1.05	0.51
– USA	34.06	1.07	0.53
Employment – European Union	33.47	0.97	0.47
– USA	32.40	1.04	0.52

Source: Aiginger and Leitner (2002)

The picture differs when employment is examined but without changing the main finding that regional concentration is declining in both regions. The USA emerges with a greater level of regional concentration than when value added is measured, although once again the difference is sensitive to the way concentration is measured. The pattern of declining concentration is maintained with the USA having the steepest rate of decline. Using employment as the concentration measure extends the European data up to 1998. The longer time period since the single-market enactment continues to show no tendency towards spatial concentration.

The European experience presented by Aiginger and Leitner (2002) does not match with the expectations of new economic geography. Support for the lack of conformity can be found in other studies. Hallet (2000), also using value-added data but with a more detailed industry analysis including some services and a time series from 1980 to 1995, confirms a decline in concentration within Europe. An OECD (2000) study based on employment data for 17 industries covered 172 regions in the USA and NUTS-2 regions for selected European (and other) countries. The time period covered varied between countries but typically at least stretched from the 1980s to the mid-1990s. Of the seven European countries included, Italy, Spain and Portugal were found to have levels of regional specialization similar to or higher than the USA. Neither was a trend toward increased regional specialization confirmed. Rather, it was concluded that national and regional employment profiles have become more similar in recent decades (OECD 2000: 60).

The expectation of new economic geography has not been confirmed but the outcome is not necessarily in conflict with the underlying theory. The trend to deconcentration in the USA and Europe may indicate that transport costs have reduced further than anticipated. As noted above, new economic geography envisages a U-shaped relationship between transport costs and concentration. An initial fall in transport costs encourages concentration. An ongoing decline is expected to ultimately cause dispersion due to the improved access peripheral locations obtain to core markets. As well, it is possible that market integration in Europe is not having a significant impact on labour mobility (although this still leaves the need to explain why specialization appears to be declining in the USA). On the other hand, the empirical evidence may indicate how location processes are more complex than can be accounted for by the range of influences considered in new economic geography.

There is evidence from Europe that economic integration and increased trade lead to regional diversification rather than specialization (Peschel 1982). The evidence predates European market integration but more recent studies have also claimed that product-market integration within Europe will lead to more intra-industry trade (see Martin and Sunley 1996: 279). This outcome is consistent with a trend to regional industrial structures becoming more similar over time.

Prior to the establishment of the internal European Market the consensus was that successful firms would become larger. An estimate that the average firm size in European manufacturing would increase by around 8 per cent was given in one influential study (Braunerhjelm *et al.* 2000: 20). In some sectors, an increase in average firm size of more than 30 per cent was projected. In the service sector, where national markets were initially more closed than in manufacturing, and where substantial economies of scale exist, even greater firm growth was possible. Subsequently, data have suggested that average firm size has actually declined. The reality may be different given organizational trends in favour of outsourcing non-core activities, so that firms may shrink in overall employment while increasing the value of final sales (Cooper and Burke 2002). Similarly the growth of inter-firm alliances and supply-chain partnering effectively extend the boundaries of organizations. As well, the impact on firm growth may become more marked over time as market integration feeds back on demand patterns, making consumers more similar across European countries (Braunerhjelm *et al.* 2000: 21). The outcome need not be that all surviving firms are larger. Opportunities will remain for small, niche producers to supplement the large firms or work for them as subcontractors and suppliers.

A bipolar distribution of firms within industries, with a few accounting for most production, does not fit with the firm assumptions of new economic geography. Large organizations have more capacity and reason to sustain a dispersed geography of production than the small, monopolistic competitors. Establishing branch plants and subsidiaries makes possible the diffusion of technology to equalize productivity differences between places. Strategically there may be advantage in maintaining production in multiple locations, for example to reduce labour power and reduce risks to the security of production. Practically, the emergence of large organizations through mergers and acquisitions are likely to create organizations with dispersed and idiosyncratic geographies of production. In contrast, the patterns of specialization predicted in new economic geography are based on internal economies of scale increasing the incentive for firms to concentrate on one site.

The comparison between Europe and the USA can also be used to draw attention to the role of immobile factors of production, especially physical space. Judged by land availability and land-use regulation, physical space is generally more of a constraint on economic activity in Europe than North America. Land constraints are recognized by new economic geographers as a potential centrifugal force but they do not form part of the core model. In the UK, for example, an inverse relationship between the degree of urbanization of a region and its manufacturing employment growth has long been apparent (Fothergill and Gudgin 1982). One interpretation of this trend indicates that the lack of space within established urban areas has encouraged employment growth to concentrate in newer industrial areas (Fothergill *et al.* 1985). The urban–rural shift was particularly pronounced in the UK but it has been an aspect of mature urban systems that needs consideration in the explanation of changing location patterns.

Conclusion

To date, new economic geography provides no clear endorsement for the emergence of business clusters as an aspect of competitive industrial economies. As one prominent new economic geographer has put it, this branch of economics is still in the Wright Brothers' phase of learning how to fly (Fujita cited in Stelder 2002). The core model built by Krugman (1991a) remains the main guide as to the direction of future flight. As with any model building, the complexity of economic life is reduced to a small number of variables and processes. In Krugman's view, the existence of gaps and emphasis on some variables at the expense of others is not a grave problem or serious limitation. The role of a model is to capture the core of real-world patterns. If it proves inadequate in this task, there is opportunity to modify the assumptions and vary the mix of variables. On this basis, it may be unfair to focus on the content of the initial model especially given the extensions and modifications that are being made (Brakman *et al.* 2001: 322). A contribution to understanding is being made by attempting to explain agglomeration without taking it for granted. Other accounts seeking to establish the importance of clustering, without the methodological rigour of mathematical economics, tend to assume processes are important and then search for evidence to confirm this.

This chapter has summarized how new economic geography approaches the examination of industry clusters. Four ways that the contribution to the assessment of business location differs from that made typically in studies of business clustering are identified.

First, the focus of model-building effort has been on large-scale agglomerative tendencies and the distribution of activity within an urban system rather than the specialization of individual locations. A settlement hierarchy in which places differ according to the range of economic activities they accommodate is the form of specialization addressed in the core model. Little additional insight has been generated into the origins of localized clusters. At the geographical scale of most interest to this book, there is little advancement on the standard Marshallian trinity of labour-market pooling, supply of intermediate goods and knowledge spillovers as the explanation for clustering (Krugman 1991a: 70). The main thrust of new economic geography has been to explain why countries are typically characterized by a highly uneven distribution of economic activity. At this level of agglomeration, people may need to change residence when they change jobs and are unlikely to maintain regular personal contact across all employers. These considerations, together with modelling preferences, have encouraged attention on only small processes generally thought to be associated with clustering.

Second, there is no reference to many of the strategic firm behaviours that other accounts of business clustering give considerable attention to. In particular, there is no inclusion of the blurring of firm boundaries created through participation in business networks. This omits the role of outsourcing in encouraging firms to locate in clusters. It also stands in contrast to the importance of transnational organizations as participants in clusters with more complex location strategies than the single-site organizations that populate agglomerations in new economic geography.

Third, the model building assumes that firms are entirely footloose and, by extension, so are the clusters that they build. Agglomerations, once established, are expected to survive even under conditions that would not cause them to form in the first instance but a point is envisaged when they may 'melt away'. Indeed once the 'sustain point' (marking the threshold up to where an agglomeration retains an advantage) is reached, change is expected to be rapid as firms, industries and even cities are always free to move as there are no sunk costs. The assumption of firm mobility is a modelling device. The rapid opening-up of new industrial areas, such as Southeast Asia and the so-called 'sunbelt' regions of older industrial economies, suggests it is not entirely unfounded. Even so, the flexibility needed for new economic geography contrasts with the frequently made argument that clusters are 'embedded' in and made possible by social and cultural conditions that link contemporary growth to past histories of economic development. For Krugman, an idea such as embeddedness is too intangible and gives too much scope for the analyst to make assumptions *a priori*, rather than demonstrating their significance through interaction with other model variables.

Fourth, new economic geography has tended to avoid the advocacy of one spatial outcome over another. Fujita, Krugman and Venables (1999: 348) explain their reticence to draw policy conclusions as recognition of the need to demonstrate further the power of the analysis before prescribing it. Specifically, it is acknowledged that the spatial structure of an economy is in perpetual flux between the relative influence of external economies that foster concentration and the congestion diseconomies that favour dispersion. Considerable further work is required before it will be possible to know what the optimal arrangement of economic activity should be. Meanwhile, it is worth noting that, at least thus far, an expected outcome of economic concentration is the increased divergence of regional growth rates. In other words, locations with an adverse employment experience are not expected to recover their lost employment and catch up with more favoured locations. More likely than recovery, workers move away from areas of decline to more buoyant employment locations. A locality whose industries are faring badly has little capacity to attract alternative industries as they, at least initially, will be disadvantaged by the absence of the external economies found in existing concentrations. Consequently, a locality with an industry in decline may simply shed jobs without the downward pressure on the price of capital and labour stimulating a recovery to its former level of employment (Krugman 1993b: 248). In this sense, although clustering is frequently advocated as a basis for regional development, in new economic geography it is associated with heightened exposure to region-specific shocks and greater disparity in regional growth rates.

6 Clusters in developing countries

The tendency for businesses to cluster in low-income economies is much higher than in high-income economies. There is no precise measurement to indicate the scale of the difference but it is known that clusters are common in a wide range of developing countries and sectors (Humphrey and Schmitz 1995). Moreover, developing-country clusters typically exhibit a more extreme form of concentration than in developed economies. They are often centred around a single community that has a clear economic specialization on a single activity, such as basket ware, dying, weaving or metal work. Unlike the ambiguity surrounding the identification of clusters in developed economies, there is no question about the existence of clusters in developing countries. In many cases the specialization has a long unbroken history. Equally, new clusters can be found. In India, for example, an incipient biotechnology cluster in Hyderabad has been reported that complements an existing concentration of software services (Dyer and Merchant 2003). In the same country, Panipat is cited as a cluster of 700 carding machines that were transferred from Prato, Italy (UNIDO 2000). The machines make shoddy yarn from recycled wool, an activity no longer viable in Italy. A long history of public-agency assistance to clusters also makes the developing-country experience of interest, as this chapter will review in the case of Indonesia.

The revival of interest in business clustering has been a stimulus for investigating the developing-country experience. Principally, it has encouraged researchers and industry development agencies working in low-income countries to reconsider cluster potential in the light of the claims about Italian industrial districts and other high-profile examples (van Dijk and Rabellotti 1997; Schmitz and Nadvi 1999). This chapter takes the opposite perspective and focuses on the lessons from developing-country experience for cluster promoters in high-income economies. A perception of the attachment of developing-country clusters to inefficient economies perhaps explains why they have been overlooked in much of the contemporary debate about cluster advantages. This outlook has partly been encouraged by a tendency for the literature on developing-country clusters to emphasize their potential role in stimulating business growth and economic transformation (Schmitz 1995a). Similarly there has been an emphasis on identifying a continuum of clusters from those embedded in the informal sector to those involving 'advanced' producers (Altenburg and Meyer-Stamer 1999). On the other hand, the emphasis on identifying transitions in cluster characteristics is potentially of wide interest. As seen in the case of Italy's industrial districts, the evolution of business organization within clusters is a challenge that many clusters face. Indeed it has been argued that the 1990s saw increased similarity of developing country and Italian clusters (Schmitz and Nadvi 1999: 1504). As the chapter will illustrate, detailed case-study evidence has been a hallmark of the research into developing-country clusters. This evidence shows how clusters change with growth and why growth eludes most clusters. These experiences should be considered in the advocacy of clusters wherever situated.

At the outset, as implied from the identification of a continuum, it needs to be acknowledged that there is not a developing-country experience. At one extreme, in most sub-Saharan African cases clustering has had minimal impact on the progress of industrialization (McCormick 1999). At the other extreme, there are clusters in Latin America and Asia that have been a vanguard for economic modernization. In the case of Taiwan and South Korea, some small firms in computer-industry clusters have grown into global corporations and played a significant role in propelling their economy's transition to high-income status (Levy and Kuo 1991; Mathews and Cho 2000). On a lesser scale, these regions have many clusters that have moved from serving local to international markets, sometimes sustaining their competitiveness in the context of decreased domestic-trade protection (Rabellotti 1999). The distinguishing features of clusters that appear to succeed in promoting enterprise growth will provide much of the discussion for the chapter.

The chapter commences by outlining a model of cluster development in low-income economies and the general conditions that are needed to transform them into environments capable of supporting business growth. This discussion draws attention to the internal differentiation of clusters, so challenging the tendency to assume clusters comprise groups of similar enterprises with common interests (Rabellotti 1999: 1581). A case study of business clusters in Indonesia is then presented. Indonesia's particularly pronounced and well-documented occurrence of business clusters partly explains the selection. It also offers the opportunity to reflect on over 20 years of experience from industrial-development agencies in seeking to lever economic advantage from clusters. This experience includes cumulative adjustment to programmes but a largely unsuccessful outcome that has led to the redirection of industrial-development support away from clusters. The final part of the chapter considers the impact of globalization on developing-country clusters, drawing on experience from Pakistan and Brazil.

A model of cluster emergence and growth

The critical test of clusters in low-income countries has been whether they accelerate economic modernization compared with a dispersed pattern of industrial location. Evidence about the contribution of developing-country clusters exists mainly in case studies of individual clusters at one point in time. From these cross-sectional profiles, a stylized account of how clusters develop and transform themselves into centres of enterprise growth has been proposed (Schmitz 1995a). This model emphasizes how the advantages obtained by a cluster vary with the stage of development. It is an idealized account as the growth experiences of clusters vary widely (Schmitz and Nadvi 1999: 1504). A context for this model is the wider appreciation of the role that cottage industry and small-scale enterprise plays in developing economies (Box 6.1).

In summary, the model proposes that the advantages first brought by a cluster are gained simply by virtue of a location within its geographical reach. At this stage, cooperation within clusters is unplanned and each participant has equal access to the economies of agglomeration. Greater advantage is obtained when the relationships between participants are based on joint decisions. Planned action brings greater benefit to the cluster but these additional advantages accrue mainly to those who directly participate in the forms of cooperation that result. Some clusters, probably most, never achieve significant planned action and survive without becoming sites of industrial growth.

Box 6.1 Business transitions in developing economies

Micro-enterprises that become small firms are the exception in developing economies. The great majority of micro-enterprises do not grow and remain dependent on family labour that may be unpaid. At the same time, the micro-enterprise sector may not decline in absolute importance when the economy starts to modernize. Until economic development is well entrenched, micro-enterprise activity tends to fluctuate with the perform-ance of the national economy. During times of growth, small firms benefit from new market opportunities and this results in their employment expansion. During economic slowdowns, small firms struggle to hold their ground and shed labour. Declining employment increases the pressure on people to start their own enterprises, even though these may generate only a mar-ginal income, or rejoin a family business. Consequently, micro-enterprise retains more importance than once assumed, maintaining the existence of many clusters but without indicating the existence of incipient business clus-ters with potential for enterprise growth. Graduation from micro-enterprise operator to small-firm owner is rare. Small firms start in the small-firm sector rather than with a prior existence as an informal enterprise.

Source: Liedholm and Mead (1999)

Within clusters that exhibit planned action, differences emerge between enterprises with respect to their size, resources, markets and pursuit of growth. Planned action is primarily a matter of negotiation between selected enterprises and is frequently stimulated by the ability of some enterprises to serve new markets. It accentuates differentiation because it brings additional advantages over the exclusive reliance on unplanned advantages. At this point two main outcomes arise. The cluster may wane as planned action becomes more selective and the most success-ful cluster participants become large enterprises that reduce their dependence on cluster resources. A more likely outcome is that the cluster will become focused around a few dominant enterprises. In either event, sustaining participation in the cluster will depend on public-agency intervention that promotes wider opportunities for planned action than arise through private negotiation. By diffusing opportunities across enterprises that are unable or unwilling to join private planned action, there is more likelihood of the cluster sustaining a diversity of interconnected enterprises than otherwise would be the case.

This stylized account raises a number of key questions about clusters.

First is the need to explain how unplanned advantages alone can support a cluster. Unplanned advantages at the outset of a cluster are linked to the resource constraints facing industrialization efforts in low-income countries. Clustering reduces the impediments to industrialization in a context of modest financial and human-capital availability, and limited prior experience of commercial enterprise. Industrialization raises the efficiency of economic activity but depends on initial investment in production capacity and in services to support production. Clustering reduces the scale of effective investment by enabling resources to be shared. Investment is divided into smaller steps than where production commences in isolation or among dissimilar activities (Schmitz 1995a). For example, when the first-movers undertake related activities in close proximity, individual enterprises and the immediate environment adapts to the collective presence. Producers do not have to acquire equipment for the entire production process; they can concentrate on a specific task and leave others to complete the process. The environment adapts to an emerging core of producers by attracting customers, traders, workers with related skills, and suppliers of inputs and services. Environmental change stimulates further enterprise creation. Where specialized suppliers of raw materials and components are close by, there is less need to store inputs. Similarly, small amounts of human capital increase in value as complementary skills become more available than they were. Specialized workshops to repair and upgrade equipment further reduce the barriers to entry.

The unplanned way that clusters gain their initial advantage is a further reason for the frequency with which they occur. For example, gaining access to market linkages does not rely on coordinated action. Traders may appear simply because they heard of the existence of the cluster

(McCormick 1999: 1533). People learn from each other while observing each other's production processes and through their negotiations with traders. People modify their own activities in response to individual preferences and calculations and in the process add to the collective strength of the cluster. One person's decision to specialize on a particular task, or to move into a service role, gives opportunities to others. The key outcome is that investment decisions are broken into small steps that impose manageable risks. In effect:

> . . . the enterprise of one creates a foothold for the other, that ladders are constructed which enable small enterprise to climb and grow. It is a process in which enterprises create for each other – often unwillingly, sometimes intentionally – possibilities for accumulating capital and skill.
>
> (Schmitz and Nadvi 1999: 1506)

Reduced risk helps understand why activity does not disperse among isolated producers. The initial stimulus bringing activity together is less well understood than why it stays in place but it seems to arise from something more than serendipity (Box 6.2).

Box 6.2 A cluster's first step

The first step in the emergence of a cluster is the hardest to generalize about. At some stage a person or group of persons started an activity that subsequently became a community specialization. Agricultural specialization or localized commodity resources may be the explanation, by giving rise to processing opportunities or supporting a population concentration that can be served with basic consumer goods or both. Development alongside a rural economy enables activities to be linked to the agricultural-production cycle. Production patterns can be made complementary to seasonal and daily variations in farming to provide secondary sources of income and flexible supplies of labour. Agriculture and agro-processing frequently share equipment, production facilities and accommodation. Rural locations may also be favoured by the free use of environmental resources, in the form of materials and land as well as in the capacity to pollute.

Resource advantages seem a logical starting point for a cluster but resource disadvantages have been linked to the origins of some clusters. In the case of Indonesia, for example, it has been suggested that acute poverty can stimulate the initiation of a cluster. People moving out of isolated locations due to drought or other natural disasters come together in some central place. Loss of linkage to previous subsistence activity forces a focus on some alternative activity. It also appears that ubiquitous activities are less likely to be associated with clusters than are activities with a comparatively small total labour force. Large numbers of dispersed producers make it hard for a cluster to gain momentum.

Source: Weijland (1999)

Unplanned advantages amount to the external agglomeration economies usually associated with clusters: labour-market pooling, intermediate input effects, technological spillovers and market access (McCormick 1999). These economies help clusters grow as long as markets, technology and industry organization remain unchanged. Agglomeration economies on their own will not enable a cluster to ride out major changes in their external environment (Box 6.3). This assessment contrasts with the perspective in high-income countries that stresses how clusters are built on agglomeration economies alone.

Whether there are any limits to the potential formation of clusters is a second question addressed in the stylized model of developing-country clusters. Two prerequisites are proposed. Enterprises must be connected to trade networks and have some basis for trusting each other. A gap in either of these requirements will stymie a cluster's ability to mobilize financial and human resources.

Without the diversification of markets beyond their immediate locality, clusters will struggle to attain significant scale. As well as the wider market, it potentially gives connection to consumers with bigger budgets than in their home community and chance to learn how to meet their preferences (Poot *et al.* 1990). Clusters attract traders by reducing the cost of organizing transactions but the strength of this incentive will vary. Not all incipient clusters are well placed to connect to trade networks. Even in a country such as Indonesia, where trade networks are highly developed, clusters are unequally connected to distant markets. Rural clusters that are well connected to distant markets by traders have higher incomes than those without good connections (Weijland 1994: 107). Physical geography is an influence on which clusters get connected. Trading networks can be wide and complex. They may stretch into remote areas, especially where they involve small traders with rudimentary transport that can navigate

---

Box 6.3 The limits of unplanned advantage

The unplanned advantages of clusters draw out the less exceptional and more frequently occurring entrepreneurs by making it possible to advance in small steps. The accumulation of capital and skills is correspondingly small. It may be too small to promote a spontaneous process of deepening specialization and too small to withstand major changes in product or factor markets. When taking large steps, there is an incentive to contemplate joint action to reduce the exposure to risk. Through joint action, it is possible to achieve upgrading that responds to market challenges. It depends on clusters attracting or developing truly visionary entrepreneurs with large amounts of capital and a willingness to take large risks. Such persons are rare but necessary for enterprise growth.

Sources: Schmitz (1999); Schmitz and Nadvi (1999)

difficult terrain. Accessible locations are, nonetheless, advantaged over isolated ones. The presence of traders with attachment to the area they serve is a further source of difference among clusters. Traders who live in the neighbourhood of their clients are likely to be acquainted with them and to develop stable and mutually supportive relationships (Weijland 1999: 1517). In contrast to Indonesia, the poor distribution networks in East and Southern Africa have been identified as reasons for the comparatively weak development of clusters in this region (Pedersen 1997).

The existence of effective sanctions and trust are a second and related condition for cluster emergence and survival. Specialization brings a high level of interdependence between individual enterprises. In the absence of well-developed legal systems for contract enforcement, it is important that producers trust each other and have the assurance that neighbouring enterprises will operate in accordance with expectations. To some degree the emergence of clusters in small communities provides a likelihood of trust. For example, it has been suggested that a key advantage of rural industry clusters is that small producers often have family connections to each other that facilitate social control (Burger *et al.* 2000). More generally, in small communities it is hard for trust breakers to remain undiscovered and so the risk of informal sanctions can encourage conformity to expected behaviours. On the other hand, other aspects of the community's structure may not be supportive of a cluster.

In low-income communities, traditional social relations are often dominated by patronage relationships, status in the socio-political hierarchy, land ownership and traditional family bonds. Individuals entering the cluster activities may need to disengage themselves from the obligations imposed by inherited community structures. As any such disengagement may be viewed as a threat to the traditional authority structure, clusters are likely to face constraints on their development. In the context of shoe making in India, for example, it has been shown how distrust between producers and traders has constrained cluster development (Knorringa 1996). Similarly ethnic divisions have been identified as reason why clusters have often brought limited development in parts of Africa (Mitullah 1999). In contrast, racial division has been an advantage in Indonesia where entrepreneurs are predominantly from a racial minority (Chinese). This encouraged patronage from the racial elite on the grounds that the minority would not challenge their political authority (Mackie 1992: 44).

Once formed, a significant transition point is the appearance of consciously pursued joint action. Key questions here concern the distinction between planned and unplanned action and the evidence that enterprise growth depends on planned joint action.

The defining characteristic of planned action is that it relies on deliberate decisions to collaborate with others. This distinction is not entirely clear cut. Setting up a business in a cluster may be envisaged as a decision to collaborate. If labour is employed, for example, the risk of losing employees to a competitor is greater than when working in isolation. The critical difference may not, therefore, be the presence of a decision but the capture of benefits from the decision. Deciding to join a cluster brings benefit to the entrant and other members of the cluster, by extending the labour pool or scope for specialization. The benefits of planned action may spill over to others in the cluster but they are gained primarily by those directly involved. The ability to capture the gains from cooperation is presumably one reason why this source of collective efficiency has more importance for the cluster's growth than unplanned cooperation. Equally, it means that the performance of individual enterprises diverges according to their capture of the benefits from joint action.

Depending on the number of participants and direction of cooperation, four characteristic forms of joint action are said to be associated with the most successful clusters (Schmitz 1997). Bilateral action involves two enterprises working together, for example in the sharing of equipment. If the enterprises are engaged in similar activity, the cooperation is horizontal; if they specialize at different stages of the production chain, the cooperation is vertical. Multilateral action involves groups of enterprises joining together in some form of association to further a common purpose. Commercial transactions are within the scope of joint action provided that they are based on some degree of mutual obligation, such as the sharing of information or a long-term commitment. Indeed, improvements in supplier–manufacturer relations are the most widely documented forms of joint action (Schmitz and Nadvi 1999: 1508).

Not all forms of joint action are of equal significance to the transformation of a cluster. Multilateral cooperation is generally thought to have most potential impact, as through support for a trade association that assists technology transfer or through collective investment in shared equipment or infrastructure. Bilateral cooperation is easier to obtain and most frequently the source of a cluster's transformation. The transformative power of bilateral cooperation is based largely on evidence that enterprises engaging in some form of joint action grow faster than their neighbours in the cluster that do not engage in joint action (Box 6.4).

Participation in joint action contributes to cluster participants becoming different to each other. The final question addressed to the cluster-development model is how it reconciles increasing internal heterogeneity with the survival of a cluster.

As the challenges facing a cluster's growth increase, the willingness or ability to join joint action, or both, intensifies differentiation between cluster enterprises. In clusters that have become exposed to international competition, for example, multilateral action can be resisted by larger producers who see opportunity to respond individually to the pressures being faced (see the case study of the Sinos Valley in the final section of the chapter). Such tension was in conflict with the prior assumption that

Box 6.4 Joint action and enterprise performance

The perceived importance of planned joint action in supporting cluster growth comes from evidence of positive and statistically significant relationships between increases in enterprise cooperation and improvements in enterprise performance. This evidence is open to interpretation and leaves a gap in the stylized account of developing-country clusters.

The forms of joint action identified mainly relate to cooperation within the context of commercial transactions, such as information sharing, credit or promises of an ongoing relationship. The existence of cooperation is generally not measured directly but taken from self-declared descriptions of business relationships. Ambiguity may exist in determining the difference between cooperation and constraint. A buyer, for example, may offer assistance to a supplier but make this conditional on the supplier refraining from serving other markets. Even where there is no such ambiguity, the existence of cooperation with improved performance leaves uncertainty over the direction of causality. Cooperation may be an outcome rather than a cause of performance success. Confidence in market growth may, for example, motivate a willingness to offer long-term supply relationships. Similarly participation in a trade association in a successful cluster is open to interpretation. There may be greater willingness to participate among already-growing enterprises as they have the resources to attend meetings or support other activities that do not bring immediate rewards. The absence of counter-factual evidence is potentially a further information gap. Without cooperation, enterprises may have had other ways of obtaining the same resources and these alternatives may provide greater flexibility than cultivating cooperation with another enterprise. Finally, the evidence about business cooperation and performance does not differentiate between intra-cluster cooperation and that between individual enterprises inside and outside the cluster.

Sources: Nadvi (1999); Schmitz (1999)

mature clusters would be characterized by well-established collective institutions pursuing strategies that brought cluster-wide benefits. It is now accepted that the ideal outcome cannot be assumed to arise. In its absence, the model identifies public agency intervention as the mechanism for resolving internal difference. Public agencies, it was believed, had capacity to widen the access to joint action beyond that arising through private initiative alone. Further evidence is now causing some caution in making this claim. The challenge some clusters face from globalization may be too great for state mediation to resolve, even in clusters where there is a willingness among cluster participants to accept public intervention (Schmitz and Nadvi 1999: 1509). The case of Sialkot (Pakistan) and the Sinos Valley illustrate some of these doubts and their experiences are reviewed in the final part of the chapter.

An uncertainty remains in the fate of clusters that develop high levels of internal difference and that face external challenges to their established market. Larger and more successful enterprises might result in the gradual demise of a cluster. Such an outcome is considered unlikely on evidence that successful firms rarely decide to move out of the cluster in which they started (Schmitz 1999: 1630). This judgement may need to be revised. In Indonesia, as discussed in the following section, enterprise migration out of clusters has been observed.

Evaluating the model

Gaps and uncertainties remain in the stylized account of developing-country clusters beyond the questions already raised. There is, for example, little reference to the relationship between a cluster and its external environment. Without assessment of how industry and market conditions shape the opportunities for growth, the power of a cluster can be exaggerated. For example, Schmitz and Nadvi (1999: 1506) suggest that the Taiwanese computer industry is the best demonstration of a cluster facilitating investment in small risk-reducing steps. Such an interpretation is incomplete without reference to the larger restructuring of electronics production that presented the Taiwanese cluster with opportunities for growth (Box 6.5). Greater attention than hitherto given to the external conditions facilitating cluster development is emerging. One stimulus for this has been recognition of the influence of global-commodity chains on cluster development (see the discussion of the Sinos valley in the final part of the chapter). Similarly, as seen in the Indonesian case study below, the role of external buyers in controlling opportunities for a cluster is becoming clear.

Box 6.5 Taiwanese bootstraps

By the mid-1990s, Taiwan supplied between two-thirds and three-quarters of the world's production of motherboards, mice and keyboards for use with personal computers. It had also become home to some of the world's largest suppliers of personal computers. A variety of interpretations of this success have been presented:

- State economic policies promoted export-led growth from the 1960s through removing controls on trade, supportive exchange-rate policies, taxation incentives (including the establishment of export processing zones) and by relaxing constraints on foreign investment. Crucially, it maintained close control on foreign direct investment. Applications were assessed case-by-case to discourage investment that might displace local enterprise. Local content requirements and import controls were used to promote linkages between foreign investors and local enterprise. This selectivity and control contrasts with the position in Singapore, another East Asian tiger economy, where openness to foreign investors crowded out indigenous enterprise.

- Various actions of the Taiwanese state are generally identified as crucial in the development of its computer industry. Joint venture investments were responsible for the start-up of semiconductor manufacture. A former premier (Y S Sun) facilitated a network of overseas Chinese engineers in the USA to bring skilled workers to the semiconductor industry. The government planned and funded Hsinchu science-based industrial park that provided infrastructure and investment incentives to high-technology enterprises.

- Taiwan's dominance of personal-computer assembly was possible because of shifts in the organization of buyer–supplier linkages in the consumer-electronics industry. Increased standardization and simplification of technology encouraged sellers of computer equipment to establish buyer-driven commodity chains that make extensive use of subcontracting in Asia. At the same time, rapid advancement in the technology on which computers are based facilitated exponential market growth.

- Local enterprise has developed in a peculiar political and social context. A Chinese Nationalist government took hold of Taiwan after the rise of communism in China and continued into the 1990s. It ruled over an island split between 'mainlanders' (settlers arriving to escape communism) and the original Taiwanese residents ('islanders'). Islanders preferred to rely on their own resources and foreign capital rather than become dependent on a state that they mistrusted and that did not seek their inclusion. This provided an entrepreneurial environment conducive to the development of subcontracting linkages with foreign businesses.

The role of passive agglomeration economies in facilitating a stepwise upgrading of enterprise in Taiwan needs to be assessed against these diverse contributors to Taiwan's economic success. Given multiple advantages and an unusual opportunity to gain a foothold in a new industry, it may be viewed as a misleading example of the impact of clustering.

Sources: Numazaki (1993); Hobday (1995); Wong (1995); Robins (1998)

A further limitation of the model is the lack of differentiation between clusters. The emphasis on identifying stages of development has tended to overlook how the scope for change may vary between types of cluster. For example, many developing economy clusters originate in the processing of local resources. Under conditions of non-sustainable resource harvesting, these clusters have a limited life. Similarly, a differentiation is required between artisan-based clusters and those based on mechanical forms of production (Box 6.6). The model is directed at understanding how clusters can become the basis for enterprise growth and international competitiveness. Most developing-country clusters are associated with rudimentary forms of production that display many characteristics of the informal sector (see the case study of palm sugar, Box 6.7). As discussed above, there is generally no transition from this scale of enterprise to participation in the modern sectors of the economy.

The stylized account of developing-country clusters has gaps but two points of contrast with the corresponding account of clusters in high-income countries are relatively well supported:

- Agglomeration economies impart limited capacity to manage changes in a cluster's market or product characteristics: deliberate joint action is needed to make successful adjustments to external challenges.
- Deliberate joint action is associated with enterprise growth but ultimately it may become a constraint on the ability of the cluster to retain a common purpose: without common objectives, the capacity to withstand intensified competition is in doubt.

Box 6.6 Cluster varieties in developing countries

A review of clusters in India made a primary distinction between artisan-based rural clusters and those existing in industrialized sectors of the economy. The artisan-based clusters were the most numerous (around 2,000 compared with 138 industrialized clusters), making products with simple hand tools and occasionally with rudimentary machinery. Their clusters consist of micro-enterprises with few linkages other than those with buyers who use their relative financial strength to exploit artisans. Clusters tend to be overcrowded with enterprises due to a 'herd instinct'. Crowding accentuates the ability of buyers to keep prices low.

Clusters of industrialized activities were distinguished according to the relationships between cluster enterprises. On this basis:

- 55 per cent of clusters were horizontal. Enterprises carried out similar activities and marketed their own output.
- 12 per cent of clusters were vertically integrated. Enterprises were connected through contracting relationships, mainly between small establishments that do not have the capacity to complete finished goods on their own.
- 5 per cent of clusters were based on large units. These are built around one or a few large enterprises that provide opportunities to surrounding small enterprises, either to provide inputs or that make use of the output of the large enterprises.
- 28 per cent of clusters exhibit some mixture of the other types of cluster.

This profile indicates that in most clusters enterprises work directly for customers, rather than operating within localized subcontracting networks.

Source: UNIDO (2000)

Clusters in Indonesia

Indonesia provides an interesting case study of developing-country clusters as small-scale industry shows a pronounced tendency to cluster in this populous country (220 million). Uneven performance is equally of interest to the propensity to cluster. Some clusters have become home to internationally competitive exporters, many are dormant and some have 'remained so poor and stagnant that one might wonder whether their producers would not be better off elsewhere' (Weijland 1999: 1520). A further attraction of the Indonesian experience is that an official record of clusters or so-called *sentra industri* has been maintained by the Ministry of Trade and Industry. *Sentra industri* are defined as geographical groupings of at least 20 similar small enterprises, or less if some of the enterprises export all or some of their production. On this basis, there are around 25,000 clusters in Indonesia providing employment for perhaps close to two-thirds of all persons working in cottage and small-scale manufacturing (Sandee and ter Wengel 2002). This includes clusters found in urban and rural areas. Examined as a proportion of rural settlements, around 10,000 villages have registered a *sentra industri* amounting to 14 per cent of all villages (Weijland 1999). Such frequency is, for example, ahead of India (see Box 6.6) which has over four times the population of Indonesia.

The uneven performance of clusters has occurred at a time of rapid industrialization and economic growth from the mid-1980s to the late 1990s. The size distribution of firms in the manufacturing sector appeared to remain unchanged over this period and this has been seen as a sign of the dynamism of small-scale enterprise (Hill 2002). The employment share of large and medium-sized enterprises remained unchanged, that of small firms (5–49 workers) rose marginally and the share accounted for by cottage industry fell modestly. Especially in the case of the cottage industry sector, data quality may be poor. The most reliable statistics cover enterprises of 20 or more employees and these show small enterprise holding ground in the economy. One interpretation acknowledges that this achievement occurred when the policy environment was increasingly conducive to doing business (Schiller and Martin-Schiller 1997). One particular success, for example, was the growth of effective banking facilities for small-scale enterprise such as that provided by Bank Rakyet Indonesia (Perry 2003).

In contrast to explanations based on the overall environment for enterprise growth, innovation by clustered enterprise has been claimed as a significant factor in the strength of the small-business sector (Sandee *et al.* 2000: 187). This argument relies on evidence that clusters are conducive to efficient enterprise. To date, the evidence comes mainly from micro-level studies that identify a variety of experiences rather than a uniform advantage in clustering (Hill 2002: 168). Before looking at some of these results, further description of Indonesia's clusters is helpful.

Enterprises within *sentra industri* typically employ two or three workers at most. There is little variation in typical employment between the main industrial activities generating clusters (Sandee 2002: 67). The preponderance of micro-enterprise is consistent with the manufacturing sector as a whole: in 1996, almost two-thirds of employment was in establishments of fewer than 20 workers. In contrast, the less than 1 per cent of establishments that employed 100 or more workers generated a third of manufacturing employment with vastly higher levels of labour productivity than the micro-enterprise sector. The marginal economic character of cluster activities is especially pronounced among the activities that most frequently give rise to a cluster.

A statistical profile of rural clusters in Central Java in the late 1980s, derived from the government record of *sentra industry*, remains one of the most detailed sources of evidence on Indonesia's clusters. Central Java still accounts for 40 per cent of all Indonesia's village-based clusters and so this region gives a good profile of rural clusters. The most numerous clusters are based on activities that have the lowest investment costs and lowest gross output (Table 6.1). Bamboo weaving, ceramics, palm sugar and other activities have the lowest investment needs. Some opportunities exist to specialize in comparatively high-value products (Box 6.7) but generally they are marginal activities that are carried out by rural households in the

Table 6.1 A profile of rural clusters in Central Java 1989

Product	Share of all clusters (%)	Enterprises per cluster	Investment per enterprise (Rp. 1,000)	Gross output per enterprise (Rp. 1,000)
Palm sugar	17.8	120.0	27.6	599
Ceramics	1.4	64.8	17.1	680
Weaving bamboo	21.5	69.4	11.8	751
Batik	3.3	96.7	117.8	1,536
Roof tiles	4.7	65.0	148.7	1,814
Tailoring	3.0	18.3	97.5	1,977
Bricks	6.2	41.5	87.1	3,147
Farm tools	1.2	33.4	154.3	3,273
Krupuk	5.6	59.1	76.8	4,340
Textile weaving	0.8	45.2	51.9	4,404
Tempe	10.7	28.0	38.6	4,854
Furniture	4.5	38.9	112.7	5,187
Other products	14.9	44.0	177.2	5,474
Leather	0.4	35.4	241.7	9,761
Tahu	2.4	33.6	299.5	11,853
Garments	0.8	47.1	731.6	13,143
Embroidery	0.8	86.3	385.7	46,482

Source: Adapted from Weijland 1999: 1522.

Note
US$ = Rp. 1,780 (1989).

Box 6.7 Sugar clusters

Palm-sugar processing is one of the most frequent activities on which clusters exist in Java, Indonesia's most populous island. It generates a marginal income for most participants, no more than a few US dollars a day. It survives by being a part-time activity that can be carried out at any time of the year or day when better-paid work is not available. Typically a household division of labour is involved: men collect tapped sugar from trees; women supervise the cooking and evaporation process. Hamlet collectors combine the output of several producers and on-sell to village collectors who supply local outlets. The survival of the activity has been helped where producers have moved into higher-quality production, enabling wider markets to be served. This requires high standards of sterilization of the receptacles that are used to collect and process sugar. More cash outlays and more labour time are needed than with traditional palm sugar. This is assisted by working for buyers who provide credit in return for exclusive supply agreements. Buyers consolidate production and sell it to supermarkets and the food and pharmaceutical industries. The marketing chains for both low- and high-quality sugar encourage clustering because of economies in the collection of sugar.

Source: Burger *et al.* (2000)

---

absence of more rewarding income-generating opportunities (Sandee 2002: 67). In contrast, embroidery and garments enterprises are based on comparatively high investment and can provide sustainable incomes. In either case, most clusters have a long history providing the basis for meaningful comparison of their impact.

Data derived from the 1989 *sentra industry* survey have been used to relate enterprise and cluster size to investment and gross output. Weijland (1999) summarizes the results for clusters based on three contrasting activities: bamboo weaving, *tahu* (fermented soybean) production and garment making. These activities are representative of activities with differing entry requirements, in terms of financial investment and skills, and the market area over which outputs are sold. Enterprise and cluster value-added and investment were compared with enterprise and cluster size with the following findings:

- The scale of employment or investment had no impact in improving the value-added of bamboo enterprises; in fact there tended to be a negative relationship. Size of the cluster, measured by the number of enterprises and total investment, did have a positive relationship with the value-added for the cluster as a whole. This was interpreted as indicating some benefits from clustering in otherwise dismally poor activities.

- *Tahu* production had characteristics that were the opposite of bamboo weaving. Individual enterprises tended to gain by increasing their employment and investment, but the size of cluster appeared to have little impact on enhancing value-added.
- Garments had a complex pattern. Enterprises gained more from increasing their employment than did clusters; while the reverse applied to investment. Investment brought significantly larger gains for the cluster as a whole than for the individual enterprise.

These results suggest that cluster advantages vary with the industry forming the cluster. Bamboo weaving is a traditional craft using little or no machinery and supplying a saturated market. There is limited scope for individual enterprises to grow. Working in a cluster appears to improve individual enterprises but the activity remains a marginal source of income. Buyers can divide orders among multiple weavers and achieve economies in collecting products. *Tahu* is a perishable product that requires swift, quality-controlled production for delivery mainly to local markets. Individual enterprises may have comparatively well-equipped kitchens, although many producers have modest equipment, but the product does not suit equipment sharing. Clustering appears to have little impact on performance partly as the product is not susceptible to order sharing or subcontracting. Garment production is based on small enterprises utilizing comparatively expensive equipment. Utilization of equipment can be maximized through specialization and dividing orders among subcontractors. As well, operating in a cluster improves the capacity to link to distant markets without the need for individual producers to invest in marketing.

Obtaining advantage from a cluster, therefore, appears to depend partly on the activity on which it is based. This finding is not inconsistent with the case that has been made for the importance of clustering. Researchers who believe clustering is a source of enterprise growth point to the clusters that have achieved significant technological upgrading rather than claiming all clusters can grow (Sandee and ter Wengel 2002). In particular, the development of subcontracting is critical to cluster growth. Subcontracting permits specialization between enterprises and provides opportunity for resource sharing and joint learning. This contribution would be significant in Indonesia. Investigations in the 1980s found that subcontracting was limited, fluid, sometimes characterized by opportunistic behaviour and not a basis for enterprise growth (Thee 1994).

Subcontracting networks strengthened as Indonesia's industrialization deepened after the 1980s (Hill 2002: 170). Urban-based, modern-sector firms played the key role in upgrading subcontracting networks, as in the case of the motorcycle industry (Thee 1997). Evidence that clusters contribute to participation in upgrading through subcontracting is mixed.

A detailed study of Ceper, the 'village of foundries', provides evidence that the important linkages for cluster enterprises are to businesses outside the cluster (Sato 2000). Located in Central Java, Ceper has close to 350 metal-casting enterprises and history dating back several centuries. Its modern form dates from the 1980s when the number of furnaces more than tripled and the use of machine tools became widespread. In the late 1990s, the cluster accounted for almost a third of Indonesia's annual metal-cast production. Enterprises were of three types:

1   A top tier of about ten large foundries with integrated machining and assembling processes, sometimes augmented by subcontracting to lower-tier foundries in the cluster.
2   Medium-sized enterprises with machine tooling, enabling processing of cast products, and accounting for around 70 per cent of the industry's employment.
3   Small home-based foundries specializing in casting and accounting for around 60 per cent of cluster enterprises.

In the case of all types of enterprise, production is mainly to satisfy specific orders. These orders may come from an assembly business (in which case, semi-processed components are supplied); a wholesaler or retailer (in which case final goods or replacement components are supplied); or an end user such as a factory or a public-works project seeking equipment parts.

Sato's survey of a sample of Ceper enterprises found that all types of business in the cluster had direct links to customers outside the cluster. These linkages were important sources of enterprise development, although this partly depends on the inclination of particular buyers and the nature of individual trading relationships. Overall, it was concluded that enterprises favoured integration over specialization and that linkages with firms outside the cluster were preferred over ties to their neighbours:

> The firms seem to feel uncomfortable with (or reluctant to be forced into) being in the lower layer of a vertical division of labour within the cluster. They are not inclined openly to exchange market or product information on their orders with other firms in the cluster. As a result, every firm has a wide product range, and development of intra-cluster specialisation and division of labour is limited.
>
> (Sato 2000: 159)

This assessment concluded that passive search and reach effects were the main significance of clustering. Ceper's high accessibility to the wider economy, facilitated by centrality to a number of urban markets, transport connections, trade and information networks, was suggested to explain the outward orientation of cluster enterprises. These connections were significant because the cluster served the domestic market. There is evidence of intra-cluster subcontracting where exporting is important, as in the case of the Jepara furniture industry.

The Jepara wooden-furniture cluster has been one of the most successful clusters documented (Sandee *et al.* 2000). It employs close to 60,000 people in over 3,000 enterprises, located in more than 100 villages. Micro-enterprises dominate but there are more than 100 establishments that each employs over 100 workers. Furniture production in Jepara started in pre-colonial times but its modern prominence dates from the 1980s. Increased economic affluence in Indonesia expanded the domestic market for quality furniture. Leading producers from Jepara sought to capture this demand by setting up representative offices in the main cities and by establishing a satellite cluster in the Klender area of Jakarta, Indonesia's main city. Domestic production accounts for over half the cluster's employment (Sandee *et al.* 2000).

Currency devaluation in 1986 was a stimulus to exporting. By 2000, the cluster exported to 68 countries. Subcontracting networks are a feature of the cluster with some export items combining work completed by five or more subcontractors. A significant concentration of export capacity is the other side of intra-cluster subcontracting. The top ten firms control about 50 per cent of exports (Schiller and Martin-Schiller 1997: 6). Although aimed at low-income buyers, exporting required a higher quality of furniture construction, including pre-treatment of the timber to prevent warping or cracking in countries less humid than Indonesia. Foreign buyers hastened the upgrading by establishing new factories in the cluster, typically through joint ventures. A small but significant source of this investment came from Western immigrants married to Indonesians (Asian Development Bank 2001: 11). This participation introduced furniture designs geared to foreign tastes and power-driven equipment. Some producers have independent access to export trade networks but most production for exports is now controlled by foreign buyers on an order-by-order basis.

The collapse of the Indonesian currency in 1997, as part of the larger Asian financial crisis (Arndt and Hill 1999; Chang *et al.* 2001), initially provided a further stimulus to the cluster. The number of exported containers jumped from around 200 per month in 1996 to a high of 2,000 per month in 2000. Subsequently, exports have fallen and in 2002 were below 1,000 containers per month. It now appears that the currency-assisted expansion disguised longer-term weaknesses that are challenging the cluster's future prosperity. Three main problems are confronting the cluster, some of which are general to all furniture clusters and some specific to Jepara:

1   Quality control has not been maintained to the satisfaction of all foreign buyers, partly as a consequence of a large influx of workers

with no prior experience in furniture making. In response, some buyers have shifted orders to other furniture clusters inside and outside Indonesia. An outflow of workers and entrepreneurs to emerging clusters has followed.

2   Overcrowding and a relatively unfavourable location have encouraged some producers to move to other clusters in Central Java.

3   Subsequent to the 1997 financial crisis, the embargo preventing the export of unprocessed logs was lifted (in line with recommendations from the International Monetary Fund). This increased the price of furniture timber.

The potential for public agencies to help resolve these problems is unclear. In the past, its major contributions were in facilitating the conversion of a local harbour (Semarang) for container transport and improving other infrastructure. Attempts to establish a timber-buying cooperative to assist small producers were unsuccessful. In fact, public agencies have been a source of weakness through their failure to control the illegal logging of high-value timbers. The failure to ensure a sustainable source of timber is a potential threat to future production in any form (Sandee and Ibrahim 2001). Local government has taxed the industry comparatively heavily at a time when economic deregulation has reduced other sources of public revenue.

The roof-tile cluster in and around the village of Karanggeneng in the Boyolali province of Central Java is another case claimed to show the importance of intra-cluster networks (Sandee and Weijland 1989; Sandee 2002; Sandee *et al.* 2000). Throughout Indonesia, proximity to rivers or irrigated rice fields that offered a supply of clay controlled the location of tile making. Clusters have faced a transition from traditional methods to so-called pressed tiles requiring a significant increase in the use of equipment such as mixers and presses. In Karanggeneng, the change in technology took place in 1987 and by 1988 no traditional tile manufacture remained. As elsewhere, the quality expectations of large customers such as government agencies and housing developers drove the conversion. The coordinated change followed visits by groups of Karanggeneng producers to other clusters that had already made the shift and the development of subcontracting ties within the cluster.

The Karanggeneng cluster comprises around 130 enterprises that collectively provide around 1,000 jobs, although most enterprises rely on family labour. The shift to pressed tiles accentuated the inequality between enterprises. A mixer is an expensive investment in equipment that even Karanggeneng's largest producer would not keep fully utilized. Investors, therefore, had an incentive to rent out the use of their equipment. The largest enterprise operated seven presses in 2002 and employed 34 workers. It rented out another 13 presses to other producers who are used as subcontractors to help complete orders. Across the cluster as a whole the move to higher-quality production changed market relationships. Production for stock has ceased in favour of supplying specific orders. This may be explained by the increased value of completed tiles and availability of large orders from end users and building material stores. Larger enterprises undertake their own marketing. Direct sales accounted for 35 per cent of output in 2001. Most enterprises depend on brokers that charge an 8 per cent commission fee, taking a large share of the profit.

Once again, a mix of opportunities and threats to the cluster left an uncertain future. The removal of subsidies on cement has raised the price of cement-based tiles, to the advantage of clay tiles. Even so, the number of roof-tile clusters is reducing. Clay-tile production is a declining industry as the growing demand for higher-quality tiles is encouraging the concentration of production. As well as being a low-value product, access to raw materials is a frequent problem. Karanggeneng has gained government approval to access a new clay pit. In the longer term, scarcity of good-quality local clay and firewood supplies will require the cluster to diversify into ceramic production, but this involves a more radical shift in technology and skills than that already made.

These and other individual experiences point to a number of conditions shaping a cluster's ability to grow and how far growth sees an increase in intra-cluster joint action:

• Traders and trading houses are the prime movers in linking clusters to export markets. As well as providing access to new sales outlets, traders help clusters modify designs of traditional products, give advice on production improvements and may assist in financing equipment. Typically the traders having a significant impact on clusters are connected to the markets that they serve rather than the areas that they buy from. Sandee and ter Wengel (2002), for example, relate the case of rattan-processing clusters in south Kalimantan that were transformed from making low-value products for local consumers into exporters of mats to Japan. The stimulus for change is credited to a Japanese businessman who made the new specialization possible by introducing technology and product ideas. After an initial success, which saw several clusters participate in the new trade, the Japanese market has declined because of consumer resistance to the product quality. It appears Japanese buyers are reluctant to assist the clusters make the improvements in production equipment that are required. The clusters were selected for a rudimentary activity and there is now opportunity to source product from elsewhere in Indonesia where buyers can be more confident of quality production than in Kalimantan. The experience may be unusual but it illustrates how traders may promote upgrading without developing long-term commitment to the clusters they trade with. In this context, the development of home-grown buying organizations is significant although they tend to be restricted to handicraft sectors. For example, the Indonesia's People's Handicraft Marketing Service (Pekerti Nusantara) handles output from over 60 clusters (Sandee and Ibrahim 2001: 25).

- The linkage to export markets may provide more likelihood of intra-cluster subcontracting than where the cluster supplies domestic markets. Export agents tend to have direct relations with only a few suppliers in a cluster. As production is controlled by the allocation of orders, lead suppliers may use subcontracting to manage uneven order flows. In contrast, linkages to domestic urban markets may be established directly by individual cluster enterprises. There is some suggestion that this will depend on the ease of transport and communication links but that generally clusters enterprises favour direct ties to buyers over working as subcontractors.

- The need for investment to upgrade production and a preponderance of micro-enterprise gives rise to some instances of joint action. Technology raises the minimum scale of efficient investment, sometimes above the level that even the cluster's largest enterprises can achieve. In this context sharing of production capacity becomes a necessary response. Reciprocal arrangements are frequently an outcome in which investors rent capacity on equipment to independent enterprises that become subcontractors. Risks are reduced for subcontractors who avoid the need for investment in equipment. Larger enterprises similarly reduce their investment risk and are further advantaged by controlling the allocation of work between their own capacity and that of others. This is a significant way that clusters can provide short, manageable steps toward industrialization. The scale of the achievement needs to be judged against its long-term sustainability and the outcomes for subcontractors. Some cluster experiences indicate sharing investment may be a temporary phase of development as demands for production efficiency and quality control require concentration in large enterprises.

- Cluster development is intimately connected to larger transformations in economic development. Indonesia has benefited from the larger economic transformation of Southeast Asia that became one of the world's leading emerging markets post-1970 (Chia 2003). This transformation came about through the enormous investment in the region by multinational enterprise and the increased openness of markets. Indonesia now has wealthy neighbours with demand for cluster products, either in the form of mass marketed clothing or handicrafts that are bought by affluent consumers. Indonesia's own economic growth has stimulated domestic demand as, for example, in the expansion of urban housing. As well, an exposure to foreign tastes brought about through international tourism has been significant to some clusters (Asian Development Bank 2001). The Bali garment-industry cluster is a prime example of this connection (Box 6.8).

Box 6.8 The Bali garment cluster

The Bali garment-industry cluster grew spectacularly in the 1980s. Foreign tourists, mainly surfers wishing to support a recreational lifestyle for themselves, saw commercial opportunities in Balinese garments and its indigenous design capacity. They were able to act as market intermediaries, connecting Balinese producers to retail outlets overseas, in the process dispersing important information on suitable design and production methods. As the island's reputation diffused, marketing links developed quickly. The industry changed from a seasonal, home-based activity to a putting-out system and subcontracting networks coordinated by the larger producers.

The first wave of foreign entrepreneurs were largely Australian and with little previous experience in the garment industry. A recession in the early 1980s saw many of the original buyers exit the trade. A second wave of foreign buyers had more sophisticated business, production and design skills. Many of these were American tourists looking for entrepreneurial opportunities. They helped producers improve quality and move into higher-value designs. Further expansion came as Balinese producers started to put out work to workers in East Java. This gave access to a larger workforce and reduced the risk of designs being copied by competitors, a growing source of antagonism between producers.

In the mid-1980s many of the second-wave buyers moved out. A new set of immigration officials reportedly sought higher bribes than those that they had replaced and this provoked many buyers to depart. Subsequently importers in overseas countries tightened their quality-inspection procedures in response to ongoing concerns. Several Bali-based producers attempted to improve quality by shifting to factory production. By this stage Bali's reputation as a producer of low-quality goods had locked it into competition with other low-wage Asian economies.

Source: Cole (1998)

Cluster successes of themselves do not indicate the viability of a bottom-up approach to economic development.

To date, evidence of a third stage in cluster development promoted through public-agency intervention is patchy. There has been considerable effort by public agencies to support cluster development, through both a cluster-wide strategy (Box 6.9) and through help to individual clusters. Generally, intervention that has sought to prescribe a mode of organization or cooperation has had limited impact. Thus efforts over many years to organize cluster participants into business groups for the purposes of providing credit, marketing and training support have generally not resulted in clusters forming cooperatives as intended by the programme (Weijland 1999; Sandee and ter Wengel 2002). Similarly investment in common service facilities such as processing equipment have rarely worked

Box 6.9 BIPIK – Indonesia's cluster programme

BIPIK (Project for Guidance and Development of Small Industry) was set up in 1980, aided by the United Nations Development Programme. It started with 12 villages and was expanded to 120 villages when the first results seemed promising. The programme aimed to encourage the technological upgrading of clusters so as to improve their capacity to supply national or even international markets.

BIPIK encouraged clusters to develop a group organization. Groups gained eligibility for programme assistance. Help most frequently involved training courses provided by extension workers and the demonstration of new equipment. Where funding provided by donors allowed, new equipment was sometimes gifted to selected producers to accelerate its wider take-up in the cluster.

The programme's budget was typically around US$1,000 per cluster. The programme sought the widest coverage of clusters with the best business prospects. By 1998, over 12,000 clusters had received assistance or around half the potential recipients. Resource constraints generally precluded follow-up support to the clusters visited although service centres were established in around 100 clusters. The service centres gave producers access to equipment beyond the investment reach of individual businesses.

Two separate programmes worked along BIPIK. A 'foster-parent' scheme sought to link larger firms, mainly state enterprises, with cluster enterprises. Small-scale handicraft cooperatives (KOPINKRA) were encouraged among clusters specializing in textiles, garments and tourist products. Cooperatives were seen to be a way of strengthening marketing capacity among home-based enterprises and of improving access to the banking system.

BIPIK was actively supported for 20 years up to the mid-1990s. Reviews showed BIPIK's assistance was effective where the cluster had already started to develop. Typically the change started when buyers or traders suggested new products or designs for definite orders. This gives cluster participants reason to seek technical and financial services and an immediate ability to utilize training and new equipment.

Buyers and traders can provide effective business-development support given their interest in ensuring orders are completed to standard and ability to provide advance payment. In this case, public support may help widen the range of customers served. Efforts to promote formal organization of the cluster generally failed, even in dynamic clusters. Producers favour flexible forms of joint action that are responsive to changing needs and opportunities. Typically, cluster transformation relies on one or a few leading firms whose preference is to work independently of any externally imposed structures. Joint action tends to be informal and not assisted by efforts to form cooperatives or business associations.

BIPIK was wound down as donor agents sought to move away from intervention aiming to reach the maximum number of clusters in favour of more intensive help to clusters with potential for development.

Source: Sandee (1998)

(Asian Development Bank 2001: 12). To encourage use of such facilities in ways that promoted cooperation and shared learning, facilities typically remained in public ownership and charged nominal user fees. Budget constraints led to equipment becoming outdated and service quality deteriorating. Separate schemes to promote business linkages and technical upgrading appear to have been no more successful than the other interventions. In this case, efforts to link clusters with a new market that public agencies deemed to offer advantages sometimes overlooked suppliers' preference to work with their existing customers (Asian Development Bank 2001: 12). For example, clusters targeted as potential subcontractors to large-scale vehicle manufacturers frequently preferred to keep their existing role as suppliers to numerous small vehicle-repair workshops in nearby large cities. Existing customers tended to be price rather than quality conscious. Switching to serve a single customer with rigorous quality expectations was unattractive. In essence, cluster interventions have generally failed to meet their objectives either because the clusters targeted do not have the capacity for growth or because policy interventions have not addressed cluster weaknesses effectively (Tarnbunan 2005).

Cluster support has been most effective when assistance coincides with a transition in the cluster (Sandee 1998). Support does not lead to high growth, but high growth leads to the use of public services, especially those offering credit or marketing assistance to help individual enterprises widen their customer base. For example, an evaluation covering a woven cloth cluster identified high participation in training provided by a public agency. The training gave guidance in identifying fashion trends and making new products to buyer specifications. Buyers of fashion clothing expect producers to be adaptable to new designs and so the training had immediate relevance to buyers facing these demands.

Clusters and globalization

A strong case for the benefits of clusters in promoting developing-country industrialization has been built from examples of clusters that have adapted to the demands of customers in high-income countries. This section looks at two cases where this transition appears to have been made: the Sialkot surgical instrument cluster in Pakistan (Nadvi 1999) and the footwear industry in the Sinos Valley, Brazil (Schmitz 1995b, 1999). Both examples have been drawn on by international-development agencies to justify their support to clusters (see Humphrey and Schmitz 1995). This influence exists despite uncertainties over the resilience of these clusters to globalization.

Sialkot, with a population of around 660,000, is among Pakistan's leading centres of manufactured exports. Its exports are concentrated in three sectors: sports goods, leather garments and stainless-steel surgical instruments. In recent years, it has been the centre of international attention because of the use of child labour in the manufacture of soccer balls (Save the Children Fund 1997). The surgical-instrument cluster is not free of child labour but quality management, rather than employment conditions, has been its recent challenge. In 1994, the Food and Drug Administration (FDA) of the USA restricted imports of Pakistani-made surgical instruments. This represented a major crisis for the cluster since the USA was the main market served. It followed a similar restriction in 1989 and indicated a worsening situation. The earlier embargo was made in reaction to product-quality concerns; in 1994, the concern had widened to quality assurance and demands that Pakistani exports show evidence of good manufacturing practices. Nadvi (1999) provides an account of the crisis that indicates how producers overcame the ban and recovered sales. He argues that operating as a cluster facilitated resolution of the crisis although some weaknesses in the performance of the cluster are recognized.

Nadvi (1999: 1609) estimates that the Sialkot surgical-instrument cluster comprises around 300 producers, surrounded by over 1,500 process specialized subcontractors and around 1,000 other supporting establishments such as those involved in international logistics. At the cluster's core is a division between two market segments. One involves production of high-quality, reusable instruments made with imported stainless steel and primarily exported to Europe; the other manufactures disposable instruments from locally produced stainless steel made from recycled and scrap metal. In the USA, demand for disposable instruments grew as a response to the rising cost of sterilization and concern of contamination from reused instruments. The quality of the metal used was the first source of concern for the FDA. A risk of rust and breakage was alleged. This was addressed by producers through discussions with their locally based steel suppliers and resolved by the early 1990s.

The FDA's action in May 1994 suspended exports pending exporters obtaining certification that they had 'good manufacturing practices'. By December 1994, one large firm in Sialkot had obtained such certification. More significantly, as evidence of cluster competitiveness, the Surgical Instrument Manufacturers' Association (SIMA) negotiated government support to appoint a quality-assurance consultancy from the USA. This firm provided training to help producers attain the FDA certification. By January 1997, 75 producers had qualified to export with the total doubling over the following year as a result of the training assistance. As well as the role of SIMA, the crisis was seen to increase inter-firm cooperation to provide increased quality assurance. Prior to the import restrictions, information exchange between buyers and suppliers and assistance to subcontractors was already frequent in matters related to production organization and product quality. Post-1994, information exchange and cooperation to improve quality increased between producers and local suppliers.

Management of subcontracting became more demanding as a consequence of the FDA requirements, particularly with respect to the documentation to be completed at each production stage. A small decline in the use of subcontracting resulted in favour of internalizing tasks such as polishing and grinding. Many subcontractors were unaccustomed to quality-assurance systems and exporters had to assist their subcontractors make significant adjustments to their working practices. In this context, the survival of subcontracting suggests recognition of its contribution to the overall functioning of the cluster. On the other hand, firms started to use fewer subcontractors than previously and to bring some previously out-sourced work in-house. As well, some large producers did make a substantial cutback in the use of subcontractors.

Turning to the relationships with foreign buyers, the independent certification of producers may mean that buyers see less risk in 'arm's length' relationships than previously existed. This has been one outcome for Sialkot, although with some variation between buyers. One large buyer, for example, ceased the technical assistance previously provided to its dozen large suppliers. Purchase volumes remained similar but it concluded suppliers now had alternative sources of support and consequently its quality-control support was cut back. At the same time, some producers have sought to diversify their customer base as a way of avoiding dependency on a single market. Suppliers tied to a single large buyer are often asked to agree to exclusive supply arrangements without being rewarded with higher prices or opportunity to diversify into higher-value products.

Buyers' competitive stance to the cluster after the quality-assurance clampdown is indicative of how the revival of trade to the USA has not been an unqualified endorsement of the cluster's strength. It might, nonetheless, be seen as evidence of the third phase in cluster development when a public agency intervenes to spread participation in joint action. SIMA's successful acquisition of government funding to support quality-assurance training enabled local producers to gain FDA certification. Critically for the stylized account of cluster development, the ability of SIMA to negotiate the support was an outcome of change in the association's executive committee to be more inclusive of the interests of small companies in need of training assistance. Without this help, large firms only would have been in a position to purchase help. On the other hand, the relationship between individual buyers and Sialkot suppliers weakened as certification widened the choice of suppliers. In terms of its larger future, Sialkot has not succeeded in upgrading its manufacturing to the point where its producers deal directly with brand-name suppliers. Most of the clusters' buyers are distributors or wholesalers rather than manufacturers. This results in lower prices and exclusion from potentially important sources of technological and manufacturing assistance.

The footwear cluster in the Sinos Valley is an interesting contrast to Sialkot because here the cluster has survived despite a weakening of its collective associations and without any decisive public support. The Sinos Valley and the larger Brazilian footwear industry have first to be understood in the context of the emergence of buyer-driven commodity chains (Gereffi 1994). As with other labour-intensive consumer goods, there has been a major relocation of production from the high-income markets where the goods are sold to comparatively low-income production locations. This transition has been controlled by large retailers, brand-named merchandisers and trading companies. Their preferred strategy is to contract production to independent suppliers. Buyers typically differentiate their suppliers according to the extent to which they are free to contract with competing buyers and according to the allocation of high- and low-value products. In the Sinos Valley, linkage into buyer-controlled commodity chains emerged in two main stages.

At the end of the 1960s, importers from the USA began scouting Brazil for shoe suppliers. According to Schmitz (1995b), the Sinos Valley was singled out among other concentrations of the footwear industry because of its range of input suppliers as well as finished good manufacturers. The Valley's initiative in supporting an organization that promoted a annual national shoe fair in the Valley is also credited with raising importer interest. Exports took off, helped by the first buyers often being manufacturers so there was no immediate opposition in the USA from producers with displaced capacity. By 1990, 80 per cent of footwear sales in the USA came from imports compared with 20 per cent in 1960 (figures cited in Schmitz 1995b: 14). In the Sinos Valley, around 20,000 pairs of shoes were produced annually in the late 1960s, all for the domestic market. By 1984, production had grown to around 160,000 pairs with roughly 100,000 of these exported. Schmitz (1995b) sees the responsiveness of the Sinos Valley to the market opportunities that arose as evidence of the advantage obtained by a cluster.

In the 1990s growth slowed and the Sinos Valley, along with the larger Brazilian shoe industry, had to meet three challenges. First, buyers redirected orders for low-value footwear to new centres of production where costs were lower than Brazil, notably China, requiring established producers to raise quality. Second, buyers introduced 'just-in-time' order scheduling that required producers to supply smaller batches of shoes with shorter delivery times between order and completion than previously. Third, exporters had to cope with macro-economic instability manifested in periods of high inflation and exchange-rate instability. The cluster met these challenges to the extent that by 1997 it had returned to the export level of 1990 based on improvements in the quality, speed and flexibility of production. On the larger test of the cluster's need to demonstrate 'strategic cooperation' on top of the spontaneous economies of clustering, Schmitz (1999) concludes the cluster largely failed. This was seen in the unsuccessful effort to obtain collective support for a 'Shoes from Brazil Programme' (Programa Calçado do Brasil, 1994). This programme was conceived originally in dialogue involving all the relevant national industry associations and was intended to lift the Brazilian footwear industry out of competition with other low-wage economies. Through cooperation in the investment of design capabilities and a Brazilian brand image it was hoped to give producers greater control of the commodity chain than obtained when working as contractors for foreign buyers. Schmitz (1999) emphasizes the resistance of the five largest enterprises to the programme as the cause of the programme's demise and the failure to shift the cluster into the 'high road of globalization'.

The Sinos Valley experience supports the need to recognize stages in the development of clusters. During the period of export growth, the cluster flourished as foreign buyers provided a link to new markets as well as help in upgrading production. In the more recent phase of intensified competition with other shoe-producing countries, the same buyers are identified as a problem for the cluster. In Schmitz's (1999: 1647) assessment, the majority of Sinos Valley export manufacturers are unable to contemplate production relationships outside of their existing ties with buyers. To do so would bring suppliers into direct conflict with the buyers on whom their enterprise depends. At the same time, buyers have proved to have a weak attachment to their suppliers when the option of using cheaper suppliers arose. Beyond the constraints on individual enterprises, buyers accentuated differences between cluster participants and fragmented its organization. For example, shoe exporters wanted easier access to inputs and equipment than local suppliers believed appropriate. Suppliers of processed leather wished to export to competing countries while local manufacturers presented this as against the interests of the cluster. Large exporters were tied closely to their buyers and perceived their interests lay in protecting this relationship whatever the larger consequences for the cluster.

As noted in the model of cluster development, Schmitz (1999: 1646) speculates that government intervention may be needed to mediate conflicts and foster upgrading. In the case of the Sinos Valley, he suggests that government mediation may have resolved intra-industry conflicts and made possible the upgrading promised by the Shoes from Brazil Programme. Meanwhile, a small number of firms identified by Schmitz perhaps point to a different development trajectory for the cluster. A recent increase in exports to other Latin American countries is due largely to enterprises that worked exclusively for the Brazilian market. Supplying the local market required expertise in design and marketing that was not needed by enterprises working for foreign buyers. Consequently, remaining outside the relationships that boosted the cluster has ultimately provided some enterprises an opportunity for growth denied those locked into the cluster. There are enterprises that supply multiple markets, including the USA, and so the constraints imposed by buyers may be challenged. Even so, the concentration of market power among a few buyers has been identified as a key obstruction on the path to a higher position on the value chain:

> The reason is that buyers are interested in manufacturers upgrading production but rarely in them acquiring their own design capability, developing their own brand names, or establishing their own marketing channels ... Producers acknowledge openly: 'não vendemos, somos comprados' (we do not sell, we are bought).
>
> (Schmitz 1999: 1647)

Two extreme interpretations arise from the experience of the Sinos Valley and Sialkot. One response is that unless the constraints imposed by globalization are overcome it is hard to sustain that clusters offer a development advantage. The opposing response stresses how globalization, in the form of buyer-driven commodity chains, imposes considerable constraints on development that clustering gives the best prospects for overcoming. The first of these interpretations is encouraged by the ongoing challenges facing both clusters. The second interpretation may be supported from the different experiences of Sialkot and the Sinos Valley indicating circumstances in which clusters may retain an advantage:

- The Sinos Valley had a particular disadvantage compared with Sialkot because of greater buyer negotiating power and greater fragmentation of business interests. For buyers of disposable surgical instruments, Sialkot remains an important source of production whereas the footwear industry is more easily established in competing locations. As a consequence, suppliers of metal in Sialkot are more dependent on the cluster than are the suppliers of leather to the Sinos Valley producers. Moreover, Sialkot is helped by its dual specialization in disposable and reusable instruments that connect the cluster to different markets.
- The form of the challenge imposed by globalization is a further differentiating influence on the capacity to respond. The Sinos valley has been affected by gradual processes of change in which initial opportunities evolve into constraints but without a decisive transition being identified. In contrast, Sialkot faced a single shock that had the effect of uniting interests within the cluster. Within a month of the FDA action, the cluster's trade association had begun formulating a collective response on behalf of Sialkot's exporters. This swift response occurred despite previous evidence of widespread dissatisfaction and disinterest in SIMA as the cluster's collective voice (Nadvi 1999: 1611).
- The adjustments putting Sialkot back on track were modest compared with the unrealized changes implied by the Shoes from Brazil Programme. Nadvi's account of Sialkot identifies a change of elected per-

sonnel within the cluster's trade association was nonetheless crucial. A change from one large-firm representative to another may be comparatively easy to achieve unlike a shift from large- to small-firm control. Exporters had to take a role in assisting subcontractors but it seems an option also existed to move production in-house and for individual enterprises to reduce the number of subcontractors given work.

Conclusion

The accounts of developing-country clusters differ from those most frequently presented on clusters in high-income countries. They emphasize the need to examine trajectories of cluster development rather than assuming that advantages are sustained over time. Globalization is more likely to be seen as a threat to the survival of clusters rather than a potential source of competitive advantage. The differentiation of interests within clusters is more likely to be stressed than unity, both in terms of a variety of enterprise sizes and dependencies on the benefits generated by the cluster. The role of collective participation in industry or community associations is more likely to be noted for its demise rather than as an ongoing source of strength. Without public-policy intervention, questions are raised about the capacity for clusters to survive whereas in developed economies clusters are viewed frequently as examples of private-sector-led competitive advantage.

Divergent interpretations are not necessarily in conflict. The development context may be viewed as creating separate cluster experiences. The great mass of developing country clusters built on informal enterprise may be seen to have little in common with a cluster in a high-income economy. On the other hand, informal-sector clusters are not the source of the stylized model of developing-country clusters. Most research has focused on the smaller group of clusters in the modernizing sectors of the economy. As well, four reasons suggest that the developing-country experience deserves consideration:

1   Taking the 'classic' description of Italian industrial districts as a benchmark for developed-country clusters, one conclusion is that clusters in the 'north' and 'south' increasingly deviate from the ideal type in similar ways. In particular, both exhibit levels of internal heterogeneity that constrain cluster-wide cooperation.
2   Transitions in the internal structure of successful developing- and developed-country clusters are found. There is much in common between the way Italy's industrial districts evolved and how developing-country clusters are affected by planned joint action.
3   The influence of commodity-chain organization is felt in both developed- and developing-country clusters, although with some difference in its impact. Developing-country clusters tend to exist at the

supplier end of buyer-driven commodity chains, making them especially dependent on the shifting strategies of organizations that
control the commodity chain. Equally, opportunities in developed-
country clusters are shaped by the relationship with a larger commodity chain over which the cluster participants may have little influence.

4   Business performance in the most successful developing-country clusters is catching up with that in high-income clusters. For example, in
the Sinos valley producers have been judged as close to their Italian
competitors in terms of quality, speed and flexibility (Schmitz 1999:
1646).

Accepting the significance of developing-country experience, the distinction between spontaneous and deliberately pursued cluster advantages
deserves reflection. Among those who have studied developing-country
clusters, there is a broad consensus that cluster development is based on
'shifting gears' from passive to active sources of collective efficiency. Case
studies show that the clusters generating enterprise growth exhibit an
increase in planned joint action, whether in the form of participation in
cluster associations or, more typically, in bilateral cooperation between
buyers and suppliers. Equally of interest is the evidence that this cooperation need not be based on intra-cluster linkages.

A further message from the developing-country experience is the need
to examine a cluster's ability to maintain growth. Understanding the
potential for sustainable development requires examination of both the
consequences of changes within the cluster and the external conditions
shaping the form that cooperation takes. For example, the linkage to
external buyers may initiate a process of upgrading. If a condition of this
upgrading is the loss of product design and independent marketing, the
long-term capacity for growth may be weakened. Hence, a further important message from the study of developing-country clusters is the need to
study how external opportunities shape local responses in clusters. In the
interim, public agencies need to recognize that the propensity for clustering does not mean that they warrant being a specific regulatory target or
policy goal.

7 Promoting clusters

Local economic-policy ideas are frequently based on the 'enthusiastic borrowing' of perceived best practice rather than detailed understanding of what works and when (Irwin 2003). Cluster policy is a pronounced case of this. In many industrial countries, efforts to promote business clusters are now a central part of regional, innovation and business-development policies administered by public agencies (Isaksen and Hauge 2002; Raines 2002). Indeed, at the start of the new century it could be claimed that few other ideas had the same level of appeal among local economic-development practitioners as did the promotion of clusters (Martin and Sunley 2003). One sign is the number of states and provinces in North America and Western Europe with ambition to build clusters in the same high-tech activities (Enright 1999). The aspiration to imitate Silicon Valley, the locality cited frequently as the model justifying intervention is reflected in the christening of valley projects around the world. In the United Kingdom, there is Motorsport Valley; in France, the Paris Optics Valley and the Mechanic Valley in Midi Pyrénées; in Belgium, Flanders Multimedia Valley and DSP Valley (microelectronics); in Germany, Materials Valley in the Rhein-Main area; in Sweden, Strängäs Biotech Valley and Dalarna Crystal Valley; in Denmark, Medicon Valley; in Poland, Plastics valley; in Lithuania, Sunrise Valley (lasers); in Japan, Sweet Valley (software) (Sölvell *et al.* 2003: 16; Ecotech Research and Consulting 2004; Perry 2004b).

National coordination of cluster initiatives has been recommended to reduce the zero-sum competition encouraged by the duplication of cluster projects (Isaksen and Hauge 2002: 45). On the other hand, the popularity of cluster promotion can disguise a wide range in actual policy activity and purpose. Interventions as diverse as science-park development, tax incentives for research and development, vocational training, web sites providing information on employment and training opportunities, business mentoring, inward investment marketing and supply-chain integration have all been associated with best practice in cluster development in one recent government published guide (Ecotech Research and Consulting 2004). The scale of the cluster that is the target of promotion, its degree of economic specialization and geographical extent are equally variable. One survey of cluster initiatives, for example, ranged from projects encompassing a single activity in a provincial town to projects in which a single cluster covered multiple industries located across a whole country (Sölvell *et al.* 2003). Such elasticity underscores that much of what is now presented as a cluster initiative represents activity that has long gone on and that does not need attachment to a cluster to justify its continuance. Established policy measures are being presented as cluster projects without a change in actual activity and new interventions designed without agreement on how existing, let alone potential, clusters are to be identified (Martin and Sunley 2003).

Policy diversity is inevitable as the significance of business clustering can be interpreted in different ways. Nonetheless, it is important to confine discussion within practical limits that recognize: (i) exemplar clusters are exceptions rather than a template for other localities to copy; (ii) industry and organizational characteristics affect the potential for cluster intervention; (iii) cluster promotion needs to consider the distribution of benefits among businesses and communities. This chapter explains these three constraints and then examines the results of public-policy efforts to assist business-cluster formation and growth in New Zealand. The projects are predominantly small scale but the policy experience focuses on a central claim in the debate about clusters: namely, local economies benefit from encouraging their business communities to collaborate as well as compete with each other. The case study reports how firms in different sectors and locations responded to the encouragement to join a cluster and the implications for designing cluster initiatives. Previous surveys of cluster initiatives tend to report the verdicts on cluster progress by those responsible for managing them and have combined judgements on projects of varying scale and context (Isaksen and Hauge 2002; Sölvell *et al.* 2003). The New Zealand evidence concentrates on comparable projects and asks why organizations join, the terms of their engagement and how far the activity encouraged is consistent with public-agency objectives. Prior to discussing the New Zealand experience, further discussion is provided of the constraints on cluster policy as this helps justify the relevance of the policy experience.

Cluster-policy objectives

The more that the label of 'cluster' has acquired political and policy significance the more difficult it is to specify the boundaries and composition of a cluster. A tension exists between any attempt to pin clusters down to a specific interpretation and policy makers' concern to avoid targeting assistance too narrowly. One reflection of this is the use of methods for identifying clusters that ensure as many regions as possible are identified as having clusters worthy of attention (Martin and Sunley 2003: 25).

Indeed by constructing clusters from linked activity, as recommended by Feser and Bergman (2000) and Porter (2003) (see Chapter 4), it becomes possible to ensure that every local economy has a cluster to nurture. Inevitably many localities will be missing the full representation of activities identified in a national cluster template. Public agencies may then claim a role in helping to fill the gaps, although this may not necessarily be recommended by those responsible for the mapping design. It invites the other main policy risk of zero-sum competition as local agencies each seek to fill out their value chains.

National coordination might help to reduce excessive cluster identification and ensure that local initiatives are complementary to each other (Department of Trade and Industry 2001). Realistically, cluster analysis will remain an art and a science that precludes the possibility of such technocratic perfection (Feser and Luger 2003). Many researchers will continue to claim the appropriateness of their particular way of defining and identifying clusters, all of which will have some claim to being tenable. Policy makers will, therefore, continue to be able to select their definition of an industry cluster, the methodology for measuring location concentration, the assumptions about spatial scale and other attributes of cluster development. This flexibility, properly used, can strengthen cluster analysis. An analogy with cost–benefit analysis, a technique that became popular in the 1970s and 1980s as a way to understand the complex trade-offs between up-front investments and long-term benefits, can be drawn (Feser and Luger 2003). It was promoted originally as a technique to provide objective and precise judgements on development proposals. Experience proved that the judgements were sensitive to data inputs that were often incomplete and surrounded by assumptions. Today the technique is regarded as a mode of inquiry rather than an analytical tool generating precise cost–benefit ratios. So cluster analysis is viewed appropriately as more of a mode of inquiry than a technical methodology that offers a precise way of defining the economic landscape (Box 7.1). As Feser and Luger (2003: 16) argue: 'cluster analysis is simply not capable of producing a single right answer about the industries and businesses a region should seek to support or grow'.

A mode of inquiry perspective on clusters may be unattractive to policy makers. Their preference is for clear and unified definitions that link policy to an accepted trademark suggesting objectivity and reputation (Rosenfeld 2003). It also challenges the ability to emulate established clusters, which is arguably the main influence that encourages policy makers to have interest in clusters. The fascination with the growth of high-profile clusters and encouragement to believe that these experiences can be replicated elsewhere have made clusters an end point rather than merely a starting point for discussions about economic development as recommended by the mode of inquiry perspective. To aid this conversion, it is necessary to examine why cluster experiences are not transferable and why it may not be desirable to attempt to make them so.

Box 7.1 Cluster policy as a mode of inquiry

The existence of dynamic external economies unites contemporary interest in business clusters. A mode of inquiry perspective is flexible as to the geographical scale at which these external economies are searched for, the methodology employed to reveal them and the assumptions about stages or timing of cluster development that are used to distinguish potential, emerging and mature clusters. The common thread is a search for and documentation of the key groups of interdependent businesses in a local, regional or national economy. Industry interdependencies help to reveal the strengths and weaknesses of an economy.

Treating cluster analysis as a mode of inquiry makes it flexible to the policy issues of particular interest. Indeed, as there is no single methodology, policy interest must be relied upon to determine the choice of approach. Policy-led cluster analysis can simply reinforce predetermined positions. Appropriate signalling that the interdependencies revealed are a product of the method followed, rather than a precise way to define the industrial landscape, guards against misuse.

The mode of inquiry perspective recognizes that research will not resolve cluster ambiguities. Business interdependence manifests itself in many ways and knowing which confer most productivity or innovation benefits is resistant to investigation. There is uncertainty in knowing how to deal with co-location that is not exploited or recognized by firms and consequently whether the potential for interdependence is of interest or only actual evidence of interdependence.

Cluster analysis is merely the modern expression of established tools of regional inquiry such as input – output analysis, occupation analysis, location quotients and regional economic accounting. The innovation is application to groups of interdependent business and industries.

Source: Feser and Luger (2003)

Exemplar clusters

As noted in the Introduction, much of the inspiration for cluster policy has been driven by the perception that Silicon Valley, Italy's industrial districts and other high-profile clusters provide a guide as to what can be achieved in other localities. This simplifies the origins of clusters that have attained international recognition and overlooks some uncertainty as to the key components that have driven their formation.

Many of the clusters that have excited policy interest are located in economically advantaged regions, as with England's Motor Sport Valley, the Öresund medical cluster spanning Denmark and Sweden, and biotechnology in Rhône-Alpes (Lagendijk 1999). Such clusters are associated typically with investment in public institutions sustained over many decades (Benneworth 2002). The origins of the present cluster of biotechnology around the university city of Cambridge in eastern England, for example, have been traced to significant public investment in a number of agricultural research stations that commenced in the 1920s (Wilkie 1991). Similarly, it is unsurprising to find that Baltimore has a medical-technology cluster given the proximity to the National Institute of Health (Benneworth 2002). That institute is responsible for allocating around US$20 billion of research funds annually in addition to its own US$1 billion research expenditure. High levels of selectively disbursed public funds have contributed to the modern-day reputations and capabilities that give capacity to influence the location of economic activity. For this reason, exemplar clusters centred on public institutions are necessarily exceptions. As pointed out from the experience of Sophia-Antipolis, it is simply not possible to multiply the benefit of accumulated exceptional levels of public funding over many locations (Longhi 1999).

It has been argued that even if the whole experience cannot be replicated, elements of the experience can be applied elsewhere (Benneworth *et al.* 2003). In practice, even among other IT clusters experiencing high growth a large gap tends to remain between them and Silicon Valley (Box 7.2).

Box 7.2 Silicon Valley stays ahead

As well as Silicon Valley during the 1990s, locations in England, Ireland, India, Israel, Scandinavia, Taiwan and other regions within the USA experienced spectacular rates of growth of information and communications technology businesses. Even so, Silicon Valley in the 1960s has more in common with new clusters elsewhere than Silicon Valley today, including evidence that the influences that get a cluster started differ from those that keep it going.

Getting started depends on building the 'economic fundamentals' needed for an industry or technology and finding a spark of entrepreneurship to exploit the opportunities. New clusters (like the youthful Silicon Valley) offer less support to new enterprise creation and growth than does a mature cluster. In the early phases of development, modest benefits arise to individual start-ups from the presence of other firms and supporting infrastructure and institutions such as venture capital.

Established markets are hard to break into, requiring new clusters to focus on technology and market gaps that have not already been exploited by any other cluster. The semiconductor industry in the incipient Silicon Valley; internet and network security in Ireland and Israel; for India, specific opportunities from YK2 and the introduction of the euro currency; for Scandinavia and Taiwan, hardware and equipment devices. Getting to the point where a cluster stakes a claim on a new technology depends on years of firm and market-building effort and long-term investment in education and skill development. Identifying a technology with such exceptional market opportunity involves luck as well as foresight.

Cluster policy seeking to emulate Silicon Valley tends to focus on supply-side attributes such as agglomeration economies rather than demand conditions. Clusters of innovative activity do not respond well to being directed, organized or jump-started. There is no substitute for hard 'old economy' work of company building and regional investments in educational institutions and other mechanisms for accumulating technical capabilities.

Source: Bresnahan *et al.* (2001)

A difficulty is to know what the important components of the cluster experience have been. As seen in the case of Silicon Valley, competing claims exist about the attributes that have contributed most to the locality's advantages but whatever explanation is prioritized none worked in isolation from other supporting attributes.

- The impact of sustained public investment is seen in the spur that the Second World War and the Korean War gave to the build-up of the electronics industry in California, the accumulation of expertise in Frederick Terman's electrical-engineering department in Stanford University and the decision of various key companies to settle in the area before the semiconductor revolution took off (Prevezer 1998).
- The willingness of Silicon Valley entrepreneurs to participate in dense social and professional networks and to regard technology knowledge as a public good have been judged as critical to the cluster's take-off (Saxenian 1994). These attributes were crucial in spreading information and diversifying the range of technological and marketing alternatives explored, avoiding the 'lock in' to a specialization that befell Route 128.
- The role of labour-market intermediaries in shaping the structure and dynamics of work and employment has been highlighted in interpretations that view Silicon Valley as primarily a labour-market phenomenon (Cappelli 1999; Benner 2002). Developing a workforce attuned to rapid changes and unpredictability in the labour market relied upon a wide range of intermediaries including temporary-help firms, employment agencies, recruiters, labour contractors and membership-based associations. These agents responded to initial demands for flexibility but then moulded the behaviour of workers and employers to the needs of an information-economy labour market.
- Venture capital is a key institution in accounts that stress the importance of finance in facilitating the development of new activities with a high risk of failure (Kenney and Florida 2000). North America's lead in IT innovation as a whole has been linked to its system of business funding that is more supportive of new industry creation than the relational banking associated with some European countries and Japan. Within Silicon Valley, it is claimed that venture capitalists are

entrepreneurial and knowledgeable about scientific and technological advances (Prevezer 1998).

- In Silicon Valley, the influence of lawyers has extended beyond the 'official charter' normally defining the activities of legal firms. More than legal advice, lawyers have been crucial to the overall organization of business relationships, acting as 'gatekeepers to withhold community resources from inappropriately constituted deviants', as 'proselytizers to promote community transactions among uninitiated novices' and as 'matchmakers to sort and steer transaction seekers' (Suchman 2000: 94).

Other research points to contingent influences that restrict the opportunity to replicate the development experience. The greenfield location created a new community in which 'nobody knows anybody else's mother' and the absence of intervening affiliations encouraged shared associations around the project of advancing a new technology (Saxenian 1994; Cohen and Fields 1999). Others point out the importance of recognizing that only 20 per cent of information-technology professionals are women in the 'Valley of the Boys' (Cooper 2000: 379). As well as labour-market intermediaries, a newly constituted masculinity that rationalized the loss of work–life balance was needed to comply with the dedication expected by employers.

Distinctive features of semiconductor technology, the core innovation associated with Silicon Valley's emergence, further constrain the ability to replicate its experiences. The basic technology was invented at the birth of the industry, allowing diffusion to new enterprises at a reasonable price (Freeman 1982). In the early phases of the semiconductor industry, university basic research lagged behind the work by industry (OTA 1984; Daly 1985). This was an inducement to concentration. University expertise tends to be highly dispersed whereas business investment in the early phases of a new industry is comparatively mobile, facilitating clustering around an initial centre of expertise (Sharp 1990). The significance of such influences is seen through comparison with biotechnology (Oakey *et al.* 1990).

In computing, the key links and information flows were between engineers in different companies; in biotechnology, the important relationships have been between the science base and companies (Prevezer 1998: 128). In the case of biotechnology, partly because of the need for regulatory approval, a long-time frame from scientific discovery to commercial application results in a particular relationship between established companies and new start-ups. Incumbents with activity potentially affected by biotechnology innovations could maintain a 'watching brief' over prospective competitors knowing that breakthrough companies would need the assistance of a large-firm partner to bring their innovation to market (Oakey *et al.* 1990). Thus it was not until the 1990s that commercial products started to emerge from the new biotechnology discoveries arising from scientific advances in genetics and molecular biology of the early 1970s (Audretsch 2001). Commercialization proceeded as large pharmaceutical companies selectively took up the products of biotechnology start-ups and began to make strategic choices about their own investment (Sharp 1999).

In computing, the 'time window' between invention and innovation was frequently narrow, encouraging close geographic location between large established companies and new ventures. In biotechnology, research alliances between geographically dispersed organizations have been more characteristic of the industry than starts-ups clustering around established participants. A further difference exists in the relationships to markets. Computing-related activity tends to divide according to the technology involved. Each specialization may serve a range of end markets, encouraging geographical clustering among producers rather than with end users. In biotechnology, activity tends to divide according to technology focus and its market application. This results in clear linkages between new biotechnology companies and selected consumers of their end products and a further inducement for biotechnology to locate among many dispersed and comparatively small clusters (Prevezer 1998: 129).

The comparative development of computing and biotechnology makes it hard to know what policy lessons might be taken from clusters in either sector. The full context of Silicon Valley's emergence and growth draws attention to its uniqueness and dangers of viewing it as a model that can be cloned (Kenney 2000: 12). Equally, the ability to find biotechnology clusters in many regions reflects features particular to this activity rather than incipient concentrations that public policy can grow into new Silicon Valleys (Box 7.3).

Industry characteristics and clusters

A feature of much policy discussion is the assumption that cluster development can be applied to any concentration of activity. One sign of this is the design of policy assuming a uniform trajectory in cluster development from embryonic cluster, through phases of establishment and maturity prior to decline (Ecotech Research and Consulting 2004). This approach concentrates on designing interventions according to the perceived stage of cluster development. The identification of when it is possible to promote firm collaboration whilst retaining competition and rivalry among those same firms is downplayed. Thus advice in respect of embryonic clusters tends to focus on how to mobilize awareness of the cluster potential, generating interest in participating in its establishment and on investigation of actions to bring the cluster together. The implicit assumption is that there is always scope to generate benefit from inter-firm collaboration. The challenge is to identify a starting point and business champions to drive a change in business behaviour.

Box 7.3 Biotechnology excites clusters

The association of biotechnology with leading-edge technology has made it a frequent target for cluster-promotion policies, as in the case of Scotland. Scottish Enterprise, the development agency for Scotland, commissioned Michael Porter's consultancy firm (Monitor) to put in place a mechanism for advancing four clusters including biotechnology. The scope, picture and resource needs of the cluster were developed first. This vision was taken to stakeholders and business leaders willing to participate in action planning of the steps to be taken to activate the cluster.

In reality the extent of biotechnology activity in Scotland remains a challenge to building a cluster that will significantly accelerate business growth. Companies spun out of research institutions are not long established and biotechnology activity is dispersed across product areas with different markets (transgenics, biopharmaceuticals, agro food and bioenvironmental). Scottish Enterprise claim that a cluster of 180 companies exists. Under close investigation, as few as 40 geographically and scientifically dispersed companies exist.

In the United Kingdom, the southern English county of Surrey with 37 companies has another relatively large concentration of biotechnology activity. There is great variety in the types of firms and few research centres. Neighbouring firms have little interaction with each other despite the existence of Southern BioScience, a regional industry association. Firm networks go outside the region as in the case of one of the county's leading drug-development firms that has research partnerships with academics in London, Scotland, elsewhere in Europe and North America.

The United Kingdom's major biotechnology concentrations are around the university cities of Oxford and Cambridge, with approximately 50 and 60 core firms in the late 1990s. Both locations benefit from the presence of several research facilities of national and international significance. Links between the science base and biotechnology companies and with big pharmaceutical companies outside the cluster were more important than between firms locally, although in the case of Cambridge the Eastern Region Biotechnology Initiative seeks to encourage local interaction.

The United Kingdom is home to most of Europe's top entrepreneurial biotechnology companies. Most are not yet profitable and most have partnerships with big pharmaceutical companies to license any technologies that become ready for distribution to the market. Meanwhile much biotechnology activity remains inordinately dependent upon public investment in research.

Source: Cooke (2001)

The influence of Italy's industrial districts, which encompass a range of manufacturing activities, is frequently given as justification for the optimism in building collaboration whatever the business environment. These districts, it is suggested, show the possibility of cooperation even in the context of business communities with intense competitiveness. In reality, opportunities for combining competition and cooperation are sensitive to the precise production and marketing environment operated in, as shown in a comparison of business clusters in France, Italy and England (Bull *et al.* 1991). The Italian district of Como was distinguished by its strategic relationships based on firm specialization whereas other clusters made less use of neighbouring firms and gained less benefit from doing so when they did. The research concluded that there was limited scope to replicate the business relationships found in Como. It implies a need for firms to change their customer base, away from mass-market retailers, and a significant increase in the specialization of individual firms. The Italian experience is frequently interpreted as demonstrating how this can be achieved but in practice the same constraints are observed there too.

A case study of two of the biggest shoemaking districts in Emilia-Romagna, Fusignano and San Mauro Pascoli, shows how apparently similar business communities are associated with contrasting combinations of cooperation and competition (Nuti and Cainelli 1996). Fusignano developed in response to the demand for cheap articles by tourists visiting the Adriatic 'Riviera'. San Mauro Pascoli has its origins in a number of medium-sized firms specializing in top-quality women's footwear. Both districts are populated by a large number of small firms (Table 7.1), but in San Mauro Pascoli firms with over 100 employees are more important than in Fusignano. This difference has tended to widen as medium- and large-sized firms have become scarcer in Fusignano than once they were. San Mauro Pascoli's large firms tend to control production involving a network of firms. This locality specializes in top-quality women's shoes which, apart from slight differences in style and market destination, are a relatively unvarying product. With the focus on quality some firms have specialized in component manufacture, for example soles and heels. The larger producers seek strategic associations with such specialists as a way of balancing the demands of quality and skill retention. With products that are relatively price inelastic what matters is the reliability of production partners. Subcontractors have become exporters (with export sales accounting for around a quarter of their output), indicating significantly more entrepreneurial capacity at this tier of the district than in Fusignano.

In Fusignano 'conventional' subcontracting is dominant: most firms are self-contained except for a few minor tasks that are given out to subcontractors. Their middle- to low-quality products are made with technology that requires comparatively large amounts of fixed investment. Managing uneven market demand and avoiding the need to add to internal capacity are the main motives for subcontracting. Contracting links tend to be without commitment to a long-term association, are made and broken according to prevailing needs and opportunities, and (unlike San Mauro Pascoli) may involve subcontractors located outside the district. Shoe firms in Fusignano are faced with a market of increasing uncertainty and

Table 7.1 Profile of two Emilia-Romagna shoe-making districts (1992)

	Total employed[1]	Share (%) of firms making		Employment concentration[2]
		shoes	components	
San Mauro Pascoli	1,243	22.3	77.7	49.5
Fusignano	666	66.2	33.8	72.2

Source: Brusco *et al.* (1996).

Notes
1 Total employed in the footwear industry.
2 Ratio of people employed in small firms (less than 50 employees) to all employees in footwear production.

shrinking size and are employing subcontracting mainly as a cost-reduction strategy.

The micro-comparison of two districts is reflected in a larger transformation that has seen archetypal districts such as Como and San Mauro Pascoli become a declining minority (see Chapter 4). The changing picture of Italy's industrial districts challenges their idealized depiction as models for combining competition and collaboration (Paniccia 2002). Most districts have seen an increased dominance of their specialization by a few enterprises whose operations span beyond their home region (Brusco *et al.* 1996; Cossentino *et al.* 1996; Dei Ottati 1994) and a loss of production capacity alongside increased concentration on design, marketing and operations management (Burroni and Trigilia 2001). One interpretation argues that such evolution reflects the limited capacity for innovation among archetypal districts (Gottardi 1996; Nuti and Cainelli 1996).

During the period when the industrial districts first gained attention they were able to grow on the basis of 'downstream' innovation. Marginal adaptations in product design and materials were often sufficient to keep pace with fashion in the shoemaking or apparel industry. The industrial district was well suited to making this type of change as it relied mainly on craftsmanship, which was well developed within small firms, and did not rely on heavy investment or coordination with upstream activities (such as raw material processors or machine-tool manufacture). While opportunities for market growth existed on this basis, firms could operate with informal relationships and opportunistic marketing strategies. Being part of a cluster helped. Market intermediaries (import/export agents) could concentrate on sourcing sales contracts with the comparative ease of locating a supplier within the cluster they worked with. This approach was not suited to a period of slower growth and significant technological change, such as the adjustment to computer-integrated manufacturing. A less informal way of working was required and this led to organizational change, generally along the lines of greater vertical integration of production and more reliance on external linkages than in the past

(Cossentino *et al.* 1996). A further outcome is that many of the business-support agencies lost their importance. Today they can provide fewer services to the firms they were set up to help and spend more time selling themselves as models of development to government agencies outside Italy (Box 7.4).

Claims about cluster advantages arose originally in relation to concentrations of small scale enterprise under local ownership. Subsequent investigation has faced the reality that many business communities are

---

Box 7.4 Collective service agencies under pressure

Industrial districts are frequently claimed to be distinguished by their 'real-service' centres. Unlike business support that is available from commercial providers or public agencies that are widely available to be drawn upon, real-service providers alter firms' behaviour, capabilities and effectiveness. An assessment of this claim needs to recognize two levels of improvement: (i) bringing firms up to a specified performance benchmark; (ii) facilitating a change in how firms learn about problems and act on the information collected. The second of these forms of improvement is most demanding, implying considerable time and effort and high levels of trust in the advice provided by the service agency.

Achieving the second level of improvement has been made harder by the changing external environment in which industrial district firms operate:

- The flow of information from outside to inside the industrial district is increasingly through a small number of nodes controlled by group enterprises.
- Important forms of knowledge come increasingly from outside the district, adding to the internal firm capabilities needed to translate new knowledge into action.
- Firms' strategic information needs are increasingly specific to individual enterprises. In the past, real-service providers responded to information bottlenecks that could be generalized to a significant number of firms.
- The information capable of driving business success is increasingly specialized. To protect specialized understanding, successful firms may limit the information that they are prepared to share with a real-service centre given the risk of it transferring to their competitors.
- Maintaining the effectiveness of real services requires ongoing investment to continually develop and enrich the understanding needed to respond to issues challenging firm competitiveness.
- The pressure to introduce private-sector funding models into real-service-centre activity increases the likelihood of firms seeking only services that can be linked to immediate needs. In other words, firms are more likely to buy what they know than to make risky investments based on unfamiliar knowledge from unfamiliar sources.

Source: Glasmeier (1999)

populated by a high proportion of overseas owned enterprises (Box 7.5). This is a particular challenge as the presence of multinational subsidiaries can affect many cluster characteristics (Peters and Hood 2000: 75). As seen in Chapter 4 (Box 4.2), one response is to exclude branch plants of foreign-owned firms from cluster analysis on the grounds that they are a sign of competitive weakness (Porter 1990). An alternative perspective sees overseas ownership as enhancing cluster capabilities, although the precise extent to which this occurs and the forms of benefit obtained will be influenced by the characteristics of the cluster and of the overseas-

---

Box 7.5 Foreign ownership and clusters

The city state of Singapore depends on the electronics sector for over 40 per cent of the manufacturing sector's value added and over 10 per cent of GDP. Foreign companies account for over 90 per cent of total value added in the main product groups, in some cases 100 per cent. The activities located in Singapore by multinational companies have limited opportunity for indigenous entrepreneurship:

- Home-country R&D: Singapore has attracted little of the R&D capacity of MNCs. Close involvement with the main design centre is important to suppliers seeking involvement in high-value component or assembly sub-contracting. Without access to the core R&D process, Singapore SMEs are relegated to comparatively routine low-value production such as circuit-board assembly and packaging.
- End of cycle product mandates: where Singapore has been allocated a product mandate by its corporate HQ it typically covers 'mature' products subject to only superficial changes in product design. For these types of products, cost competitiveness is critical and amongst the study sample the outcome was high-volume, internalized mass production with little requirement for externalized sourcing.
- Cost-orientated activity: Singapore's origins as a manufacturing base selected for production-cost advantages continues to shape subcontracting opportunities, even where organizations have ceased to view the region primarily as an export platform. Production-cost sensitivity is reflected in the ongoing relocation of activity to low-wage production sites. This tends to result in the periodic reconstitution of supply needs in Singapore, resulting in a corresponding dislocation of local supply linkages, helped by increased industrial skills in other Asian economies.
- Technology: inward investment has tended to comprise activities that can operate with long-distance supply linkages or whose local input needs involve simple technology. Limited linkage development can thus be seen as partly a process of Singapore being selected as an investment site by organizations that are not reliant on a localized supply base, although they may have an interest in seeing more of one develop.

Source: Perry and Tan (2000)

owned participants. For example, a study of IT activity in Stockholm judged that foreign subsidiaries strengthened the cluster by increasing the visibility of innovations made by local firms (Birkenshaw 2000: 111). This benefit was contingent upon foreign-owned firms being as committed to their investment in Stockholm as local investors.

Existing policy experience reinforces the challenge to promoting collaboration among businesses. The failure of the 'hard business networks' programme developed originally by the Danish Technological Institute and then taken up in many other countries is one comparatively well-documented case (Chaston 1996; Arzeni and Pellegrin 1997). The programme gave support to encourage small groups of business to work together, ideally for the purpose of expanding exports. The programme used 'brokers' to assist identify and manage the networks, and offered financial support to joint activity. An assumption was that small firms would wish to join a network to make it easier and less risky than entering export markets alone (Ffowcs Williams 1996). By sharing resources and undertaking joint investments, it was envisaged that small firms would compete as if they were a large firm while still retaining their own identities and core competencies. In practice, the results indicate that such possibilities need to be balanced against the motivations for being in business and the difficulty of maintaining agreement over inputs and returns from a venture on which individual participants are likely to have differing degrees of dependence. Getting small firms to cooperate is highly problematic wherever you are. Even in Denmark it has been observed that attempting to accelerate cooperation amongst businesses that have little prior familiarity with each other was likely to be fraught with 'serious problems' (Henriksen 1995). Cooperation amongst firms operating in different parts of the value chain proved especially hard to initiate and sustain. At the outset there may be few areas of common experience, different perspectives on the aspects of their business critical to performance or possibly a history of adversarial relationships with the businesses in their value chain. When projects are identified, implementation exposes networks to even greater challenges. Perhaps inevitably firms will have different dependencies on the network and different perceptions of the potential returns and barriers to 'going it alone'. The evidence in Denmark was that once public subsidies were withdrawn networks rapidly ceased to function (Huggins 1996; Amphion Report cited in Ingley and Selvarajah 2000).

Other policy experience in New Zealand was obtained from attempts to build industry groups for export cooperation. Among the outcomes it appeared that what groups would cooperate about varied with the balance of large and small firms in the group (Box 7.6). Cluster advocates tend to present collaboration as 'win-win' activity: firms can still compete and gain the advantage of sharing resources. Experience indicates that it is often more realistic to view collaboration as a form of resource commitment

---

Box 7.6 Industry structure and export cooperation

During the early 1990s, Trade New Zealand (since merged and now operating as New Zealand Trade and Enterprise) gave support to industry-based business cooperation directed toward export growth. The programme was developed following an investigation into New Zealand's competitive weaknesses led by Michael Porter. The policy responded to that report's suggestion that competitive advantage derives from clusters of related activity rather than enterprises working in isolation. At its peak, over 30 'joint action groups' existed, typically each with 20 to 30 members. Sustaining the groups proved difficult and most lapsed with the withdrawal of financial support.

While they existed, the focus of group activity varied according to the balance of large and small firms in the industry. Groups comprising comparatively similar-sized organizations were most likely to work collectively as expected by the programme's designers. In 'dualistic industries' comprising a few dominant firms and a large number of small firms, joint activity relied on large firms having some strong reason to engage with firms whose experience of and capacity for exporting was considerably less than theirs. Typically, this was either when there was a threat of new entry into the industry or when the industry as a whole was under severe pressure. In the former case, large firms sought to protect their established marketing strategies. In the case of industry-wide pressure, large firms were motivated to help small firms survive so as to protect the industry's supply base.

Source: Perry (1995)

---

that may or may not be available and that may or may not fit with the business environment operated within. There is a need to develop specific understanding of the conditions that allow cooperation but sufficient information exists to indicate that the opportunities are limited.

Clusters for all

There is awareness that high-profile clusters can encompass communities that do not share equally in the prosperity (Crang and Martin 1991; Benner 2002). The growth of industrial concentrations can encourage congestion, increased land costs and labour shortages, and these outcomes tend to fall first on those gaining least benefit from the core activity of a cluster. Firms with lower margins may be forced out of the area along with workers on lower incomes who find it more difficult to afford housing in the cluster. Such distributional outcomes are not reflected in the advocacy of clusters for economic development. This is a significant omission as cluster intervention is unlikely to spread opportunities to individuals in low-skilled jobs, small enterprise or economically distressed regions unless it is specifically designed to do so (Rosenfeld 2003).

It may be argued that distributional issues can be addressed by other interventions, cluster policy left in tact and that a sufficient test for cluster intervention is its ability to enhance overall competitiveness and business growth. On the other hand, Rosenfeld (2003) suggests that the promotion of clusters without consideration of the distributional outcomes risks widening economic differences in at least four ways:

- Clusters create a capacity for industry participants to network and learn from one another but for non-participants they can increase the barriers to gaining access to opportunities within the industry. The more that clusters are defined by formal membership and the more that business activity depends on personal networking, the higher the hurdles can become for outsiders to gain entry. For example, it is suggested that while social capital is not necessarily absent from low-income communities it is less likely to be linked to power and influence than in high-income communities.
- Clusters based on locally owned enterprise, creating opportunities in a local community, might be trawled for expertise by outside firms who subsequently abandon the cluster in a reduced state. Such a process is reported in the case of a telecommunications cluster in northern Denmark. Of five outside multinationals attracted to the locality in the 1990s to gain access to its particular expertise, three had closed their operations by the end of the decade having expropriated knowledge from the cluster for application elsewhere (Lorentzen and Mahnke 2002).
- Unless confined to businesses within short and inexpensive travel time of each other, distance will become an impediment to participation. Typically, small companies have few discretionary funds and little free time to travel to become active members of associations that offer unclear benefits to their business. Even where they do, large firms may require that decision-making influence is related to organizational size. Issues addressed and opinions expressed by the cluster may favour the already best resourced organizations.
- Cluster promotion can be linked to a preference for 'new economy' activities, as defined by the research and knowledge intensity of companies. Even if there is not an overt link, the propensity for clustering among new industries at the incubator or take-off stage (Glasmeier 2000) can lead cluster promotion to favour information technology, life science and other new industries. Growth of these activities can increase economic inequality and relegate less-educated people to low income jobs in the services purchased by highly paid professionals.

Rosenfeld's (2003) recommended actions to enable clusters to reach and serve the interests of weaker economies and small businesses were drawn up in the context of the United States where there are particular dimensions to economic inequality. A general message was that an inclusive cluster policy would need to operate with lower entry requirements than one which left distributional outcomes to be addressed by other interventions. This would include a willingness to loosen the definition of clusters to include any activity which could take advantage of relationships and externalities. In a rural community, for example, any activity in which separate enterprises specialized might be taken up as a cluster. The example is given of a small Welsh town (Hay-on-Wye) that became a cluster of 35 used-book shops.

A second general point is that conditions on the access to cluster assistance are needed to distribute benefits widely. This might include requirements for training initiatives to include representation from labour unions and for a requirement that cluster agencies include participation from 'third-sector' organizations with interests in the environment, civil society and equity. This proposal was made with some optimism that businesses can be encouraged to diversify their objectives beyond profit. That assessment may apply to large organizations with the capacity for stakeholder management and 'triple bottom line' reporting. More generally, giving influence to campaign groups is likely to deter business participation. Flexibility in cluster definition may be more of an issue for policy makers. As Rosenfeld (2003) points out, widening the application of so-called cluster strategies conflicts with the preference for a precise definition that imparts a specific status to resulting interventions.

Policy experience in New Zealand

New Zealand's approach to promoting business clusters may be regarded as inclusive. It has operated without rigorous entry criteria, has captured activity in a wide range of activities, has supported initiatives in comparatively high- and low-income regions, and made specific provision for 'special interest' clusters including those based on Mäori enterprise. These characteristics go some way to satisfying Rosenfeld's (2003) requirements for expanding the opportunities arising from cluster strategies. On the other hand, public-agency support assumed that clusters would generate significant impacts on business growth by coordinating action to address issues such as training, infrastructure and procurement. A 'cluster-building toolkit' prepared to support the main cluster-promotion programme noted the goal of trying to convert existing concentrations of activity into localities with more of the characteristics of Silicon Valley and the Italian industrial districts (Cluster Navigators 2001). Six particular experiences are of general interest among the results of trying to build clusters: (i) motivations for joining a cluster; (ii) conditions on co-operation; (iii) the need to go national; (iv) facilitator dependence; (v) need for a leader; (vi) missing clusters. Before explaining these outcomes, it helps to understand the context in which the experience occurred.

Policy context

New Zealand is a small economy predominantly reliant on agriculture-commodity exports. Its population of 4 million is one-third concentrated in the Auckland region located in the north of the North Island. The majority of the country is thinly settled, especially the South Island where half the one million population are located in and around the major city of Christchurch. It is predominantly an economy of small enterprises but in the early 1990s it was estimated that in most industries four firms could account for at least 60 per cent of industry output (Hayward 1996). During the 1990s, the economy went through a significant change in regulation as many controls on business activity were removed (Dalziel and Lattimore 1996: Silverstone *et al.* 1996). These reforms opened domestic industry to more competition from imports and foreign investment but also reduced foreign-exchange and other restrictions that had hampered offshore investment. As part of the adjustment to a more open economy than it had been, various public agencies have sought to encourage business cooperation particularly for the purpose of developing export markets. These projects generally indicated a high interest in joining business networks although often it proved hard to sustain membership (Perry 2001).

Based on Nordic experience, it has been suggested that small economies such as New Zealand should benefit from 'shared trust' (Maskell *et al.* 1998). Just as in a village compared with a city, it may be difficult to act opportunistically without being sanctioned, so in a small economy the pressure to 'play by the rules' is said to increase (Maskell 1998: 198). Shared backgrounds and the likelihood of participation in joint activity (social, political or professional), in the past if not the present, means that information flows quickly and widely across business communities. With confidence that disruptive or dishonest behaviour will be transparent, and that business has a common interest in punishing malfeasance, barriers to cooperation are thought to be low.

Assuming that shared trust actually exists in the way described, the New Zealand environment for business cooperation is different to that in Nordic economies. Business managers in New Zealand confirm that there is a high degree of personal familiarity and shared culture amongst participants in an industry but it is doubted that this in itself makes cooperation easy to establish (Perry 2001). The weakness of informal sanctions for punishing abuse of trust is one reason given for cooperative relations being hard to establish. As well, most managers agree that 'big players' have little interest in developing mutual-development opportunities with small firms. Overall, it may be concluded that New Zealand is not particularly distinct in its business culture affecting the willingness to act collaboratively. Some features of the country suggest that it should be comparatively easy to gain support for cluster activity, others that there would be significant resistance to overcome.

The policy support for cluster formation has come mainly from economic-development agencies linked to local authorities and from a Cluster Development Programme administered by a central-government agency (currently New Zealand Trade and Enterprise). Forms and levels of assistance vary between these programmes but some common features are evident:

- Clusters are envisaged as membership associations. This might be achieved through an informal association but public-agency preference tends to be to see groups develop some form of legal entity with a specific membership.
- Eligibility has not been based on any prior cluster mapping exercise or strict guidelines regarding the selection and scope of activity. This has allowed groups of variable significance to gain recognition as clusters.
- Public agencies give support by identifying and bringing together potential clusters and then providing administration and facilitation to help develop and maintain activity. That support may be offered in three ways: (i) dedicated support from an employee of the public agency seeking to assist the cluster; (ii) funding the position of a cluster facilitator who is appointed by and accountable to the cluster; (iii) joining the cluster as a co-member.
- The level of direct public support typically enables a part-time facilitator to be appointed and occasionally a full-time person. Cluster groups may get support for specific projects from separate business-development and trade-promotion programmes. Otherwise groups rely on their own resources collected through membership fees or one-off contributions.

This policy context has tended to result in the encouragement of a large number of clusters covering typically no more than 30 enterprises and frequently significantly fewer than this. In early 2004, it was possible to identify around 95 cluster initiatives that had received varying levels of public support and were still in existence. Of these, 42 were attached to the Cluster Development Programme and generally represented the most coherent and well-supported initiatives.

A review of 25 cluster initiatives conducted through interviews with cluster facilitators and managers in agencies providing assistance reveals a diversity of projects (Tables 7.2 and 7.3). How representative the initiatives are of all projects is not known. The selection was divided evenly between clusters supported by the Cluster Development Programme and those not. A quarter of all clusters are based on education, film production, forestry and software/IT, and these account for a third of the clusters reviewed. Even so, the main claim for the sample is that it captures experience that deserves attention regardless of knowing its incidence among other clusters. Among the clusters are some interesting initiatives (Box 7.7) but more widespread are constraints on cluster effectiveness that are discussed below.

Table 7.2 Organizational characteristics of selected New Zealand clusters (2004)

	Years established	Incorporated society or trust	Public-agency led	Other structure	Membership	Membership fees	Geographic membership	Stakeholder involvement
Canterbury Electronics	3			•	6		•	
Canterbury and Nelson Neutraceuticals	2		•		120		•	•
Earthquake Engineering	7	•			33	•		•
Health IT	3	•			38	•		•
Film Auckland	<1				n/a			•
Forestry Wairarapa	6		•		7		•	•
Kapiti Horowhenua Apparel & Textile	3		•		55		•	•
Manawatu Defence	6	•	•		30	•	•	•
Māori Consultants	1				15	•		
Natural Hazards	3.5	•			27	•	•	
Otago Southland Forest Product Group	3	•			15	•	•	•
Wood Hawke's Bay	4		•		42		•	•
Wools of Aotearoa	6			•	5			
Clusters not supported by the Cluster Development Programme								
Creative Capital	6	•			~40	•	•	•
Wellington Creative Manufacturing	1.5		•		45	•	•	•
Electronics South	1.5		•		50		•	•
Film South	5	•					•	•
International Education Manawatu	3	•			19	•	•	•

Cluster								Number of members
Manawatu IT cluster	3	•	•						n/s
Nelson Bays Arts Marketing Trust	11	•	•				•		n/a
Tertiary Education Cluster	3	•	•			•	•		7
Tourism Horowhenua	3	•	•	•		•			~30
River Road Tourism Providers	7	•	•		•				21
Wanganui Classic Car Restoration	1.5	•	•			•			8
Wanganui Overseas Student Cluster	4	•			•	•			8

Notes
Number of members refers to the number of organizations represented in the cluster. n/s indicates that membership numbers are not known; n/a indicates not a membership organization.
Geographic membership indicates whether membership is limited to organizations with establishments in a localized area: those without have national membership.
Stakeholder involvement indicates that non-business organizations such as economic development agencies, local authorities and education/training agencies participate in the cluster.

Table 7.3 Activity profile of selected New Zealand clusters (2004)

	Networking	Vision or mission	Agreed strategy	Cluster brand	Joint marketing	Lobby	Business development planning	Industry planning	Consortia bidding	Joint resource
Canterbury Electronics	•									•
Canterbury and Nelson Neutraceuticals	•						•	•		
Earthquake Engineering	•	•	•	•	•	•	•			
Health IT	•	•	•	•	•	•	•	•	•	
Film Auckland	•	•	•	•	•	•	•	•	•	
Forestry Wairarapa	•					•	•	•		
Kapiti Horowhenua Apparel & Textile	•					•				
Manawatu Defence	•	•			•					
Māori Consultants	•	•			•					
Natural Hazards		•	•		•				•	
Otago Southland Forest Product Group	•			•	•	•	•	•		
Wood Hawke's Bay		•	•	•	•	•	•			
Wools of Aotearoa		•		•	•					•
Clusters not supported by the Cluster Development Programme										
Creative Capital	•	•	•	•	•		•			
Wellington Creative Manufacturing	•	•	•			•	•			
Electronics South	•	•		•	•		•			
Film South	•	•	•	•	•	•	•	•	•	
International Education Manawatu	•	•	•	•	•		•	•	•	•
Manawatu IT cluster	•									

	Networking	Vision or mission	Agreed strategy	Cluster brand	Joint marketing	Business development	Industry planning	Consortia bidding	Joint resource
Nelson Bays Arts Marketing Trust	•	•	•	•	•				•
Tertiary Education Cluster	•	•	•		•	•	•		
Tourism Horowhenua	•	•		•	•	•	•		•
River Road Tourism Providers	•	•	•	•	•				•
Wanganui Classic Car Restoration	•	•			•	•			
Wanganui Overseas Student Cluster	•	•	•		•				

Notes

Networking indicates activity specifically to promote informal interaction among members, such as through regular membership meetings and 'show and tell' sessions.

Vision or mission indicates that the cluster has agreed a vision or mission statement (or both).

Agreed strategy indicates development of a document guiding cluster activity over the next 2–5 years.

Cluster brand indicates the development of a cluster brand identity and its use in marketing activity.

Joint marketing indicates that members participate in collective promotional activity, such as joint presentation at a trade show.

Business development indicates working with individual enterprises to address current issues faced by the business.

Industry planning is activity to address labour and physical infrastructure requirements to support the future development of cluster activity.

Consortia bidding is where groups of cluster members bid jointly for project/contract work.

Joint resource indicates any other shared investment such as the sharing of equipment or staff, an inter-firm trading system or joint procurement capacity.

Box 7.7 New Zealand cluster innovations

Electronics South has developed an on-sale component market for members. Small firms, it is believed, are often forced to buy components in larger volumes than they need. This provides a surplus that other firms might wish to buy. The market network has been established to facilitate the exchange of these surplus components.

Three members of the Canterbury Electronics Group established a joint web site for promoting employment opportunities in their companies to engineers resident outside New Zealand.

Creative Capital established a separate legal entity to allow those members wishing to participate in the Singapore market to operate as a single commercial business.

Kapiti Horowhenua Apparel & Textile cluster designed a scheme in negotiation with the local benefit agency and training providers to attract local unemployed into the apparel industry. Firms committed to employ 30 trainees but the project lapsed when redundancies created a surplus of trained workers.

Health IT has negotiated a Sector Collaboration Framework with the Ministry of Health to secure a role for the cluster in recommending and reviewing health IT standards.

Motivation for the cluster

Intervention to promote clusters assumes that they facilitate business development in ways that assist growth and community development. New Zealand's policy experience indicates that businesses may come together to defend established positions against new entrants. This outcome exists in the initial reasons for the formation of the Otago Southland Forest Products Group. It was formed to produce estimates of forest-industry investment opportunities that showed less scope for new entrants than the estimates produced by regional agencies that were keen to attract new investment. New Zealand faces a large increase in its potential forest harvest over the next 20 years but the implication for new investment opportunities attracts different assessments. For established timber processors the 'wall of wood' offers the prospect of declining raw-material cost as available timber supply increases. Forest owners might be more concerned to see processing capacity grow but they also seek to export unprocessed timber and require new investment in road and shipping infrastructure to facilitate increased exports. This context encourages much dispute over future investment priorities. The worst-case scenario for industry incumbents is that government agencies prioritize new investment in processing capacity through incentives and favoured regulatory conditions that leaves established investors at a relative disadvantage and does little to assist raw-log export capacity.

A shared concern that economic-development agencies were misinformed about the region's capacity to accommodate new investment brought the Otago Southland Forest Products Group together. Members were the region's largest companies with most existing investment at stake. Government and port representatives have since been invited to join and attend meetings. Small companies and any business not directly involved in forest ownership or timber processing have been excluded. The restricted membership is defended on the grounds that it keeps the involvement of senior executives and that this is more important than diversifying the interests represented. As well, it is argued that being a small group has helped initiate new projects such as investigations of the scope for a shared regional brand and for combining the transport operations of individual companies. From the perspective of clusters as drivers of business cooperation and growth, it remains to be seen whether these investigations are successful and, if they are, whether they produce public-good outcomes. If mainly private benefits result, support for an exclusive group motivated to curtail the region's marketing to new investors might be questioned.

Conditions on cooperation

The overt effort to control entry is most evident in the case of the Otago Southland Forest Products Group but in several groups collaboration is conditional on membership restrictions. Another forestry group (Forestry Wairarapa) operates on the basis that membership is restricted to forest owners and managers. The local economic-development agency had sought to build a cluster comprising forest and processing interests. Like Otago Southland, the economic-development agency was perceived as being too concerned to attract new investment in processing capacity and this proved a barrier to retaining participation from existing timber processors. Unlike Otago Southland, the regional industry tends to have few combined timber growers and processors. In this case, therefore, the cluster split along segments of the value chain rather than according to the scale of operation. Compared with the government priority for expanding value-added activity in New Zealand, the segment prepared to join a cluster are of less value than those not supporting the initiative. This is reflected in the scale of the activity addressed by the group such as lobbying to change the organization of rural local fire-service areas to match forest boundaries and a drug and alcohol policy to cover forestry workers.

Membership restrictions exist in other clusters too. The Tertiary

Education Cluster comprises seven public-sector tertiary establishments in Wellington that decided against an inclusive group of public- and private-sector tertiary institutions. The Canterbury Electronics Group brings together the region's six largest electronics companies. They favour separation from the region's population of around 100 small and medium-sized electronics companies. Voicing concerns over national and regional industry issues as the 'big six' is perceived as more influential than speaking individually and often preferable to joining with the rest of the regional industry. Common interests are less among firms of different size and export dependence than they are among the elite firms. As well as the time to negotiate priorities, group diversification would mean less personal familiarity and trust than exists among the big six CEOs. On the other hand, business-development cooperation is limited by their different specializations and three of the six having transferred to overseas ownership. Companies tend, therefore, to have separate supplier and marketing networks. In the case of foreign subsidiaries, chances of cooperation are restricted further by procurement decisions which may be controlled from outside New Zealand.

Need to go national

In the search for projects judged to engage enterprises with potential to generate significant revenue, the Cluster Development Programme has opened participation to national industry groups. Membership of four of the clusters examined was open to organizations irrespective of their location. This shift can be interpreted as a realistic approach to promoting collaboration in a small economy. The impact on membership may nonetheless be of concern as it heightens barriers to participation from small and medium-sized enterprises. Experience indicates some ways that this impact can be reduced but it implies a reduced applicability of clustering. Health IT is a national association most of whose 38 members have fewer than 25 employees. This is possible because firms in the sector are narrowly focused on supplying IT products and services to the healthcare industry. This requires an interest in national structures affecting IT procurement such as the national standardization of individual health records and protocols covering the communication of patient data. The contrast is seen with a neutraceutical cluster that has been joined by mainly small businesses located in two regions. Geographic expansion was to diversify membership to suppliers and processors of food crops for medical and health products. Without a strong justification for the group, long travel distances to meetings are a significant barrier to participation. Similarly, a cluster of earthquake-engineering firms has a national membership to encompass relevant industry expertise but recognizes that small-firm members from outside Wellington, where the group is coordinated, participate less than those located there (see Box 4.5).

Facilitator dependence

The number and size of individual clusters presents a misleading impression of collaborative activity. A distinction can be made between clusters that exist because of the commitment of their members and those that are the creation of economic-development agency efforts to promote a cluster and are still dependent on that agency for maintaining the group. This is not a clear distinction as until agency support is withdrawn the sustainability of the cluster cannot be known for certain. Of the 25 clusters, reflecting member motivation to get the group started, eight existed prior to public-agency involvement. In another eight cases, it appears that public-agency support remains essential to keep the initiative going. In one case, for example, the agency had not arranged a meeting of a cluster for five months (because of effort being directed to recovery after a natural disaster hit the region) and this was seen as evidence of the lack of member ownership of the initiative. Among the other nine clusters examined, some prefer that the agency remains involved. This preference may be to retain a 'neutral' partner or simply to save administration costs.

Facilitator dependence is significant for the nature of the activity pursued as well as its sustainability. Where the dependence is high, it tends to result in a cluster characterized by customized support to individual members rather than activity involving joint participation or changes in business practice. Indeed, across all of the projects actual changes in business operations are few and in this sense most projects have still to demonstrate that they are encouraging collaboration. Aside from the willingness to attend network meetings, share information for benchmarking or lobbying purposes and pay a modest membership fee of up to NZ$500 a year, collaborative activity is sparse (Box 7.7 gives the main examples).

Need for a leader

Clusters are expected to assist businesses increase export activity. To this end many cluster initiatives seek to develop a brand image and joint publicity material for use in overseas markets. Organizing collective representation at international trade shows and linking individual companies to sources of market intelligence are other frequent activities. A further hope is that established exporters will act as mentors to those without export experience. As noted above (Box 7.6), prior to the cluster initiatives 'joint action groups' had tried similar methods for increasing export activity. Most of these groups found that export cooperation was hard to sustain (Perry 2001). It typically relied on all members having little existing international experience or on those with experience identifying a new market that no member had already invested in. Otherwise, most progress was made by those groups which comprised a single lead contractor with other members as subcontractors. Having a clear leader ensured agreement over marketing strategies and reduced concern that prior market-development investment would not be lost to competitors. Some groups might start with several members capable of being the lead firm but if these firms were competitors overseas it often proved difficult to keep more than one in the group. Such experiences tended to result in a transition to relatively small, exclusive groups that eventually led to the withdrawal of government assistance (Box 7.8).

Similar experiences are already apparent among the cluster initiatives. The Earthquake Engineering cluster is focused on export-market development to a greater extent than any other cluster examined. Membership from New Zealand's largest engineering-consultancy firm has provided

---

Box 7.8 Working in groups can be hard

The Building Industry Export Group was formed to gain recognition as a 'joint action group' (JAG) to bring members increased access to government export funding and a paid coordinator. It appointed a full-time coordinator in 1993, attracted around 50 members and started with group participation in a trade show in Fiji.

Responding to a survey of member priorities, projects in Australia and Southeast Asia were then proposed. Activities for the Australian market attracted little support. In practice, members saw Australia as an extension of the domestic market and either already operated there or preferred to enter the market alone. A New Zealand identity was not seen as an asset in Australia and this discouraged further any perceived advantage in a group approach. In Southeast Asia, participation reduced as it became evident that the region had to be addressed as separate national markets. Once individual countries were targeted, the group fragmented with, for example, around six companies joining a mission to Vietnam.

After several years the group had effectively become a dozen or more subgroups each with a separate market focus. With encouragement from Trade New Zealand, some sub-groups became JAGs in their own right (including airport technologies, food systems and kitset homes). This trend suited specialists but for multi-activity companies it resulted in a loss of attachment to any single group and reduced sector-wide activity. The original group was re-launched as 'Constructive Solutions' with around 20 members, each a specialist resolving previous tensions between competitors in the original group. Even so, with varying degrees of commitment and little consistent participation, a paid coordinator was essential to keep activity going.

In the end, Trade New Zealand judged that too little of their support was being devoted to actual export promotion as compared with the effort invested in maintaining membership. After Trade New Zealand funding was withdrawn, the group disbanded.

Source: Perry (2001)

the critical resource to enter overseas markets. A collective approach has worked because the lead firm needs the specialist expertise of other members to deliver projects. The Creative Capital cluster, on the other hand, shows how small firms working together cannot make up for the absence of a lead contractor. To exploit opportunities in Singapore, a commercial entity was formed in which individual members would participate according to their interest in that market and the combination of expertise needed for individual contracts. Still lacking was the financial capital to enable that new entity to secure government contracts in its own right. This forced it to act as a subcontractor to a Singapore-based company. Over NZ$4 million of contracts were won on this basis but the position as a subcontractor exposed cluster members to the uncertainties of being dependent on other parties for project delivery and payment. Ultimately, key businesses felt that there was insufficient control and too much risk. In 2004, the decision was made to cease trading through their joint entity and the cluster has gone back to focusing on the New Zealand market (Perry 2004c).

Missing clusters

The distribution of cluster projects indicates significant gaps in the activity covered. The Auckland region accounts for around a third of the national economy but has few cluster initiatives. One reason for this is that the drift of economic activity to Auckland has given greater support for local economic projects in other parts of the country. The distribution of clusters is often, therefore, indicative of promotional effort rather than business-development potential. Similarly, in respect of land-based activity, clusters are largely absent in the food sector. In the forestry sector, the Central North Island has the largest concentration of activity and unlike lesser regional concentrations has not developed a cluster.

Education has proved to be the most 'cluster-friendly' activity as a consequence of possessing attributes that most other activities do not share. Education institutions are found throughout the country although those attracting high numbers of international students are regionally concentrated. The expansion of international student numbers has been encouraged nationally. A collaborative approach to overseas marketing was encouraged by 'export network' funding provided by Trade New Zealand prior to the start of the Cluster Development Programme. Geographically proximate institutions have many reasons to collaborate with each other beyond the subsidy for trade delegations forming export networks. It is generally recognized that their main competitor is other countries rather than other local institutions. Each education provider tends to have a point of difference from its neighbours that further reduces any preference to market overseas alone. For example, secondary schools may differ according to whether they are public or private, boarding or non-boarding, single sex or co-educational, affiliated to a religious persuasion or non-religious. There is a common interest in needing to work with their local communities to ensure international students have a positive experience and to manage accommodation standards. Through this community dependence, large institutions are linked to smaller institutions and are willing to use their resources for joint as well as individual activity. Finally, individual institutions have a common regulator (the Ministry of Education) and benefit from sharing experience in maintaining compliance to an industry code of practice.

Interpreting New Zealand's policy experience

The promotion of predominantly local, membership associations of businesses with a common-resource dependency or market represents one conception of clusters. It is consistent with a widely held view that there can be advantage in encouraging collaboration among businesses with common interests that are located in close proximity to each other. When this approach is attempted without restrictive eligibility criteria, shortcomings are evident. The threshold for a cluster has simply been a sufficient number of organizations to form a group rather than statistical analysis to identify exceptional concentrations of activity or to specify a range of activity that must be represented in the cluster. One response may be, therefore, that the policy is too low key to merit attention. A justification for taking the experience seriously is that cluster advocates tend to suggest that advantages can be obtained at any scale of concentration. Indeed, from the perspective of ensuring a wide distribution of benefit, it is recommended that entry barriers be deliberately set low (Rosenfeld 2003).

The main shortcoming evident is that defensive motivations to join a cluster initiative have been encouraged as well as outward-looking collaboration. One reflection of this is the establishment of groups with membership restricted to large organizations or those concentrated in one part of the value chain. This outcome poses a dilemma for policy intervention. It can produce groups with a relatively high level of member commitment and self-management but directed to outcomes that generate less public-good benefit than might be if membership was diversified. One response has been the formation of 'umbrella clusters' made up of representatives from sub-clusters with selective memberships. An ICT cluster was set up for this purpose by Canterbury Development Corporation, including a representative from the small firm Electronics South and the big firm Canterbury Electronics Group. This 'umbrella cluster' includes representatives of other software-linked activities and addresses resource issues for the sector as a whole. For example, strategies for improving skilled-labour supply, where both large and small firms share some common interests, are being examined. In this context, the separation of cluster groups is a mechanism for maintaining wider participation in some form of joint activity than with a single cluster but it does impose comparatively high administration costs on public agencies.

More broadly, it may be argued that defensive motivations are an important basis for cooperation and an indicator that private benefits may exceed public benefits. In the education sector, cluster projects are partly directed towards increasing community acceptance of the large number of international students being attracted and that cluster members now have a large economic reliance upon. The Health IT cluster is partly about giving member businesses influence over the setting of regulatory standards governing IT products. One motivation for this is to generate first-mover advantages for members that design products to specifications that become adopted as the industry standard. Tourism clusters can be about operators seeking to control access to a particular location. All of these projects have justification and some public benefit but they do contrast with a presentation of clusters as unambiguously spurring innovation and growth.

The sensitivity of cluster opportunities to precise industry and market characteristics is a further reflection from New Zealand's experience. The Earthquake Engineering cluster was identified above as a rare example of a cluster directed to export-market development. As well as the presence of a lead contractor, the group has had other attributes that explain its formation and continued support. Prior to the cluster there had existed a professional association of earthquake engineers that was concerned about the ageing of the profession and the potential loss of indigenous New Zealand expertise. Gaining more work outside New Zealand was identified as one way of making the industry attractive to young recruits. The option of firms becoming significant exporters in their own right was limited as overseas work opportunities for New Zealand are mainly in low-income countries on government-controlled projects funded by international agencies such as the World Bank. This means a long and uncertain process for winning contracts, imposing market costs beyond the reach of individual cluster members. The nature of the work and the specialization of member firms mean that members offer complementary skills and that there is mutual recognition of the role played by the lead contractor. Even so, 'rules of engagement' have been developed to minimize the risk of conflict. Annual membership fees have been kept low to require that firms involved in individual bids fund that activity rather than the group as a whole. When information is shared, it is expected to be in full and open for others to act upon but there is no requirement for individual members to share information on market opportunities or other industry intelligence.

Multiple influences have enabled the Earthquake Engineering cluster to maintain a cooperative approach to overseas marketing. The contrast is seen with the Canterbury Electronics Group which among the projects examined is one of the few others with a high degree of independence from public-agency support. The six members have their own international-marketing capacity, particular specializations and business relationships that preclude any direct role for the group in business growth. A collective voice to lobby government agencies, benchmarking internal operations and cooperation in human-resource activities, where members have a common challenge in recruiting and retaining skilled staff, are reasons for the group. Different judgements are possible on how far such activities justify public-funding support of the group's facilitator, especially given the separation from the region's larger population of small electronics companies. The general message is that not all forms of collaboration are of equal public benefit. Programmes implemented without precise understanding of how industry and market conditions affect the scope for collaboration need guidance on where support should be concentrated. Without that guidance, opportunity to benefit from cluster promotion is limited.

Conclusion

There are many ways that an interest in clusters may be translated into policy measures to assist business development. This chapter has concentrated on the possibility that within individual business communities collaborative opportunities exist widely. This is one frequent way that it is thought that clusters offer an advantage that policy intervention can augment by directing collaboration to activities that significantly add to business growth. As well as the widespread opportunity, the underlying assumption is that collaboration will not emerge 'naturally' or at least not in a form that maximizes business growth. Three qualifications have been raised to this case for cluster policy. First, the experiences of exemplar clusters are not a justification for believing that other localities can copy their growth or a model that can be disassembled and implemented in part with the expectation of a proportionate impact. Second, industry and market characteristics significantly affect the scope for introducing collaboration among competing businesses. For this reason, attempts to define uniform trajectories of cluster development from inception to maturity are misconceived. Third, unless attention is paid to the distributional impacts of efforts to promote business clusters there is a high likelihood of benefits being concentrated among already relatively advantaged groups.

New Zealand's policy experience is not a sufficient test of the existence of collaborative opportunity but it does have outcomes that question the value of seeking to encourage localized cooperation. One risk is that defensive forms of cooperation are assisted as much as activities promoting change and development. This is one reason the success of cluster promotion cannot be judged by the number or scale of initiatives that result: precise activity needs to be evaluated. Another reason is that initiatives may be dependent on public-agency participation and take more of the form of customized business support to individual businesses than collaboration demanding changes in individual firm behaviour. One response to New Zealand's experience is to raise the eligibility for support with the aim of concentrating help where desirable forms of business cooperation can be most encouraged. This has been recognized through a shift of support to clusters with capacity for significant income growth and to national industry clusters. Support then tends to be given to initiatives involving comparatively well-resourced organizations and to the projects that raise barriers to participation for small enterprise. A further consequence is that policy distinctiveness is lost. Efforts to promote business cooperation through national industry groups were made during the 1990s and abandoned partly from concern that membership was not inclusive.

8 Conclusion

There is no undisputed evidence that patterns of industrial location are changing in favour of clusters or that businesses that are located in a cluster gain an advantage over those that do not. For every study that purports to find evidence of the importance of business clusters it is possible to find another that concludes otherwise. This situation is unlikely to change if the debate becomes one between clusters as good and clusters as indifferent, if not bad, for business competitiveness. The concept of a regional industry cluster is open to such a range of interpretations that conclusions from any single study are unlikely to go unchallenged. Business interdependence, for example, can show itself in a wide variety of ways, including the direct links between trading parties, common usage of third-party resources or simply a shared market. They can be searched for among groups of neighbouring firms in a city district, as Alfred Marshall principally had in mind, to industry participants dispersed across a whole country or even internationally. Equally variable is the response to co-location that is unrecognized by the businesses themselves and that did not form part of the original location decision. In some research, the potential for interdependence is less crucial than actual evidence of interdependence; in other research, the opposite view is taken. Practical difficulties distinguishing varieties of agglomeration advantage are further challenges even if the conceptual issues are agreed. Determining which type of interdependence has most impact on productivity and innovation is critical to establishing their significance but practically it has so far proved impossible to do so.

Research progress requires recognition of alternative perspectives and a willingness to learn from them. This book has had a focus on trying to assess clusters as a particular location condition. From this perspective, it has considered how cluster boundaries should be identified, what influences encourage activity to cluster, the impact of location in a cluster on business behaviour and the extent of advantage obtained. Other researchers do not start from a concern of understanding clusters in the sense of localized business communities. Their perspective may be that the key aspect of clustering is the need to recognize interdependencies between enterprises at whatever spatial scale they exist or is of interest to the particular research project. Others are focused on examining the impact of relative degrees of business concentration and diversity. Each approach potentially adds to the sum of knowledge and may ultimately point to one or more perspectives being of most insight. For example, some proponents of cluster identification through the factor analysis of input–output data suggest that this is inherently more appropriate than using measures of industry concentration and locality specialization (Feser and Bergman 2000; Feser and Luger 2003). Rather than seeking to assert the superiority of one approach over another, the two approaches should be seen as having different priorities but with each having potential to learn from the other.

For the present, three main responses have been offered to the competing claims about and varieties of cluster. One response emphasizes the chaotic nature of the evidence and debate about clusters. A second response argues that cluster analysis should be viewed as an art as well as a science. A third response is to stress that clusters potentially offer advantage to activities with particular characteristics for particular purposes but that overall economic development benefits from a diversity of business environments.

Clusters as chaos

Outright dismissal of a case for promoting interest in business clusters is based on two perceived limitations with existing discussion (Martin and Sunley 2003: 28). First, that the definition of clusters is too elastic to provide a basis for making any rigorous claims about the significance of agglomeration for regional and local economic development. The concept needs to be nailed down in a way that sets specific parameters for distinguishing a cluster from lesser forms of concentration. Meanwhile, with no precise rules for establishing when a cluster exists, it has been possible to pick and mix research evidence too freely. Second, even though there is an association between some high-growth industries and a tendency for geographical concentration this is not a basis for claiming that concentration is a cause of high growth. The enthusiasm for clusters has jumped too quickly from a few particular experiences to a belief in the universal capacity for concentration to generate growth.

Given widespread advocacy of the advantages of business clusters, their depiction as a chaotic conception needs to explain why standards of acceptable research evidence appear to have dropped so low. One suggestion is that clusters provide policy advisors with a rationalization for defending local actions against the drift of much economic and business activity into a global sphere of operation (Peters and Hood 2000). This rationalization has been particularly appealing as the importance of clusters has been linked to any position along the intervention spectrum, from simply recognizing the presence of a cluster to the micromanagement of business relations among cluster participants. Such flexibility of interpretation alone is not sufficient to explain the diffusion of cluster advocacy. Knowledge dissemination processes have reinforced the appeal of clusters, particularly those linked to Michael Porter whose methods for analysing national competitiveness based on the 'diamond model' have been taken up around the world (Peters and Hood 2000: 70). Certainly, direct 'missionary' work by Porter and the associated Monitor Consultancy has formed the basis of cluster strategies in many European countries (Benneworth *et al.* 2003).

More than just the well-organized exploitation of an appealing economic analysis tool, cluster advocacy has been interpreted as an example of brand management rather than intellectual discourse (Martin and Sunley 2003: 29). Just as commercial organizations use a brand image to seek to differentiate an otherwise 'ordinary' product, the cluster label has been attached to a set of ideas that essentially are little different to standard business-agglomeration theory and associated policy recommendations. Tired academic arguments have gained a new lease of life through the 'cluster brand' partly through its skilful linkage to an image of high productivity, knowledge-rich, decentralized, entrepreneurial and socially progressive local economies being within the reach of policy makers wherever located. As a brand, cluster has five essential attributes: (i) accordance with strongly held aspirations, in this case innovation and competitiveness; (ii) expressed in language that is flexible enough to permit a wide range of interpretations; (iii) backed by authority, in this case Michael Porter's expert knowledge of competition and business strategy; (iv) capable of continual and consistent renewal to keep pace with changing environments, as achieved with cluster applications to the dot.com and knowledge economies; (v) permit practical action, in this case the replication of cluster successes.

Undoubtedly, clever marketing has been behind the influence attained by the cluster idea although the full account of the campaign has yet to be written. As well as the influence of Michael Porter, the supporting role of 'new economic geography' also needs to be included in the credits. While perhaps not intended by most proponents, this linked cluster promotion to the esoteric and rigorous world of econometrics as well as spawning influential folklore such as Miss Evans' contribution to carpet making in Dalton. The desirable destinations recommended for gaining insight into clusters – California and northern Italy – cannot be overlooked as well. An idea derived from the experiences of less attractive locations may have faced much greater difficulty gaining traction. On the other hand, it was of further help that international agencies working in low-income countries were provided with a tool that seemed tailor-made to their business geographies.

Further investigation of the branding of academic theory is justified but to focus on cluster evangelism alone overlooks that much interesting activity has been going on even if it was often misinformed about the likelihood of success. Present efforts to map clusters could be dismissed as guided by arbitrary rules or they can be accepted as a starting point for learning more about who gains from agglomeration under what circumstances. Similarly, the policy interventions seeking to encourage collaboration among independent businesses provide potential insight into how industry and market characteristics affect support for collective projects. Rather than wait for the cluster brand to exhaust its appeal, opportunity remains to investigate and redirect policy intervention.

Clusters as art and science

As the number of agencies and researchers referring to business clusters has grown so have the boundaries and composition of clusters become blurred (Rosenfeld 2003). To some observers, as just discussed, elasticity in application is a sign of conceptual weakness. A positive response is to view the widening policy application as a sign of usefulness. It is appropriate for policy interests to determine the form of clustering investigated because there is no single, objective way of identifying when a cluster exists or of specifying how one might be searched for. All that can be offered is a minimum requirement that business clusters comprise 'tight connections that bind certain firms and industries together in various aspects of common behaviour' (Bergman and Feser cited in Feser and Luger 2003: 13). These connections may exist both locally and over great distance (Feser and Bergman 2000). The science of cluster analysis is to identify all these connections so as to distinguish which activities are most closely connected with which other activities based on connections that may exist nationally (or perhaps even internationally) or locally or both.

The methods available for cluster analysis require that inferences and judgements be made. In this sense, the 'science' of cluster analysis is partly an art. Thus when a technique such as factor analysis of input–output data is used to identify relationships between industries, it is necessary to interpret the factor loadings that are produced. Presentation of results should also recognize that the approach works better for mature manufacturing businesses than for small business and service sectors. Typically national level data will be used for the analysis, relying on tenuous inferences to make applications to regions. All of which means that quantitative cluster analysis can be seriously misleading if it is assumed to be more authoritative than it is (Feser and Luger 2003: 15). Additional qualitative insight is helpful but exposes analysis to the risk of being guided by 'expert opinion' obtained from persons with interests in the use made of the information they provide. That research is partly an art means caution should be exercised in acting on the results, not that the endeavour should be abandoned. Optimistically, innovative combinations of quantitative and qualitative analysis will reduce the level of caution needed.

Policy-maker direction is a bigger 'art' to cluster analysis than methodological judgement. Their contribution is needed to identify the issues potentially to be informed by cluster insight. Policy interest may vary according to whether existing, emerging or potential clusters are of interest; whether interdependencies are sought at a localized, regional or national scale; and whether a specific form of interdependence is the focus of inquiry, such as innovation, labour-market pooling or value-chain integration. A cluster is a multi-dimensional concept and so the policy objectives must guide the methodology followed. The process must be transparent in its purpose and procedures followed with methods sufficiently documented so that limitations and likely biases are discussed explicitly. When this is done, it is argued that one of the most important uses of cluster analysis can then be support for ongoing debate among researchers, policy makers and the public about a locality's economic prospects and future (Feser and Luger 2003: 16).

Cluster analysis as art and science can be seen as a realistic appraisal of current methodological capacity. It has yet to be seen how policy makers will respond to this presentation. While encouraging of the prospect of better things to come, for the present it implies a downgrading of what is implied by a cluster. From some definite state that can be attained, policy makers are asked to accept the significance of clustering as being little more than a recommendation to build development strategies on groups of interconnected industries than on industries alone. The appeal of this recommendation is likely to be further reduced by the caution that any group identified may not actually be strongly interdependent. Feser and Luger (2003) present case studies of some policy makers apparently responding to their guidance. The endorsement claimed occurred against the backdrop of cluster-brand marketing still unchecked and it is not clear that widespread conversion to an arts and science perspective will take place. In addition, it may be questioned whether this perspective does not assume a greater level of academic agreement than actually exists. The emphasis on clusters as interconnected industries represents a leap that not all researchers are willing to make. Feser and Luger (2003: 14) regard looking at individual industries, as through the application of location quotients, as less sophisticated than the application of input–output methods. Others prefer a view of clusters that is more open to the possible form that clusters take, including both traded and untraded dependencies between industries and the advantages that may accrue from the geographical concentration of a single industry. After all, the exemplar clusters are often built on a single industry or group of similar industries.

Clusters as a contribution to diversity

The third perspective agrees that there is a long tradition to the science of clusters. That research, it is believed, has given partial endorsement of cluster effectiveness but is doubtful this justifies the policy attention currently enjoyed. Contemporary cluster advocacy tends to assume that the capacity of firms to benefit from concentration is sufficiently general as to make its promotion a desirable policy goal whatever the activity and wherever the context (Glasmeier 2000). This claim has been addressed in many decades of research about urban and regional development. The result is that some activities have been shown to have more of a tendency to cluster than others and that the history of places and industry matter for the location patterns that result. Firms in dynamic, information-intensive sectors such as biotechnology tend to be relatively concentrated, especially during the early period of industry development. Over time, successful firms age and evolve through a combination of local expansion, branch openings, the restructuring of core activities, alliances with others or perhaps disappear entirely. Similarly, locations evolve as firms move in and out and activities grow or decline in importance. The result has been labelled 'diffuse development' (Glasmeier 2000: 565).

Within the pattern of diffuse development, some companies can benefit by clustering with others that make similar or closely related products. In some classifications this has been referred to as the development of 'industrial complexes' and which gives rise to localities with a strong industry association, such as iron and steel districts, motor-vehicle-assembly towns or chemical regions. These types of activity gain localization advantages from their close proximity and ability to influence the provision of specialized services and a labour market rich in skills and knowledge relevant to the core industry. There are other companies that operate successfully in a location amidst a broad range of activities and that might even benefit from the proximity to unconnected businesses as well as the services supplied to industry in general. Development for these companies is assisted more by urbanization economies than localization economies.

Overall there is much evidence produced by economists indicating that the cities which grow faster and are more adaptable to economic change are those that accommodate a diversity of industries. As discussed in Chapter 3, such evidence is complex partly as urbanization and localization need not be mutually exclusive. A metropolitan region may have a diverse economy overall but for individual activities to come together as clusters within diversity. On the other hand, many economists would argue that if localization economies are important they should be reflected in an advantage locating only among the activities localization benefits are shared with. Pulling against any such tendency is the evidence from many industry sectors that innovation is assisted by a location amidst diversity.

Ultimately, much of the case for clusters assumes that firms more easily learn from firms with whom they are in close proximity and that localized learning can be highly effective for business growth. The availability, circulation and absorption of information are certainly critical to the long-term survival and adaptability of business. Glasmeier (2000: 566) sees no reason to believe that firms located in a cluster should gain a learning advantage over firms that operate in isolation of their industry peers. Firms, wherever they are located, have limited capacity to learn, being organizations built around routine and action legitimized more by past experiences than anticipations of the future. Indeed, to the extent that clustering produces uniformity in the sources of knowledge and a lack of attention to developments going on elsewhere, it may even be detrimental to learning. This assessment is a reminder to consider the actual behaviour of firms. Experiences such as Silicon Valley are not created by firms suddenly becoming quick learners but rather rely on conditions and resources accumulated over a long time.

Structures can nonetheless play a role. In some circumstances it is possible that clusters may gain an advantage, but this will depend on external circumstances. In recent times, the dramatic loss of Japan's advantage in many industries is an illustration of how organizational structures can suddenly become a liability. Chon (1997) illustrates this in the case of the semiconductor manufacturing equipment industry. Originally close integration of the production of semiconductor manufacturing equipment with the manufacture of semiconductors was a source of strength to Japan's electronics sector. The direct transfer of knowledge about trends in the market for semiconductors helped equipment producers innovate more quickly than their competitors in the United States where equipment manufacturers were independent of users. The balance of competitive advantage changed when North American equipment manufactures reorganized through strategic alliances. Working in cooperation with competitors, high-tech manufacturers combined resources, shared risks and learned to better link their knowledge of production processes with research and development. Firms in the United States became leading suppliers of equipment to Japan and in Japan ties between equipment users and suppliers have been cut. Today, among equipment makers the need is to prioritize economies of scale with the increase in development cost associated with the sophistication of production equipment now needed to manufacture small semiconductor devices. Understanding such transitions and working out when cooperation, of what form, is consistent with competition provides an ongoing research agenda that deserves attention.

References

Aiginger, K. and Leitner, W. (2002) 'Regional concentration in the USA and Europe: who follows whom?', *Weltwirtshafitliches Archiv* 138(4): 1–28.

Almeida, P. and Kogut, B. (1997) 'The exploration of technological diversity and geographic localization of innovation', *Small Business Economics* 9: 21–31.

Altenburg, T. and Meyer-Stamer, J. (1999) 'How to promote clusters: policy experiences from Latin America', *World Development* 27: 1693–713.

Amin, A. (ed.) (1994) *Post-Fordism: A Reader*, Oxford: Blackwell.

Angel, D. (1994) 'Tighter bonds? Customer–supplier linkages in semiconductors', *Regional Studies* 28(2): 187–200.

Arndt, H. and Hill, H. (eds) (1999) *Southeast Asia's Economic Crisis*, Singapore: Institute of Southeast Asian Studies.

Arzeni, S. and Pellegrin, J.-P. (1997) 'Entrepreneurship and local development', *OECD Observer* 204(Feb./March): 27–9.

Asheim, B. (2000) 'Industrial districts: the contributions of Marshall and beyond', in G. Clark, M. Feldman and M. Gertler (eds) *The Oxford Handbook of Economic Geography*, Oxford: Oxford University Press.

Asian Development Bank (2001) 'Best practice in developing industry clusters and business networks', SME Development Technical Assistance Policy Discussion Paper 8, Jakarta: Asian Development Bank.

Audretsch, D. (1998) 'Agglomeration and the location of innovative activity', *Oxford Review of Economic Policy* 14(2): 18–29.

—— (2001) 'The role of small firms in U.S. biotechnology clusters', *Small Business Economics* 17: 3–15.

Beardsell, M. and Henderson, V. (1999) 'Spatial evolution of the computer industry in the USA', *European Economic Review* 43: 431–56.

Beaudry, C. and Breschi, S. (2003) 'Are firms in clusters really more innovative?', *Economics of Innovation and New Technology* 12(4): 325–42.

Becattini, G. (1990) 'The Marshallian industrial districts as a socio-economic notion', in F. Pyke (ed.) *Industrial Districts and Inter-firm Cooperation in Italy*, Geneva: International Institute for Labour Studies.

Benner, C. (2002) *Work in the New Economy: Flexible Labour Markets in Silicon Valley*, Oxford: Blackwell.

Bennett, R., Graham, D. and Bratton, W. (1999) 'The location and concentration of business in Britain: business clusters, business services, market coverage and local economic development', *Transactions of the Institute of British Geographers* 24: 393–420.

Benneworth, P. (2002) 'Creating new industries and service clusters on Tyneside', *Local Economy* 17(4): 313–27.

Benneworth, P., Danson, M., Raines, P. and Whittam, G. (2003) 'Confusing clusters: making sense of the cluster approach in theory and practice', *European Planning Studies* 11(5): 511–20.

Birkenshaw, J. (2000) 'Upgrading if industry clusters and foreign investment', *International Studies of Management & Organization* 30(2): 93–113.

Black, D. and Henderson, V. (1999) 'A theory of urban growth', *Journal of Political Economy* 107: 252–84.

Blair, J. (1995) *Local Economic Development: Analysis and Practice*, Thousand Oaks, Calif.: Sage.

Boeker, W. (1997) 'Executive migration and strategic change: the effect of top manager movement on product-market entry', *Administrative Science Quarterly* 42: 213–36.

Brakman, S., Garretsen, H. and van Marrewijk, C. (2001) *An Introduction to Geographical Economics*, Cambridge: Cambridge University Press.

Braunerhjelm, P. and Johansson, D. (2003) 'The determinants of spatial concentration: the manufacturing and service sectors in an international perspective', *Industry and Innovation* 10(1): 41–63.

Braunerhjelm, P., Faini, R., Norman, V., Ruane, F. and Seabright, P. (2000) 'Integration and the regions of Europe: how the right policies can prevent polarization', Monitoring European Integration 10, London: Centre for Economic Policy Research.

Bresnahan, T., Gambardella, A. and Saxenian, A. (2001) '"Old economy" inputs for "new economy" outcomes: cluster formation in the new Silicon Valleys', *Industrial and Corporate Change* 10(4): 835–60.

Brusco, S., Cainelli, G., Forni, F., Franchi, M., Malusardi, A. and Righetti, R. (1996) 'The evolution of industrial districts in Emilia-Romagna', in F. Cossentino, F. Pyke and W. Sengenberger (eds) *Local and Regional Response to Global Pressure: The Case of Italy and its Industrial Districts*, Geneva: International Institute for Labour Studies.

Buck, N., Drennan, M and Newton, K. (1992) 'Dynamics of the metropolitan economy', in S. Fainstein, I. Gordon and M. Harloe (eds) *Divided Cities: New York and London in the Contemporary World*, Cambridge, Mass.: Blackwell.

Bull, A. C., Pitt, M. and Szarka, J. (1991) 'Small firms and industrial districts, structural explanations of small firm viability in three countries', *Entrepreneurship and Regional Development* 3: 83–99.

Burger, K., Kameo, D. and Sandee, H. (2000) 'Clustering of small-scale enterprises. An analysis with special reference to agro-processing in Central Java, Indonesia', unpublished paper, FEWEB, Vrije Universiteit, Amsterdam.

Burke, R. (2002) 'Organizational transitions', in C. Cooper and R. Burke (eds) *The New World of Work – Challenges and Opportunities*, Oxford: Blackwell.

Burroni, L. and Trigilia, C. (2001) 'Italy: economic development through local economies', in C. Crouch, P. Le Galés, C. Trogilia and H. Voelzkow (eds) *Local Production Systems in Europe: Rise or Demise?*, Oxford: Oxford University Press.

Cappelli, P. (1999) *The New Deal at Work: Managing the Market Driven Workforce*, Boston: Harvard Business School Press.

Carnevali, F. (2003) '"Malefactors and honourable men": the making of commercial honesty in nineteenth-century industrial Birmingham', in J. Wilson and A.

Popp (eds) *Industrial Clusters and Regional Business Networks in England, 1750–1970*, Aldershot: Ashgate.

Casella, A. (1993) 'Discussion', in F. Torres and F. Giavzzi (eds) *Adjustment and Growth in the European Monetary Union*, Cambridge: Cambridge University Press.

Chang, H.-J., Palma, G. and Whittaker, D. H. (eds) (2001) *Financial Liberalization and the Asian Crisis*, Basingstoke: Palgrave.

Chaston, I. (1996) 'Critical events and process gaps in the Danish Technological Institute SME structured networking model', *International Small Business Journal* 14(3): 71–84.

Checkland, S. G. (1981) *The Upas Tree: Glasgow 1875–1975: A Study in Growth and Contraction*, Glasgow: University of Glasgow Press.

Chia, L. S. (ed.) (2003) *Southeast Asia Transformed*, Singapore: Institute of Southeast Asian Studies.

Chon, S. (1997) 'Destroying the myth of vertical integration in the Japanese electronics industry: restructuring in the semiconductor manufacturing equipment industry', *Regional Studies* 31(1): 25–39.

Christensen, C. (1997) *The Innovator's Dilemma*, Boston: Harvard Business School Press.

Cingano, F. (2003) 'Returns to specific skills in industrial districts', *Labour Economics* 10: 149–64.

Cluster Navigators (2001) *Cluster Building: A Toolkit*, Wellington: Industry New Zealand.

Coe, D. and Helpman, E. (1995) 'International R&D spillovers', *European Economic Review* 39: 859–87.

Coe, N. (2001) 'A hyrid agglomeration? The development of a satellite-Marshallian industrial district in Vancouver's film industry', *Urban Studies* 38(10): 1753–75.

Cohen, S. and Fields, G. (1999) 'Social capital and capital gains, or virtual bowling in Silicon Valley: an examination of social capital in Silicon Valley', Working Paper, Berkeley, Calif.: Berkeley Round Table on the International Economy, University of California.

Cole, W. (1998) 'Bali's garment export industry', in H. Hill and K. W. Thee (eds) *Indonesia's Technological Challenge*, Singapore: Institute of Southeast Asian Studies.

Combes, P.-P. and Duranton, G. (2001) 'Labour pooling, labour poaching, and spatial clustering', Centre for Economic Performance Discussion Paper 510, London: London School of Economics and Political Science.

Cooke, P. (2001) 'Biotechnology clusters in the U.K.: lessons from localisation in the commercialisation of science', *Small Business Economics* 17: 43–59.

Cooper, C. and Burke, R. (eds) (2002) *The New World of Work – Challenges and Opportunities*, Oxford: Blackwell.

Cooper, M. (2000) 'Being the "go-to guy": fatherhood, masculinity, and the organization of work in Silicon Valley', *Qualitative Sociology* 23(4): 379–405.

Cossentino, F., Pyke, F. and Sengenberger, W. (eds) (1996) *Local and Regional Response to Global Pressure: The Case of Italy and its Industrial Districts*, Geneva: International Institute for Labour Studies.

Crang, P. and Martin, R. (1991) 'Mrs Thatcher's vision of the "new Britain" and the other sides of the "Cambridge phenomenon"', *Environment and Planning D: Society and Space* 9: 91–116.

Crewe, L. and Davenport, E. (1992) 'The puppet show: changing buyer–supplier relationships within clothing industry', *Transactions of the Institute of British Geographers* 17(2): 183–97.

Crouch, C. and Farrell, H. (2001) 'Great Britain: falling through the holes in the network concept', in C. Crouch, P. Le Galés, C. Trogilia and H. Voelzkow (eds) *Local Production Systems in Europe: Rise or Demise?*, Oxford: Oxford University Press.

Cunha, R. C. (2002) 'Privatisation and outsourcing', in C. Cooper and R. Burke (eds) *The New World of Work – Challenges and Opportunities*, Oxford: Blackwell.

Dale, B. (2002) 'Self-assessment models and quality/excellence awards', in C. Cooper and R. Burke (eds) *The New World of Work – Challenges and Opportunities*, Oxford: Blackwell.

Daly, P. (1985) *The Biotechnology Business: A Strategic Analysis*, London: Pinter.

Dalziel, P. and Lattimore, R. (1996) *The New Zealand Macroeconomy: A Briefing on the Reforms*, Melbourne: Oxford University Press.

Davis, D. and Weinstein, D. (1996) 'Does economic geography matter for international specialization?', National Bureau of Economic Research Working Paper 5706, Cambridge, Mass.: NBER.

—— (1998) Market Access, Economic Geography and Comparative Advantage: An Empirical Assessment, National Bureau of Economic Research Working Paper 6787, Cambridge, Mass: NBER.

—— (1999) 'Economic geography and regional production structure: an empirical investigation', *European Economic Review* 43: 379–407.

Dean, J. and Snell, S. (1991) 'Integrated manufacturing and job design: moderating effects of organizational inertia', *Academy of Management Journal* 34(4): 774–804.

Dedoussis, V. and Littler, C. (1994) 'Understanding the transfer of Japanese management practices: the Australian case', in T. Elger and C. Smith (eds) *Global Japanization? The Transnational Transformation of the Labour Process*, London: Routledge.

Dei Ottati, G. (1994) 'Trust, interlinking transactions and credit in the industrial district', *Cambridge Journal of Economics* 18(6): 529–46.

Department of Trade and Industry (2001) *Business Clusters in the UK – A First Assessment*, London: Department of Trade and Industry.

Dewhurst, J. and McCann, P. (2002) 'A comparison of measures of industrial specialization for travel-to-work areas in Great Britain, 1981–1997', *Regional Studies* 36(5): 541–51.

Dicken, P. (1998) *Global Shift: Transforming the World Economy*, 4th edn, Guildford: Paul Chapman.

—— (2000) 'Places and flows: situating international investment', in G. Clark, M. Feldman and M. Gertler (eds) *The Oxford Handbook of Economic Geography*, Oxford: Oxford University Press.

Djelic, M.-L. (1998) *Exporting the American Model: The Postwar Transformation of European Business*, Oxford: Oxford University Press.

Donaghu, M. and Barff, R. (1990) 'Nike just did it: international subcontracting and flexibility in athletic footwear production', *Regional Studies* 24(6): 537–52.

Dosi, G. (1984) *Technical Change and Industrial Transformation*, London: Macmillan.

Dumais, G., Ellison, G. and Glaeser, E. (1997) 'Geographic concentration as a dynamic process', National Bureau of Economic Research Working Paper 6270, Cambridge, Mass.: NBER.

Dunning, J. (1993) 'Internationalizing Porter's diamond', *Management International Review* 33(2): 7–15.

Duranton, G. and Puga, D. (2002) 'Diversity and specialization in cities: why, where and when does it matter?', in P. McCann (ed.) *Industrial Location Economics*, Cheltenham: Edward Elgar.

Dyer, G. and Merchant, K. (2003) 'The birth of a biotech cluster', *Financial Times*, 14 August.

Eaton, B. and Kortum, S. (1996) 'Trade in ideas: patenting and productivity in the OECD', *Journal of International Economics* 40(3/4): 251–78.

Ecotech Research and Consulting (2004) *A Practical Guide to Cluster Development*, London: Department of Trade and Industry.

Edgington, D (1997) 'Flexibility and corporate organization in Chukyo, Japan: a study of five industries', *Regional Development Studies* 3(Winter): 83–108.

Elger, T. and Smith, C. (1994) 'Global Japanization? Convergence and competition in the organization of the labour process', in T. Elger and C. Smith (eds) *Global Japanization? The Transnational Transformation of the Labour Process*, London: Routledge.

Ellison, G. and Glaeser, E. (1997) 'Geographical concentration in US manufacturing industries: a dartboard approach', *Journal of Political Economy* 105: 889–927.

Enright, M. (1996) 'Regional clusters and economic development: a research agenda', in N. Schaefer and B. Sharma (eds) *Business Networks: Prospects for Regional Development*, Berlin: Walter de Gruyter.

—— (1999) 'The globalization of competition and the localization of competitive advantage: policies toward regional clustering', in N. Hood and S. Young (eds) *The Globalization of Multinational Enterprise Activity and Economic Development*, London: Macmillan.

EU Expert Group on Enterprise Clusters and Networks (2003) *Final Report of the Expert Group on Enterprise Clusters and Networks*, Brussels: Enterprise Directorate General, European Commission.

Feldman, M. and Audretsch, D. (1999) 'Innovation in cities: science-based diversity, specialization and localized competition', *European Economic Review* 43: 409–29.

Feser, E. and Bergman, E. (2000) 'National industry cluster templates: a framework for regional cluster analysis', *Regional Studies* 34(1): 1–20.

Feser, E. and Luger, M. (2003) 'Cluster analysis as a mode of inquiry: its use in science and technology policymaking in North Carolina', *European Planning Studies* 11(1): 11–24.

Ffowcs Williams, I. (1996) 'New Zealand: The internationalisation of competition and the emergence of networks', in *Networks of Enterprises and Local Development*, Paris: Organization for Economic Cooperation and Development.

Florida, R. and Kenney, M. (1990) 'High technology restructuring in the USA and Japan', *Environment and Planning A* 22(2): 233–52.

Foord, J., Bowlby, S. and Tillsley, C. (1996) 'The changing place of retailer–supplier relations in British retailing', in N. Wrigley and M. Lowe (eds) *Retailing, Consumption and Capital: Towards a New Retail Geography*, London: UCL Press.

Fothergill, S. and Gudgin, G. (1982) *Unequal Growth*, London: Heinemann.

Fothergill, S., Kitson, S. and Monk, S. (1985) 'Rural industrialization: trends and causes', in M. Healey and B. Ilberry (eds) *Industrialization of the Countryside*, Norwich: Geo Books.

Freeman, C. (1982) *The Economics of Innovation*, 2nd edn, London: Pinter.

Fujita, M. and Krugman, P. (1995) 'When is the economy monocentric? Von Thünen and Chamberlin unified', *Regional Science and Urban Economics* 25: 505–28.

Fujita, M. and Thisse, J.-F. (2000) 'The formation of economic agglomerations: old problems and new perspectives', in J.-M. Huriot and J.-F. Thisse (eds) *Economics of Cities*, Cambridge: Cambridge University Press.

Fujita, M., Krugman, P. and Mori, T. (1999) 'On the evolution of hierarchical urban systems', *European Economic Review* 43: 209–51.

Fujita, M., Krugman, P. and Venables, A. (1999) *The Spatial Economy*, Cambridge, Mass.: MIT Press.

Fukuyama, F. (1995) *Trust: The Social Virtues and the Creation of Prosperity*, London: Hamish Hamilton.

Gambetta, D. (ed.) (1988) *Trust: Making and Breaking Cooperative Relations*, New York: Blackwell.

Gereffi, G. (1994) 'The international economy and economic development', in N. Smelser and R. Swedberg (eds) *The Handbook of Economic Sociology*, Princeton, NJ: Princeton University Press.

Gertler, M. (2003) 'Tacit knowledge and the economic geography of context, or the undefinable tacitnesss of being (there)', *Journal of Economic Geography* 3: 75–99.

Giddens, A. (1990) *The Consequences of Modernity*, Stanford, Calif.: Stanford University Press.

Glaeser, E. (1998) 'Are cities dying?' *Journal of Economic Perspectives* 12(2): 139–60.

—— (2000) 'The new economics of urban and regional growth', in G. Clark, M. Feldman and M. Gertler (eds) *The Oxford Handbook of Economic Geography*, Oxford: Oxford University Press.

Glaeser, E., Kallal, H., Scheinkman, J. and Schleifer, A. (1992) 'Growth in cities', *Journal of Political Economy* 100(6): 1126–52.

Glasmeier, A. (1999) 'Territory-based regional development policy and planning in a learning economy: the case of "real service centres" in industrial districts', *European Urban and Regional Studies* 6(1): 48–68.

—— (2000) 'Local economic development policy', in G. Clark, M. Feldman and M. Gertler (eds) *The Oxford Handbook of Economic Geography*, Oxford: Oxford University Press.

Glassman, U. and Voelzkow, H. (2001) 'The governance of local economies in Germany' in C. Crouch, P. Le Galés, C. Trogilia and H. Voelzkow (eds) *Local Production Systems in Europe: Rise or Demise?*, Oxford: Oxford University Press.

Gordon, I. and McCann, P. (2000) 'Industrial clusters: complexes, agglomeration and/or social networks', *Urban Studies* 37(3): 513–32.

Gottardi, G. (1996) 'Technology strategies, innovation without R&D and the creation of knowledge within industrial districts', *Journal of Industry Studies* 3(2): 119–34.

Grabher, G. (1993) 'The weakness of strong ties: the lock-in of regional development in the Ruhr area', in G. Grabher (ed.) *The Embedded Firm: On the Socioeconomics of Industrial Networks*, London: Routledge.

Grabher, G. and Stark, D. (1997) 'Organizing diversity: evolutionary theory, network analysis and post-socialism', in G. Grabher and D. Stark (eds) *Restructur-*

ing Networks in Post-Socialism: Legacies, Linkages and Localities, Oxford: Oxford University Press.

Granovetter, M. (1985) 'Economic action and social structure: the problem of embeddedness', *American Journal of Sociology* 91(3): 481–510.

—— (1992) 'Problems of explanation in economic sociology', in N. Nohria and R. Eccles (eds) *Networks and Organizations: Structure, Form and Action*, Boston: Harvard Business School Press.

Gudgin, G. (1978) *Industrial Location Processes and Regional Development*, Farnborough: Saxon House.

Hallencreutz, D. and Lundequist, P. (2001) *Innovative Clusters in Sweden*, Stockholm: NUTEK.

—— (2003) 'Spatial clustering and the potential for policy practice: experience from cluster building in Sweden', *European Planning Studies* 11(5): 533–47.

Hallet, M. (2000) 'Regional specialization and concentration in the EU', Economic Papers 141, Brussels: European Commission.

Hamel, G. and Prahalad, C. (1994) *Competing for the Future*, Boston: Harvard Business School Press.

Hamilton, G. and Biggart, N. (1988) 'Market, culture and authority: a comparative analysis of management and organization in the Far East', *American Journal of Sociology* 94 (supplement): S52–S94.

Hanson, G. (2000) 'Firms, workers, and the geographic concentration of economic activity', in G. Clark, M. Feldman and M. Gertler (eds) *The Oxford Handbook of Economic Geography*, Oxford: Oxford University Press.

Harrison, B. (1992) 'Industrial districts: old wine in new bottles', *Regional Studies* 26(5): 469–83.

Hayter, R. (1997) *Industrial Location: The Factory, the Firm and the Production System*, Chichester: John Wiley & Sons.

Hayward, D. (1996) 'Industrial concentration and industry strategy', in R. Le Heron and E. Pawson (eds) *Changing Places: New Zealand in the Nineties*, Auckland: Longman Paul.

Henderson, V. (1974) 'The sizes and types of cities', *American Economic Review* 64(4): 640–56.

—— (1988) *Urban Development: Theory, Fact and Illusion*, Oxford: Oxford University Press.

—— (1997) 'Externalities and industrial development', *Journal of Urban Economics* 42(3): 449–70.

—— (1999) 'Marshall's economies', National Bureau of Economic Research Working Paper 7358, Cambridge, Mass.: NBER.

—— (2001) 'Marshall's scale economies', mimeo., Providence, RI: Brown University.

Henderson, V., Kuncoro, A. and Turner, M. (1995) 'Industrial development and cities', *Journal of Political Economy* 103: 1067–85.

Hendry, C., Brown, J. and Defillip, R. (2000) 'Regional clustering of high technology-based firms: opto-electronics in three countries', *Regional Studies* 34(2): 129–44.

Hendry, C., Brown, J., Defillip, R. and Hassink, R. (1999) 'Industry clusters as commercial, knowledge and institutional networks: opto-electronics in six regions in the UK, USA and Germany', in A. Grandori (ed.) *Interform Networks: Organization and Industrial Competitiveness*, London: Routledge.

Henriksen, L. B. (1995) 'Formal cooperation among firms in networks: the case of Danish joint ventures and strategic alliances', *European Planning Studies* 3(2): 254–60.

Hill, H. (2002) 'Old policy challenges for a new administration: SMEs in Indonesia', in C. Harvie and B.-C. Lee (eds) *The Role of SMEs in National Economies in East Asia*, Cheltenham: Edward Elgar.

Hirst, P. and Thompson, G. (1996) *Globalization in Question*, Cambridge: Polity Press.

Hobday, M. (1995) *Innovation in East Asia: The Challenge to Japan*, Cheltenham: Edward Elgar.

Holmann, D. and Wood, S. (2003) 'The new workplace: an introduction', in D. Holman, T. Wall, C. Clegg, P. Sparrow and A. Howard (eds) *The New Workplace: A Guide to the Human Impact of Modern Working Practices*, Chichester: John Wiley & Sons.

Holmes, T. and Stevens, J. (2002) 'Geographic concentration and establishment scale', *Review of Economics and Statistics* 84(4): 682–90.

Hoover, E. (1937) *Location Theory and the Shoe and Leather Industry*, Cambridge Mass.: Harvard University Press.

—— (1948) *The Location of Economic Activity*, New York: McGraw Hill.

Hudson, R. (1999) 'The learning economy, the learning firm and the learning region: a sympathetic critique of the limits of learning', *European Urban and Regional Studies* 6(1): 59–72.

Huggins, R. (1996) 'Technology policy, networks and small firms in Denmark', *Regional Studies* 30(5): 523–52.

Humphrey, J. and Schmitz, H. (1995) 'Principles for promoting clusters and networks of SMEs', Small and Medium Enterprises Programme Discussion Paper 1, Vienna: UNIDO.

—— (2002) 'How does insertion in global value chains affect upgrading in industrial clusters?', *Regional Studies* 36(9): 1017–27.

Ingley, C. and Selvarajah, C. (2000) 'Business cluster development and performance', in R. Edwards, C. Nyland and M. Coulthard (eds) *Readings in International Business: An Asia Pacific Perspective*, Frenchs Forest: Pearson Education Australia.

Irwin, D. (2003) 'The challenge to learn and share', *Agenda for Local Economic Development* 60(October): 3–4.

Isaksen, A. and Hauge, E. (2002) *Regional Clusters in Europe*, Observatory of European SMEs 3, Luxembourg: Office for Official Publications of the European Communities.

ISTAT (2003) *Quarterly Labour Force Survey October 2003*, Rome: National Institute of Statistics.

Izushi, H. (1997) 'Conflict between two industrial networks: technological adaptation and inter-firm relationships in the ceramics industry in Seto, Japan', *Regional Studies* 31(2): 117–29.

Jacobs, J. (1961) *The Death and Life of Great American Cities*, New York: Random House.

—— (1969) *The Economy of Cities*, New York: Random House.

Jaffe, A. and Trajtenberg, M. (1996) 'Flows of knowledge from universities and federal labs: modeling the flows of patent citations over time and across institutional and geographic boundaries', National Bureau of Economic Research Working Paper 5712, Cambridge, Mass.: NBER.

Jaffe, A., Trajtenberg, M. and Henderson, R. (1993) 'Geographic localization of knowledge spillovers as evidenced by patent citations', *Quarterly Journal of Economics* 108: 577–98.

Kelley, M. and Helper, S. (1999) 'Firm size and capabilities, regional agglomeration, and the adoption of new technology', *Economics of Innovation and New Technology* 8: 79–103.

Kenney, M. and Florida, R. (1993) *Beyond Mass Production*, New York: Oxford University Press.

—— (2000) 'Introduction', in M. Kenney (ed.) *Understanding Silicon Valley: The Anatomy of an Entrepreneurial Region*, Stanford, Calif.: Stanford University Press.

Kim, S. (1995) 'Expansion of markets and the geographic distribution of economic activities: the trends in US regional manufacturing structure, 1860–1987', *Quarterly Journal of Economics* 110: 881–908.

Knorringa, P. (1996) *Economics of Collaboration: Indian Shoemakers Between Markets and Hierarchy*, New Delhi: Sage.

Kotval, Z. and Mullin, J. (1998) 'The potential for planning an industrial cluster in Barre, Vermont: a case of 'hard rock' resistance in the granite industry', *Planning Practice & Research* 13(3): 311–18.

Krugman, P. (1980) ' Scale economies, product differentiation and the pattern of trade', *Journal of International Economics* 9: 469–79.

—— (1991a) *Geography and Trade*, Cambridge, Mass.: MIT Press.

—— (1991b) 'Increasing returns and economic geography', *Journal of Political Economy* 99: 483–99.

—— (1993a) 'On the number and location of cities', *European Economic Review* 37: 293–8.

—— (1993b) 'Lessons of Massachusetts for EMU', in F. Torres and F. Giavzzi (eds) *Adjustment and Growth in the European Monetary Union*, Cambridge: Cambridge University Press.

—— (1998) 'What's new about the new economic geography?', *Oxford Review of Economic Policy* 14(2): 7–17.

—— (2000) 'Where in the world is the "new economic geography"?', in G. Clark, M. Feldman and M. Gertler (eds) *The Oxford Handbook of Economic Geography*, Oxford: Oxford University Press.

Krugman, P. and Venables, A. (1990) 'Integration and the competitiveness of peripheral industry', in C. Bliss and J. Braga de Macedo (eds) *Unity with Diversity in the European Economy*, Cambridge: Cambridge University Press.

Lagendijk, A. (1999) 'Learning in non-core regions: towards intelligent clusters addressing business and regional needs', in R. Rutten, S. Bakkers, K. Morgan and F. Boekem (eds) *Learning Regions: Theory, Policy and Practice*, Cheltenham: Edward Elgar.

Lamming, R. (1993) *Beyond Partnership: Strategies for Innovation and Lean Supply*, London: Prentice Hall.

Leamer, E. and Storper, M. (2001) 'The economic geography of the internet age', National Bureau of Economic Research Working Paper 8450, Cambridge, Mass.: NBER.

Lever-Tracy, C. (1992) 'Interpersonal trust in ethnic business – traditional, modern or postmodern?' *Policy Organisation and Society* 5(Winter): 50–63.

Levy, B. and Kuo, W-J. (1991) 'The strategic orientation of firms and the performance of Korea and Taiwan in frontier industries: lessons from comparative case studies of keyboard and personal computer assembly', *World Development* 19: 363–74.

Liedholm, C. and Mead, D. (1999) *Small Enterprise and Economic Development. The Dynamics of Micro and Small Enterprises*, London: Routledge.

Lloyd, P. and Dicken, P. (1977) *Location in Space: A Theoretical Approach to Economic Geography*, 2nd edn, London: Harper and Row.

Longhi, C. (1999) 'Networks, collective learning and technology development in innovative high technology regions: the case of Sophia-Antipolis', *Regional Studies* 33(4): 333–42.

Lorentzen, M. and Mahnke, V. (2002) 'Global strategy and the acquisition of local knowledge: how MNCs enter regional knowledge clusters', Working Paper 02-08, University of Aalborg: Danish Research Unit for Industrial Dynamics.

Lorenz, E. H. (1988) 'Neither friends nor strangers: informal networks of subcontractors in French engineering', in D. Gambetta (ed.) *Trust: Making and Breaking Cooperative Relations*, New York: Blackwell.

Luhmann, N. (1988) 'Familiarity, confidence, trust: problems and alternatives', in D. Gambetta (ed.) *Trust: Making and Breaking Cooperative Relations*, New York: Blackwell.

Lundvall, B.-Å. and Johnson, B. (1994) 'The learning economy', *Journal of Industry Studies* 1: 23–42.

—— (eds) (1992) *National Systems of Innovation*, London: Frances Pinter.

Macaulay, S. (1963) 'Non-contractual relations in business: a preliminary study', *American Sociological Review* 28(1): 55–67.

Mackie, J. (1992) 'Overseas Chinese entrepreneurship', *Asian-Pacific Economic Literature* 6(1): 41–64.

Malecki, E. and Tootle, D. (1996) 'The role of networks in small firm competitiveness', *International Journal of Technology Management* 11(1/2): 43–57.

Malmberg, A. and Maskell, P. (2002) 'The elusive concept of localization economies: towards a knowledge-based theory of spatial clustering', *Environment and Planning A* 34: 429–49.

Malmberg, A., Malmberg, B. and Lundequist, P. (2000) 'Agglomeration and firm performance: economies of scale, localisation, and urbanisation among Swedish export firms', *Environment and Planning A* 32: 305–21.

Markusen, A. (1996) 'Sticky places in slippery space: a typology of industrial districts', *Economic Geography* 72(3): 293–313.

Marshall, A. (1890) *Principles of Economics*, 1st edn, London: Macmillan and Co.

—— (1923) *Industry and Trade*, 4th edn, London: Macmillan and Co.

—— (1927) *Principles of Economics*, 8th edn, London: Macmillan and Co.

Martin, P. (2001) 'The limits of outsourcing', *Financial Times*, 25 September.

Martin, R. (1999) 'The new "geographical turn" in economics: some critical reflections', *Cambridge Journal of Economics* 23: 51–81.

Martin, R. and Sunley, P. (1996) 'Paul Krugman's geographical economics and its implications for regional development theory: a critical assessment', *Economic Geography* 72: 259–92.

—— (2003) 'Deconstructing clusters: chaotic concept or policy panacea?', *Journal of Economic Geography* 3: 5–35.

Martin, R. and Tyler, P. (2000) 'Regional employment evolutions in the European Union: a preliminary analysis', *Regional Studies* 34: 601–16.

Maskell, P (1998) 'Learning in the village economy of Denmark: the role of institutions and policy in sustaining competitiveness', in H.-J. Braczyk, P. Cooke and M. Heidenreich (eds) *Regional Innovation Systems*, London: UCL Press.

Maskell, P., Eskelin, H., Hannibalsson, I., Malmberg, A. and Vatne, E. (1998) *Competitiveness Localised Learning and Regional Development*, London: Routledge.

Massey, D., Quintas, P. and Weild, D. (1992) *High Tech Fantasies: Science Parks in Society*, London: Routledge.

Mathews, J. and Cho, D.-S. (2000) *Tiger Technology: The Creation of a Semiconductor Industry in East Asia*, Cambridge: Cambridge University Press.

Maurel, F. and Sedillot, B. (1999) 'A measure of the geographic concentration in French manufacturing industries', *Regional Science and Urban Economics* 29(5): 575–604.

May, W., Mason, C. and Pinch, S. (2001) 'Explaining industrial agglomeration: the case of the British high-fidelity industry', *Geoforum* 32(3): 363–76.

McCann, P. (1997) 'How deeply embedded is Silicon Glen? A cautionary note', *Regional Studies* 31(7): 695–703.

—— (1998) *The Economics of Industrial Location: A Logistics-Costs Approach*, Heidelberg: Springer.

—— (2001) *Urban and Regional Economics*, Oxford: Oxford University Press.

McCormick, D. (1999) 'African enterprise clusters and industrialization: theory and reality', *World Development* 27: 1531–51.

McGrath, M. and Hoole, R. (1992) 'Manufacturing's new economies of scale', *Harvard Business Review* May–June: 94–102.

Micklethwait, J. and Wooldridge, A. (1997) *The Witch Doctors*, London: Mandarin.

Miles, R. and Snow, C. (1992) 'Causes of failure in network organizations', *California Management Review* 34(4): 53–72.

Mitullah, W. (1999) Lake Victoria's Nile Perch industry: institutions, politics and joint action', Institute of Developing Studies Working Paper 87, Brighton: University of Sussex.

Mogridge, M. and Parr, J. (1997) 'Metropolis or region: on the structure and development of London', *Regional Studies* 31: 97–115.

Morgan, K. (1997) 'The learning region: institutions, innovation and regional renewal', *Regional Studies* 31(5): 491–503.

Moulaert, F. and Djellal, F. (1995) 'Information technology consulting firms: economies of agglomeration from a wide area perspective', *Urban Studies* 32: 105–22.

Nadvi, K. (1999) 'Collective efficiency and collective failure: the response of the Sialkot surgical instrument cluster to global quality pressures', *World Development* 27: 1605–26.

Neary, J. (2001) 'Of hypes and hyperbolas: introducing the new economic geography', *Journal of Economic Literature* XXXIX: 536–51.

Newlands, D. (2003) 'Competition and cooperation in industrial clusters: the implications for public policy', *European Planning Studies* 11(5): 521–32.

Numazaki, I. (1993) 'Tainanbang: the rise and growth of a banana-bunch-shaped business group in Taiwan', *The Developing Economies* XXXI(4): 485–510.

Nuti, F. and Cainelli, G. (1996) 'Changing directions in Italy's manufacturing industrial districts: the case of the Emilian footwear districts of Fusignano and San Mauro Pascoli', *Journal of Industry Studies* 3(2): 105–18.

Oakey, R. (1995) *High Technology Small Firms: Innovation and Regional Development in Britain and the United States*, London: Pinter.

Oakey, R., Faulkner, W., Cooper, S. and Walsh, V. (1990) *New Firms in the Biotechnology Industry: Their Contribution to Innovation and Growth*, London: Pinter.

Oakey, R., Kipling, M. and Wildgust, S. (2001) 'Clustering among firms in the non-broadcast visual communications (NBVC) sector', *Regional Studies* 35(5): 401–14.

OECD (2000) *OECD Employment Outlook 2000*, Paris: OECD.

Ohlin, B. (1933) *Interregional and Internal Trade*, Cambridge Mass.: Harvard University Press.

O'Malley, E. and van Egeraat, C. (2000) 'Industry clusters and Irish indigenous manufacturing: limits of the Porter view', *Economic and Social Review* 31(4): 55–80.

OTA (Office of Technology Assessment) (1984) *Commercial Biotechnology: An International Analysis*, Washington, DC: Government Printing Office.

Ottaviano, G. and Puga, D. (1997) 'Agglomeration in the global economy: a survey of the "New Economic Geography"', Centre for Economic Performance Discussion Paper 356, London: London School of Economics and Political Science.

Paija, L. (2001) 'The ICT cluster: the engine of knowledge-driven growth in Finland', in P. den Hertog, E. Bergman and D. Charles (eds) *Innovative Clusters: Drivers of National Innovation Systems*, Paris: OECD.

Pakes, A. and Griliches, Z. (1984) 'Patents and R&D at the firm level: a first look', in Z. Griliches (ed.) *R&D, Patents and Productivity*, Chicago: Chicago University Press.

Panditharatna, A. and Phelps, N. (1995) 'A new industry in an older industrial region: skills, technology and linkages', *Local Economy* 9(4): 341–53.

Paniccia, I. (2002) *Industrial Districts Evolution and Competitiveness in Italian Firms*, Cheltenham: Edward Elgar.

Park, S. O. (1996) 'Networks and embeddedness in the dynamic types of new industrial districts', *Progress in Human Geography* 20: 81–104.

Parr, J. (2002a) 'Agglomeration economies: ambiguities and confusions', *Environment and Planning A* 34: 717–31.

—— (2002b) 'The location of economic activity: central place theory and the wider urban system', in P. McCann (ed.) *Industrial Location Economics*, Cheltenham: Edward Elgar.

Peck, J. (2000) 'Doing regulation', in G. Clark, M. Feldman and M. Gertler (eds) *The Oxford Handbook of Economic Geography*, Oxford: Oxford University Press.

Pedersen, P. (1997) 'Clusters of enterprises within systems of production and distribution: collective efficiency and transaction costs', in M. P. van Dijk and R. Rabellotti (eds) *Enterprise Clusters and Networks in Developing Countries*, London: Frank Cass.

Perry, M. (1995) 'Industry structures, networks and joint action groups', *Regional Studies* 29(3): 208–17.

—— (1999) *Small Firms and Network Economies*, London: Routledge.

—— (2001) *Shared Trust Strategies for Small Industrial Countries*, Wellington: Institute of Policy Studies, Victoria University of Wellington.

—— (2003) 'Bank Rakyat Indonesia', *Agenda for Local Economic Development* 52(February): 9–10.

—— (2004a) 'Earthquake Engineering New Zealand', *Agenda for Local Economic Development* 66(April): 9–10.

—— (2004b) 'Softopia, Japan', *Agenda for Local Economic Development* 67(May): 9–10.

—— (2004c) 'Creative Capital, New Zealand', *Agenda for Local Economic Development* 68(June): 9–10.

Perry, M. and Newell, J. (2004) 'Regional labour markets' in P. Spoonley, A. Dupuis and A. de Bruin (eds) *Work & Working in Twenty-First Century New Zealand*, Palmerston North: Dunmore Press.

Perry, M. and Tan B. H. (1998) 'Global manufacturing and local linkage in Singapore', *Environment and Planning A* 30: 1603–24.

—— (2000) 'Subcontracting for transnationals: buyer–supplier interaction in Singapore's electronics cluster', *Journal of Asian Business* 16(3): 27–50.

Peschel, K. (1982) 'International trade, integration and industrial location', *Regional Science and Urban Economics* 12: 247–69.

Peters, E. and Hood, N. (2000) 'Implementing the cluster approach', *International Studies of Management & Organization* 30(2): 68–92.

Phelps, N. (1993) 'Contemporary industrial restructuring and linkage change in an older industrial region: examples from the northeast of England', *Environment and Planning A* 25: 863–82.

—— (1996) 'Collaborative buyer–supplier relations and the formation of centralised networks', *Geoforum* 27(3): 393–407.

Pinch, S. and Henry, N. (1999) 'Paul Krugman's geographical economics, industrial clustering and the British motor sport industry', *Regional Studies* 33(9): 815–27.

Pinch, S., Henry, N., Jenkins, M. and Tallman, S. (2003) 'From "industrial districts" to "knowledge clusters": a model of knowledge dissemination and competitive advantage in industrial agglomerations', *Journal of Economic Geography* 3: 373–88.

Poot, H., Kuyvenhoven, A. and Jansen, J. (1990) *Industrialization and Trade in Indonesia*, Yogyakarta: Gadjah Mada University Press.

Porter, M. (1990) *The Competitive Advantage of Nations*, New York: Free Press.

—— (1998) 'Clusters and the new economics of competition', *Harvard Business Review* 76(6): 77–90.

—— (2000) 'Locations, clusters and company strategy', in G. Clark, M. Feldman and M. Gertler (eds) *The Oxford Handbook of Economic Geography*, Oxford: Oxford University Press.

—— (2003) 'The economic performance of regions', *Regional Studies* 37(6–7): 549–78.

Prevezer, M. (1998) 'Clustering in biotechnology in the USA', in G. Swann, M. Prevezer and D. Stout (eds) *The Dynamics of Industrial Clustering: International Comparisons in Computing and Biotechnology*, Oxford: Oxford University Press.

Rabellotti, R. (1999) 'Recovery of a Mexican cluster: devaluation bonanza or collective efficiency?', *World development* 27: 1571–85.

Raines, P. (2002) *Cluster Development and Policy*, Aldershot: Ashgate.

Rao, H. and Drazin, R. (2002) 'Overcoming resource constraints on product innovation by recruiting talent from rivals: a study of the mutual fund industry, 1986–1994', *Academy of Management Journal* 45: 215–40.

Richardson, H. (1995) 'Economies and diseconomies of agglomeration', in H. Giersch (ed.) *Urban Agglomeration and Economic Growth*, Berlin: Springer.

Rimmer, P. (2003) 'The spatial impact of innovations in international sea and air transport since 1960', in L. S. Chia (ed.) *Southeast Asia Transformed: A Geography of Change*, Singapore: Institute of Southeast Asian Studies.

Robertson, P. and Langlois, R. (1995) 'Innovation, networks and vertical integration', *Research Policy* 24: 543–62.

Robins, F. (1998) 'Taiwan's economic success', in K. Sheridan (ed.) *Emerging Economic Systems in Asia*, St Leonards: Allen & Unwin.

Romer, P. (1986) 'Increasing returns and long run growth', *Journal of Political Economy* 94: 1002–37.

Rosenfeld, S. (2003) 'Expanding opportunities: cluster strategies that reach more people and more places', *European Planning Studies* 11(4): 359–77.

Rousseau, D., Sitkin, S., Burt, R. and Camerer, C. (1998) 'Not so different after all: a cross-discipline view of trust', *Academy of Management Review* 23(3): 393–404.

Sabel, C. (1992) 'Studied trust: building new forms of co-operation in a volatile economy', in F. Pyke and W. Sengenberger (eds) *Industrial Districts and Local Economic Regeneration*, Geneva: International Institute for Labour Studies.

—— (1994) 'Learning by monitoring: the institutions of economic development', in N. Smelser and R. Swedberg (eds) *The Handbook of Economic Sociology*, Princeton, NJ: Princeton University Press.

Sabel, C., Herrigel, G., Deeg, R. and Kazis, R. (1989) 'Regional prosperities compared: Massachusetts and Baden-Württemberg in the 1980s', *Economy and Society* 18: 374–404.

Sako, M. (1992) *Prices, Quality and Trust: Inter-firm Relations in Britain and Japan*, Cambridge: Cambridge University Press.

Sandee, H. (1998) 'Promoting small-scale and cottage industry clusters in Indonesia', *Small Enterprise Development* 9: 52–8.

—— (2002) 'SMEs in Southeast Asia: issues and constraints', in C. Harvie and B.-C. Lee (eds) *Globalisation and SMEs in East Asia*, Cheltenham: Edward Elgar.

Sandee, H. and Ibrahim, B. (2001) 'Evaluation of SME export promotion in Indonesia', SME Development Technical Assistance Background Report, Jakarta: Asian Development Bank.

Sandee, H. and ter Wengel, J. (2002) 'SME cluster development strategies in Indonesia', paper presented at JICA workshop on strengthening capacity of SME clusters in Indonesia, Jakarta, 5–6 March.

Sandee, H. and Weijland, H. (1989) 'Rural cottage industry in transition: the roof tile industry in Kabupaten Boyolali, Central Java', *Bulletin of Indonesian Economic Studies* 25: 79–98.

Sandee, H., Andadari, R. K., Sulandjari, S. (2000) 'Small firm development during good times and bad: the Jepara furniture industry', in C. Manning and P. van Dierman (eds) *Indonesia in Transition*, London: Zed Books.

Sato, Y. (2000) 'Linkage formation by small firms: the case of a rural cluster in Indonesia', *Bulletin of Indonesian Economic Studies* 36: 135–64.

Save the Children Fund (1997) *Stitching Football: Voices of Children*, London: Save the Children Fund.

Saxenian, A. (1994) *Regional Advantage: Culture and Competition in Silicon Valley and Route 128*, Cambridge, Mass.: Harvard University Press.

Sayer, A. and Walker, R. (1992) *The New Social Economy*, Oxford: Blackwell.

Schiller, J. and Martin-Schiller, B. (1997) 'Market, culture and state in the emergence of an Indonesian export furniture industry', *Journal of Asian Business* 13: 1–23.

Schmitz, H. (1995a) 'Collective efficiency: growth path for small-scale industry', *Journal of Development Studies* 31: 529–66.

—— (1995b) 'Small shoemakers and fordist giants: tale of a supercluster', *World Development* 23: 9–28.

—— (1997) 'Collective efficiency and increasing returns', Institute of Developing Studies Working Paper 50, Brighton: University of Sussex.

—— (1999) 'Global competition and local cooperation: success and failure in the Sinos Valley, Brazil', *World Development* 27: 1627–50.

Schmitz, H. and Nadvi, K. (1999) 'Clustering and industrialization: introduction', *World Development* 27: 1503–14.

Schonberger, R. (1986) *World Class Manufacturing: The Lessons of Simplicity Applied*, New York: Free Press.

Scitovsky, T. (1954) 'Two concepts of external economies', *Journal of Political Economy* 62: 143–51.

Scott, A. (1988) *New Industrial Spaces: Flexible Production, Organization and Regional Development in North America and Western Europe*, London: Pion.

Scott, A. and Storper, M. (1992) 'Industrialization and regional development', in M. Storper and A. Scott (eds) *Pathways to Industrialization and Regional Development*, London: Routledge.

Sforzi, F. (1990) 'The quantitative importance of Marshallian industrial districts in the Italian economy', in F. Pyke, G. Becattini and W. Sengenberger (eds) *Industrial Districts and Inter-Firm Co-operation in Italy*, Geneva: International Institute for Labour Studies.

Shapiro, S. (1987) 'The social control of impersonal trust', *American Journal of Sociology* 93(3): 623–58.

Sharp, M. (1990) 'European countries in science-based competition: the case of biotechnology', in D. Hague (ed.) *The Management of Science*, Basingstoke: Macmillan.

—— (1999) 'The science of nations: European multinationals and American biotechnology', *Biotechnology* 1(1): 132–62.

Silverstone, B., Bollard, A. and Lattimore, R. (eds) (1996) *A Study of Economic Reform: The Case of New Zealand*, Amsterdam: Elsevier.

Sölvell, Ö., Lindqvist, G. and Ketels, C. (2003) *The Cluster Initiative Greenbook*, Stockholm: Ivory Tower AB.

Sorenson, O. and Audia, P. (2000) 'The social structure of entrepreneurial activity: geographic concentration of footwear production in the United States, 1940–1989', *American Journal of Sociology* 106(2): 424–62.

Staber, U. (2001) 'Spatial proximity and firm survival in a declining industrial district: the case of knitwear firms in Baden-Württemberg', *Regional Studies* 35(4): 329–42.

Steiner, M. (2001) 'Clustering and economic change: new policy orientations – the case of Styria', in B. Johansson, C. Karlsson and R. Stough (eds) *Theories of Endogenous Regional Growth*, Heidelberg: Springer-Verlag.

Stelder, D. (2002) 'Geographical grids in "new economic geography" models', in P. McCann (ed.) *Industrial Location Economics*, Cheltenham: Edward Elgar.

Storper, M. (1995) 'The resurgence of regional economies, ten years later: the region as a nexus of untraded interdependencies', *European Urban and Regional Studies* 2(3): 191–221,

Stuart, T. and Sorenson, O. (2003) 'The geography of opportunity: spatial heterogeneity in founding rates and the performance of biotechnology firms', *Research Policy* 32: 229–53.

Suchman, M. (2000) 'Dealmakers and counselors: law firms as intermediaries in the development of Silicon Valley', in M. Kenney (ed.) *Understanding Silicon Valley: The Anatomy of an Entrepreneurial Region*, Stanford, Calif.: Stanford University Press.

Sudjic, D. (1992) *The 100 Mile City*, London: André Deutsch.

Swann, G. (1998) 'Towards a model of clustering in high technology industries', in G. Swann, M. Prevezer and D. Stout (eds) *The Dynamics of Industrial Clustering: International Comparisons in Computing and Biotechnology*, Oxford: Oxford University Press.

Swann, G., Prevezer, M. and Stout, D. (eds) (1998) *The Dynamics of Industrial Clustering: International Comparisons in Computing and Biotechnology*, Oxford: Oxford University Press.

Thee, K. W. (1994) 'Indonesia' in S. D. Meyanathan (ed.) *Industrial Structures and the Development of Small and Medium Enterprise Linkages: Examples from East Asia*, Washington, DC: Economic Development Institute of the World Bank.

—— (1997) 'The development of the motorcycle industry in Indonesia', in M. Pangestu and Y. Sato (eds) *Waves of Change in Indonesia's Manufacturing Industry*, Tokyo: Institute of Developing Economies.

Tarnbunan, T. (2005) 'Promoting small and medium enterprises with a clustering approach: a policy experience from Indonesia', *Journal of Small Business Management* 43(2): 138–54.

Toms, S. and Filatotchev, I. (2003) 'Networks, corporate governance and the decline of the Lancashire textile industry, 1860–1980', in J. Wilson and A. Popp (eds) *Industrial Clusters and Regional Business Networks in England, 1750–1970*, Aldershot: Ashgate.

Turok, I. (1995) 'Multinational/supplier linkages in the Scottish electronics industry', in F. Chittenden, M. Robertson and I. Marshall (eds) *Small Firms: Partnerships for Growth*, London; Paul Chapman.

—— (2003) 'Cities, clusters and creative industries: the case of film and television in Scotland', *European Planning Studies* 11(5): 549–65.

Tyler, P. and Kitson, M. (1987) 'Geographical variations in transport costs of manufacturing firms in Great Britain', *Urban Studies* 24: 61–73.

UNIDO (2000) 'Cluster development and promotion of business development services: UNIDO's experience in India', Private Sector Development Branch Working Paper 6, Vienna: Investment Promotion and Institutional Capacity Building Division, UNIDO.

US Census Bureau (2002) *Annual Survey of Manufacturers*, Washington, DC: Bureau of the Census, US Department of Commerce.

van den Berg, L., Braun, E. and van Winden, W. (2001) 'Growth clusters in European cities: an integral approach', *Urban Studies* 12(3): 52–60.

van Dijk, M. P. and Rabellotti, R. (eds) (1997) *Enterprise Clusters and Networks in Developing Countries*, London: Frank Cass.

Vernon, R. and Hoover, E. (1959) *Anatomy of a Metropolis*, Cambridge, Mass.: Harvard University Press.

Watts, H., Wood, A. and Wardle, P. (2003) '"Making friends or making things?": interfirm transactions in the Sheffield metal-working cluster', *Urban Studies* 40(3): 615–30.

Weijland, H. (1994) 'Trade networks for flexible rural industry', in P. O. Pedersen, A. Sverrisson and M. P. van Dijk (eds) *Flexible Specialization: The Dynamics of*

Small-Scale Industries in the South, London: Intermediate Technology Publications.

—— (1999) 'Microenterprise clusters in rural Indonesia: industrial seedbed and policy target', *World Development* 27: 1515–30.

Weinstein, B. (2001) 'Regional growth theories and local economic development: some case studies', in B. Johansson, C. Karlsson and R. Stough (eds) *Theories of Endogenous Regional Growth: Lessons for Regional Policies,* Berlin: Springer-Verlag.

Whitley, R (1999) *Divergent Capitalisms: The Social Structuring and Change of Business Systems,* Oxford: Oxford University Press.

Wilkie, T. (1991) *British Science and Politics Since 1945,* Oxford: Blackwell.

Williamson, O. E. (1975) *Markets and Hierarchies: Analysis and Antitrust Implications,* New York: The Free Press.

—— (1979) 'Transaction cost economics: the governance of contractual relations', *Journal of Law and Economics* 22: 233–61.

—— (1991) 'Comparative economic organization: the analysis of discrete structural alternatives', *Administrative Science Quarterly* 36: 269–96.

—— (1994) 'Transaction cost economics and organization theory', in N. Smelser and R. Swedberg (eds) *The Handbook of Economic Sociology,* Princeton, NJ: Princeton University Press.

Wilson, J. and Popp, A. (eds) (2003) *Industrial Clusters and Regional Business Networks in England, 1750–1970,* Aldershot: Ashgate.

Wilson, J. and Singleton, J. (2003) 'The Manchester industrial district, 1750–1939: clustering, networking and performance', in J. Wilson and A. Popp (eds) *Industrial Clusters and Regional Business Networks in England, 1750–1970,* Aldershot: Ashgate.

Womack, J., Jones, D. and Ross, D. (1990) *The Machine that Changed the World,* New York: Harper Perennial.

Wong, P. K. (1995) 'Competing in the global electronics industry: a comparative study of the innovation networks of Singapore and Taiwan', *Journal of Industry Studies* 2(2): 35–61.

Wood, S. (2002) 'Organisational performance and manufacturing practices', in D. Holman, T. Wall, C. Clegg, P. Sparrow and A. Howard (eds) *The New Workplace A Guide to the Human Impact of Modern Working Practices,* Chichester: John Wiley & Sons.

Wright, P. and Gardner, T. (2003) 'The human resource-firm performance relationship: methodological and theoretical challenges', in D. Holman, T. Wall, C. Clegg, P. Sparrow and A. Howard (eds) *The New Workplace: A Guide to the Human Impact of Modern Working Practices,* Chichester: John Wiley & Sons.

Yetton, P., Craig, J., Davis, J. and Hilmer, F. (1992) 'Are diamonds a country's best friend? A critique of Porter's theory of national competition as applied to Canada, New Zealand and Australia', *Australian Journal of Management* 17(1): 1–32.

Zeitlin, J. (1992) 'Industrial districts and local economic regeneration': overview and comment', in F. Pyke and W. Sengenberger (eds) *Industrial Districts and Local Economic Regeneration,* Geneva: Independent Labour Organization.

Zeitlin, J. and Herrigel, G. (eds) (2000) *Americanization and its Limits – Reworking US Technology and Management in Post-war Europe and Japan,* Oxford: Oxford University Press.

Index

Note: page numbers in italics refer to figures or tables